Vicious Infants

A Volume in the Series
Childhoods: Interdisciplinary Perspectives on Childhood and Youth

Edited by
Rachel Conrad, Alice Hearst, Laura Lovett,
and Karen Sánchez-Eppler

VICIOUS INFANTS

DANGEROUS CHILDHOODS IN ANTEBELLUM U.S. LITERATURE

LAURA SODERBERG

University of Massachusetts Press
Amherst and Boston

Printed in the United States of America

ISBN 978-1-62534-588-2 (paper); 589-9 (hardcover)

Designed by Deste Roosa
Set in LTC Kennerley Pro and Gotham
Printed and bound by Books International, Inc.

Cover design by Deste Roosa
Cover photo: duncan1890/iStockPhoto.

Library of Congress Cataloging-in-Publication Data
Names: Soderberg, Laura, author.
Title: Vicious infants : dangerous childhoods in antebellum U.S. literature / Laura Soderberg.
Description: Amherst : University of Massachusetts Press, 2021. | Series: Childhoods: interdisciplinary perspectives on children and youth | Based on the author's dissertation (doctoral)—University of Pennsylvania, 2016. | Includes bibliographical references and index.
Identifiers: LCCN 2020053356 (print) | LCCN 2020053357 (ebook) | ISBN 9781625345882 (paperback) | ISBN 9781625345899 (hardcover) | ISBN 9781613768440 (ebook) | ISBN 9781613768457 (ebook)
Subjects: LCSH: American literature—19th century—History and criticism. | Children in literature. | Social problems in literature. | Child labor in literature. | Juvenile delinquency in literature. | African American children in literature.
Classification: LCC PS374.C45 S63 2021 (print) | LCC PS374.C45 (ebook) | DDC 810.9/3523—dc23
LC record available at https://lccn.loc.gov/2020053356
LC ebook record available at https://lccn.loc.gov/2020053357

British Library Cataloguing-in-Publication Data
A catalog record for this book is available from the British Library.

A portion of chapter 2 was previously published as "Writing the Criminal Child: Antebellum Prison Records, Parenting Manuals, and the Rise of the Incorrigible Child" in *J19: The Journal of Nineteenth-Century Americanists* 6, no. 2 (November 2018): 307–34. Copyright © 2018 C19: The society of Nineteenth-Century Americanists. Reprinted with permission. A portion of chapter 3 was previously published as "Prodigious Births: Black Infancy, Antebellum Medicine, and the Racialization of Heredity" in *Studies in American Fiction* 46, no. 2 (December 2019): 217–38. Copyright © 2019 The Johns Hopkins Press.

For Matt and Emily

CONTENTS

ACKNOWLEDGMENTS

When I think about all of the people and institutions who have contributed to this book, I am very aware that writing is not a solitary task, and I am staggered by the grace and kindness I have received. I wrote this book over the course of several positions and with the help of countless friends, colleagues, and mentors. I first began this project while in graduate school. My committee members were invaluable guides in the process and were everything I could have hoped for in advisors. Nancy Bentley offered strategic and insightful guidance as well as the rare gift of practical writing advice. David Kazanjian consistently pushed me to think more broadly and more precisely about my work. Chi-ming Yang gave generous and brilliant feedback and always gave me more to consider. I also had the honor of meeting scholars and friends whose readings and thoughts have shaped my own. Sunny Yang and Don James McLaughlin deserve special thanks for having read and commented on much of the material in this book. I also want to thank Omari Weekes, Sierra Lomuto, Aundeah Kearney, Mary Zaborskis, Marina Bilbija, Kalyan Nadiminti, Julius Fleming, Ana Schwartz, Bronwyn Wallace, Sal Nicolazzo, Jazmín Delgado Flores, Evelyn Soto, Clare Mullaney, and many others. I owe them all a great deal.

I also received crucial support as a fellow with the McNeil Center for Early American Studies, a time that was invaluable for its interdisciplinary structure and the conversations with and research done by other fellows. My research was further supported by a short-term fellowship at the Winterthur Museum and Library, and I am grateful for the research assistance of librarians there and at the Historical Society of Pennsylvania. Earlier and shorter versions of work from this book appeared in *J19* and *American Literature*. I appreciate the time and recommendations that the editors and reviewers for those journals contributed to this material.

The academic market being what it is, the manuscript came with me to several homes. I did further work on this text while holding visiting positions at Washington College and Franklin & Marshall College. I am indebted to my colleagues at those institutions, especially Courtney Rydel, Shari Goldberg, and Peter Jaros for their hospitality and advice. I am completing it from the University of Southern Indiana. I am grateful for the conversations and contributions of all of my colleagues there and for the faculty development award that supported this work.

A number of conferences and seminars have provided important interlocutors, including the childhood teleologies workshop at C19 facilitated by Anna Mae Duane and Karen Sánchez-Eppler, and the Childhoods of Color conference hosted by the University of Wisconsin-Madison's Center for the History of Print and Digital Culture and organized by Brigitte Fielder. Matt Becker has been a terrific editor, and I am grateful to him and to the anonymous reviewers at the University of Massachusetts Press whose feedback has greatly improved this text.

Throughout all of this, I have also been supported by the immense kindness of friends and family. Helen, Janani, Dena, and Alex are extraordinary friends. I appreciate the warmth and welcome of the Hagerty family. Without the support of my parents and sister, I would never have undertaken this work, much less completed it. Finally, to Matt, you deserve more than thanks.

Vicious Infants

INTRODUCTION

In 1758, Carl Linnaeus set out a taxonomy of the human population. A revision of the system he had first published in 1735, Linnaeus's tenth edition of *Systema Naturæ* classifies humans by the racial categories that were then beginning to be consolidated—proposing different human species for African, American, European, and Asian peoples with a collection of physical traits describing each—but the system also includes two subspecies that operate much less conventionally.[1] One, *Homo monstrous*, acts as a catchall for racialized groups whom he believed to be physically distinct from the larger categories. Each of these smaller groups, which include the so-called Patagonian giant and the dwarf of the Alps, are assigned a specific region and a set of common characteristics, such as size or timidity.[2] The remaining type, *Homo ferus*—or, to use a more common term, the feral child—works more strangely. Although he offers three shared traits of four-footedness, muteness, and hairiness within the species, Linnaeus's chief definition of *Homo ferus* comes, unlike all the other species of humanity, as a list. That list is comprised of six cases: the Bear Boy of Lithuania (*Juvenis Ursinus lithuanus*), the Wolf Boy of Hesse (*Juvenis Ursinus Hessensis*), the Irish Sheep Boy (*Juvenis Ovinus hibernus*), Peter of Hanover (*Juvenis hannoverans*), the two Pryenean Boys (*Pueri Pyrenaici*), and Jean of Liège (*Johannes Leodicensis*).[3] Apparently trusting his readers' familiarity with the feral children whom he references, Linnaeus provides no information about any of these cases beyond these names, nor does he give any further information about the group as a whole.

How do seven children scattered across Europe, most of whom never met one another, constitute a coherent group? And, more pointedly, what intersection of reproduction and population is Linnaeus relying on when he so quickly assumes that the grouping will be clear to his readers? *Systema Naturæ* anchors the other taxonomic categories of humanity into a stable geography and more recognizable kinship; they are the people who have lived in an area, reproducing their supposedly unique traits across the generations. They represent, in other words, a version of what Alys Eve Weinbaum has termed "the race/reproduction bind," or a model of race that inheres within heterosexual reproduction.[4] Put differently, Linnaeus most often envisions a relationship between population and reproduction that is so common that it is often invisible or, at the very least, treated as common sense.

The unfamiliarity of *Homo ferus*, however, provides a way into the strange linkages of reproduction, population, and childhood. Nothing as simple as ancestry or location defines the feral child. One of their few common traits instead seems to be their disconnection from the predictable patterns of life around them; they are a population defined by their estrangement from the populations around them. The basic premise of genealogy asserts that a group—whether a family, race, or nation—can be recognized and traced over time, even as its individual members are entirely replaced by new individuals. Linnaeus's feral children function in almost perfect opposition to this, defined by their being individual examples and their discontinuity with previous generations. What it means to live as a feral child or how an adult might recognize one is left entirely unexplained. In this respect, the feral child is not precisely the archetype of a certain kind of subject; its function is closer to being the trace left by a system of reproduction with its own source of coherence distinct from geography or genealogy. In other words, the grouping of *Homo ferus* provides a model for deriving population from reproduction.

While it is an extreme case, this image of feral children is not alone in bearing this representative weight. As I will demonstrate across *Vicious Infants*, visions of childhood index different visions of reproduction, whether social or biological, and therefore often served as markers of the imagined coherence or lack of coherence of the communities to which they belonged. The minimal coherence of the feral child as a category (as a list of individuals named together into a species) mirrors their disconnection from genealogy. They are removed from families and therefore from the social world in general. Yet feral children are not the only children whose childhoods have been defined by the presence or absence of sociability. By sociability, I mean the degree to which children are allowed to serve as synecdoche for their community as a whole. Sociable children become a kind of shorthand for interconnection by reminding adults of themselves as children or of their own children or their neighbors' children. As I will argue throughout this text, one of the defining features of antebellum childhoods is the ability or prescribed inability to abstract from the one to the many. From the vantage point of the twenty-first century, Americans tend to think of the most privileged children as being the ones allowed the greatest individuality and granted the most unique and elaborated interior lives. Yet sociability prioritizes and prizes their ability to serve as a general template for society. The most prized and protected child can also be the most generic. Because it was also a trait that many white readers and writers saw as inextricable from whiteness, affluence, ability, and normative gender, the refusal to ascribe sociability to the many children outside these categories also worked as an erasure of their families or a rewriting of their genealogies to exclude them from national belonging.

By the antebellum period, childhood had crystallized as a key symbol of the relationship between the individual and the larger social world. Long before Linnaeus imagined the possibility of a feral population from a constellation of remarkable children, the balance between liberal individualism and the necessary continuity of a social world had been the rhetorical work of more conventional childhood. John Locke made his foundational claim for liberal individual freedom by managing the relationship between a newly born subject and the established social and political world into which they were born. As the apparently pre-cultural being that Locke had earlier described as the *tabula rasa* (blank slate), the child promises evidence that adult subjects have an intrinsic claim to liberty. Locke writes, "Saying that 'begetting of children makes them not slaves to their fathers' as certainly sets all mankind free as his affirming the contrary makes them all slaves."[5] In this promised freedom from previous generations is the presumption of a radical innocence of history; each birth, for Locke, represents an escape from history, and therefore offers an erasure of systemic history from private life. However, as that pre-cultural tabula rasa, Locke's version of the child was also primed to be a generality, a subject distinct from but formally equal and socially identical to all other subjects. Locke's child, in other words, formed a means to think about the liberal individual in the multiple. While Lockean childhood was a highly influential model, it also was not the only one; other versions of childhood were connected to, or excluded from, their own versions of community.

Ideas about sociability are inextricable from ideas of child development. By insisting on repetitive patterns of birth, growth, and maturation, sociable childhoods blurred into the living mass that is population. This is a temporal imagination—the much more explored futurity in U.S. childhood—but it is also a synchronous ability to feel social connections between oneself and one's child or a child next door or a child in a different state. Through their focus on sociability, narratives about childhood thus provided a language with which to imagine reproduction at the scale of population. Aligning developmental arcs to generalize from the one to the many also provided a way to exclude groups of people on the grounds that they developed differently or failed to develop at all. Following on this idea, I link what Kathryn Bond Stockton has termed "growing sideways," or the deviation from normative paths of development whether by choice or compulsion, with biopolitical life at the largest scale.[6] Sociability, though, also focuses us on the host of other childhoods that are defined by their relationship to sociability—the children cut off from the crowd or made into exceptions supposedly too rare for national inclusion. The promise of lives lived in parallel trajectories, and so in community, also creates distinct developmental paths meant to marginalize and therefore racialize.

At its core, *Vicious Infants* argues that the antebellum period had a far more extensive and more variable range of childhoods than is usually discussed. As such, it pushes against any singular type of antebellum childhood, to which one is either admitted or refused, and toward a broader vocabulary of multiple childhoods that each have their own relationship to civic and family life. Scholars working in Black girl studies and Indigenous girl studies have proven not only that race and gender closely influence what types of childhood were available to children, but also that Black and Indigenous girls and adults collaborated to create new categories of childhood.[7] Building from this vital work, I argue that the consolidation of childhood into a single model has been a messy business accompanied by a host of rejected or submerged alternatives here termed "antisocial." These are childhoods that often go unnoticed because they are so far from what we conventionally recognize as childhood, most notably because they are cruel social narratives that harm the children they label. Yet, sentimental conceptions of childhood do not begin to address the host of antebellum children who were never imagined as the future of the nation, except as a future to be warned against and avoided. At the same time that images of childhood purity and preciousness saturated U.S. culture, regulations binding children under systems of indenture, imprisonment, and slavery were also taking their greatest hold, sparking other stories of children as dangers to be managed. Instead, *Vicious Infants* offers a counter-history of childhood that focuses on its function as social threat in the antebellum United States. These childhoods governed a maturing subject's trajectory toward or away from adult inclusion, marking some children as too fundamentally antisocial to acquire rights as adults. In other words, for many antebellum Americans, the children inhabiting a nation were not necessarily its future citizens and might even be a danger to its future stability.

The challenge of the conventional answer—that such a childhood is no childhood at all—is that it overwrites the ways that juvenile bodies never eligible for sentimental childhood were nonetheless classified and defined by their youth. The antebellum period saw the increasing attention to Black childhood under slavery as it became a point of explicit management for plantation owners. In order to guarantee a steady supply of people who could be legally enslaved once the international slave trade had been deemed illegal, enslavers learned to deploy the category of childhood as an investment strategy, producing a comparatively young labor force. According to Marie Jenkins Schwartz's estimates, more than 40 percent of those enslaved during the antebellum period were under the age of fifteen and a third were under ten.[8] Childhood under these circumstances took on a double-edged nature, wherein futurity could shift into the actuarial terms of investment and return, and, as Wilma King notes, measures of age often slipped into measures of labor potential.[9] Similarly, as Dawn Peterson has demonstrated, the adoption of Native children by white families was a central tactic in the United States' theft of Native lands, functioning both as part political negotiation and, for white settlers, as a moral justification for land theft.[10] The status of more protected white children shifted, too, as industrial demands for the cheap labor of child workers led rural families to send their children away to work in urban areas and produced a legal redefinition of children as contractual agents in their own right, in order to allow hiring to go on at a distance from parents.[11] The result was a wave of displaced children with new economic opportunities but dubious family ties, a legally uncertain access to personhood rights such as contractual consent and private property, and the mobility necessitated by temporary labor. A host of new categories came with this turmoil, from "street Arab" to "juvenile delinquent," to narrate children who had become objects of suspicion by leaving the domestic sphere.

Far from being irrelevant to such subjects, childhood operated as a dimension of power through which children's property, labor, and freedom could be appropriated by the state. Antisocial childhoods had the capacity to injure and dispossess those subjects whom they claimed, as well as to control which groups were legible as cohesive and continuous. As both Anna Mae Duane and Robin Bernstein have shown, sentimental forms of childhood focused respectively on vulnerability and innocence enacted to reinforce racial lines by claiming a need to protect white children.[12] While discourses of sentimental childhood racialized by contrast—imagining a white subject who is worthy of childhood and a subject of color who is not—there were also other models of childhood that marginalized children themselves, most often by dismissing such children as exceptional or unusual cases. By cutting these children off as reproductive flukes or social isolates, models of antisocial childhood also recast them as outside of the "natural" population of the United States.

The question of how to constitute a population was not an abstract question in the antebellum era. It was an immediate legal issue based in the specificity of U.S. settler colonialism. While much of the work on potentially antisocial children has emerged from the field of British literature to examine figures like the criminal orphans of Charles Dickens or the "watercress girl" of Thomas Mayhew, U.S. portrayals of childhood have their own specificity as a means to confer or contest political inclusion.[13] The United States' roots in settler colonialism meant that geography did not act as a simple register of belonging. This is partly because the desire to claim land held by Native peoples in the west incentivized the government to extend sovereignty over the mobile settlers—and thereby to the areas they entered—without extending citizenship rights to the Native Americans who continued to live there, and partly because the slavery-based economy of the nation required a legal separation between the concepts of residency and citizenship. While Great Britain's empire created its own racial hierarchies, the space of the island itself provided an anchor point for that racism as a symbolic source of purity and identity for British subjects, albeit one that was rhetorically constructed, continually contested, and subject to much anxiety.[14] The United States organized its racism on far more domestic terms while maintaining looser geographies in hopes of future colonization.

As a result, U.S. legal thinking relied far more on intergenerational bonds as a way of establishing belonging and citizenship. In 1790, Congress established citizenship's ability to be conferred by parentage, structuring American nationality by *jus sanguinis* (right of blood) by recognizing genealogy as a component of citizenship. This law, entitled "An act to establish an uniform Rule of Naturalization," enacted three principles: long-term residents might receive citizenship through federal naturalization; the children of these residents would also be naturalized by this process, provided that they are under twenty-one; and the children born to U.S. citizens traveling abroad receive U.S. citizenship as a birthright.[15] The goal of such laws is to define what legal scholar Kristin A. Collins has called the "parent-child citizenship transmission" and thereby to stabilize national identity over time.[16] As the law established, children marked a critical relay between generations of Americans, ensuring that travel—or conquest—could not disrupt the United States' sovereign claim on a family and that the recognition of new citizens established their descendants as new chains of future citizens. This genealogical component also explicitly racialized the transmission of citizenship. Naturalization of a resident subject, and the accompanying incorporation of the resident's children into the nation, applied to "any alien, being a free white person."[17] Collins describes the force of such limits as amounting to a form of population control, writing that it worked to "regulate the actual reproduction—and racial composition—of the citizenry."[18] Put differently, antebellum ideas about how strongly and in what ways children are connected to their parents were inextricable from ideas of race and from the lifelong ability to access rights.

All of which is not to say that there was a stable relationship between genealogy, birthplace, and citizenship in the antebellum period. To the contrary, as Carrie Hyde has argued, the qualifications for and limits to citizenship were surprisingly undertheorized by early nineteenth-century law. Instead, as she argues, literature and other forms of speculative thinking played a central role in providing popular, often contradictory, definitions of citizenship.[19] Martha Jones, too, has demonstrated the foundational work of African American writers proposing and defining birthright as the basis of belonging, well before the Civil War.[20] Literary depictions of children as belonging to or being cut off from the civic body were a significant part of this public debate, shaping popular notions of kinship and its boundaries. The Fourteenth Amendment offered a clearer official definition in 1866, establishing at least a technical right to citizenship for anyone born within the country's borders. (It was, perhaps not incidentally, followed by a surge in the popularity of rebellious child characters, including Jo March in 1868 and Tom Sawyer in 1876—children who could defy social norms safe in the new stability of their belonging.[21]) Though children have of course continued to be flashpoints of debate over questions of national belonging and government power, during the period from the nation's inception through the Civil War, they were uniquely central to debates about the relationship between individuals and the social body. These conversations draw from legal discourses, but they also extended to extralegal conceptions of community on scales ranging from the individual to global population patterns, a trajectory this text follows.

As a result, while Charles Dickens was writing about loveable pickpockets, relatively secure in the sense of their ultimate Britishness, U.S. writers imagined children who very well might not be part of the nation at all. Thus, as Kenneth Kidd observes, during this time, the scene of European stories about feral children begin to shift toward more distant imperial spaces, displacing these fears of child wildness onto bodies coded as foreign or primitive.[22] In contrast, as racial hierarchies began to be consolidated as an internal element of national society, new categories of non-assimilated or unassimilable childhood multiplied throughout the most domestic sites of nineteenth-century U.S. literature.[23]

One of the most canonical examples of antisocial children in U.S. literature is *The Scarlet Letter*'s Pearl, the illegitimate child of Hester Prynne "born outcast of the infantile world."[24] Pearl is shunned by her Puritan community because of her social status, but Nathaniel Hawthorne also invests her with a more essential removal from her world. Her eyes possess "a strange remoteness and intangibility" that register a level of difference from even her mother, who finds her "intelligent, yet inexplicable, so perverse, sometimes so malicious . . . that Hester could not help questioning, at such moments, whether Pearl were a human child."[25] Hawthorne's catalog of traits—intelligence, inexplicability, perversity, and malice—is not the diametric opposite of the sentimental child. It is instead a version of childhood that has an opposite orientation toward adult authority, which can neither contain it nor understand it. The effect is not freeing in any direct way. Under examination by the governor and religious orders, Pearl refuses to declare that she was created by God, but instead insists that she was "plucked by her mother off the bush of wild-roses that grew by the prison-door."[26] Pearl's proposal of an alternative genealogy echoes the fact of her birth outside of socially sanctioned reproduction and symbolically aligns her with the pleasure of roses over the punishment of prisons. Most immediately, though, Pearl's declaration nearly leads her to be taken into custody, separated from her mother, and presumably set to labor as an apprentice for another family. Only intervention from Dimmesdale, her guilt-ridden father, prevents the then-three-year-old girl from forcibly becoming a ward of the state.

Hawthorne is relatively admiring of Pearl's freedom and there are widely accepted arguments that she is based partially on his own daughter, Una.[27] However, Pearl also acts a literary mirror for broader discourses that were increasingly coming to see childhood's futurity not as a promise but as a threat of social upheaval. One commentator on these forms of vicious infancy was Charles Loring Brace, the philanthropist who would later become famous as the major force behind the so-called Orphan Trains that shipped children westward. His warnings, first published in 1854, about urban poverty and in particular the urban poverty of children born to Irish and German immigrants display a similar ambivalence about the social disconnection of the children whom he wished to educate:

> It should be remembered, that there are no dangers to the value of property or to the permanency of our institutions, so great as those from the existence of such a class of vagabond, ignorant, ungoverned children. This "dangerous class" has not begun to show itself, as it will in eight or ten years, when these boys and girls are matured. . . . They will vote. They will have the same rights as we ourselves, though they have grown up ignorant of moral principle, as any savage or Indian. They will poison society. They will perhaps be embittered at the wealth, and the luxuries, they never share. Then let Society beware, when the outcast, vicious, reckless multitude of New York boys, swarming now every foul alley and low street, come to know their power and *use it!*[28]

Fear, rather than pity, drives his warning that New York was infested with an "outcast, vicious, reckless multitude" threatening to overrun it. The peril that this "dangerous class" offers to Brace is not a specific menace so much as it is the internal threat to the known social order and particularly to that predictable continuity of sovereignty that he terms "the permanency of our institutions." As the conventional language of reproductive futurity takes on the character of apocalyptic prophecy, what seem like children—and therefore harmless, trivial, and above all apolitical—will rise up into rights-bearing adults, because to the eyes of the state, they are citizens as much as anyone else. Brace's warning is that these future citizens will have no loyalty to the laws and class hierarchies into which they have been born, and thus no reason to continue them; their lack of recognizable socialization places them as far outside national tradition as "any savage or Indian." The fear of these vagrant children, then, lies in the idea that they are the future, but a future with no affinity to the present and guaranteed only to appear to observers like Brace as a place of disorder and unpredictability.

Returning to Pearl, a reading of her ability to scare her mother alongside Brace's jeremiad on the homeless children of New York alongside the taxonomies of antisocial childhood points to a pervasive history of childhood as a perceived threat to existing systems of power. These examples are easy starting points in part because their whiteness grants them some proximity to more recognizable languages of childhood—note that Brace's ultimate threat is that white children might be racialized into becoming like Native Americans, a threat that precludes recognition of Native American children as children—but narratives of supposedly antisocial children pervade white descriptions of children of color, particularly Black children. These narratives acted as justifications of often brutal control. I certainly chose my title, "Vicious Infants," in part for its apparent contradictoriness, but more importantly because it registers a real and historically codified type of child. As a criminal designation, vicious infancy stripped subjects of their ability to participate in a social world outside of institutional control, potentially for as long as they could be classed as minors.[29]

Theorists of sovereignty have long seen more conventional versions of childhood as ideal territory for conservative utopian thought. Because its futurity is bound up in adults thinking back to their own memories, the futures projected on children can easily take the form of an idealized regression back to a supposedly purer past. That is, adult thinkers often present childhood as a known entity, having been children themselves, and therefore assume that its trajectories into the future can be fully managed—albeit through a regimen of painstaking corrections. As Michel Foucault wrote of nineteenth-century Europe, "the education of children was the fundamental utopia, crystal, and prism through which problems of conduction were perceived."[30] Through childhood, adults in power dreamed of sculpting subjects to their own specifications. Studies of childhood have accordingly concentrated on the dual uses of childhood as contact point and warrant for governmental power, in that the perceived vulnerability of the child to external forces serves both as an opportunity for social conditioning and a justification for a "protective" control. Lee Edelman, Elizabeth Freeman, and Lauren Berlant have each argued that the relentless futurity associated with utopian visions of the child is used to narrow the present desire of adults into heteronormative channels.[31] This version of childhood serves a site on which the future may be inscribed; once designated as the fragile vessel of that perfect future, it becomes a pretense for policing the present.

Moreover, childhood's importance in U.S. national discourse reflects and reinforces a sense that the only way of thinking about time that matters is a linear futurity based in straight, biological reproduction. As Jack Halberstam explains these connections between generational rhythms and state power, the ongoing movement of "values, wealth, goods, and morals" from parents to children "connects the family to the historical past of the nation, and glances ahead to connect the family to the future of both familial and national stability."[32] By intertwining childhood, biological reproduction, and state structures of power, the nation creates a sense of naturalized continuity located in the family and then claims that continuity for itself. Childhood, in other words, has been a place where authority could claim endurance and cohesion, shifting its power from the individuals of the present to an open-ended population stretching into the future. However, as José Muñoz has commented with devastating understatement, "The future is only the stuff of some kids. Racialized kids, queer kids, are not the sovereign princes of futurity," noting that Edelman in particular "accepts and reproduces this monolithic figure of the child that is indeed always already white."[33] The importance of childhood to the construction of population did not extend protection to all children; it made violence against marginalized children a higher priority for the state, in order to enforce the boundaries of population.

This history of using childhood vulnerability to justify governmental power extends to the origins of the United States and has always worked in conjunction with white supremacy. As Holly Brewer argues, minors in the early republic were seen as unable to provide legal consent, helping to spur the development of a more strictly delimited private sphere to shelter them and providing language for the comparative equality of adults.[34] That language, however, was immediately deployed to argue that the children of white U.S. Americans needed to be saved from racialized threats of violence or, in pro-slavery tracts, from labor. In her readings of Native American captivity narratives and other narratives of racial menace to white families, Duane suggests vulnerability as the defining term of childhood.[35] Likewise, Bernstein notes the emergence of innocence to separate the supposedly delicate white children from the coerced labor assigned to their Black counterparts.[36] In both cases, such texts argued that this protected childhood extended primarily or exclusively to white children and that the way to save these white children was to inflict violence onto people of color.

However powerful this version of childhood was, it was immediately and consistently challenged by authors of color, who created their own definitions of childhood. Nazera Sadiq Wright has argued, for example, that African American authors throughout the nineteenth century created portraits of Black girlhood that emphasized strength, courage, and resilience, redefining what girlhood could be.[37] Work in Black children's literature has also pushed beyond the traditional categories of historical archives and of children's literature to give fresh visions of what African American children read and wrote and of how they lived.[38] Native American authors like Charles A. Eastman and Zitkala-Ša published children's literature for audiences that included white children but centered Native American stories and traditions as valuable and formative. Such writers were doing more than claiming the conventions of childhood; they were rewriting them. In this regard, I scout the limits of sentimentalism to consider which children are beyond the transformational force of pathos, but I also push against the presumption that sentimentalism, even broadly defined, was the only discourse dictating antebellum cultures of childhood.

The majority of this text tracks the racialization, marginalization, and rhetorical othering of marginalized children, especially Black children, in literary and official writing. It does so because it is important to understand the harms that these narratives have done in order to better trace and ameliorate their legacies. However, the implicit cost of studying these texts is to risk recirculating and reproducing their injuries. I study this archive in the belief that the harms of these texts already persist in the world in many forms and that examining antebellum narratives grants us a better understanding of these historical continuities. Just as importantly, it also helps us recognize strategies of resistance to these narratives. Another limit of this project is that it tells us less about the perspective of historical children themselves than about the adult cultures they confronted. This is not a desire to signal that these perspectives went unrecorded or are wholly lost to us; even in these archives of adult writing, hints of child subjectivity peek through. Rather it is a matter of better understanding and more fully recovering these perspectives by examining the world they encountered.

Childhood studies cannot place its center in even a putatively singular subject. Returning to one of the origin points of the field reveals the fundamental plurality of visions of children. The angelic child never existed without the delinquent, the apprentice, the prodigy, or any of the other frameworks for childhood that this project might have considered but for which it lacked the space. Instead, these figures—which are themselves so invested in attempts to think about the antebellum United States as a heterogeneous set of populations with discontinuities, exceptions, and difference—point to childhood as an object of study in which multiplicity must be a central feature of not only its content, but also its methods. In other words, the stories that the field tells must be messy, fragmented, and partial, reflecting the interplay between activism for living or historical children and criticism of rhetorical childhoods as well the limits of adult scholars to reach across the boundaries of age.

OVERVIEW

Narratives of childhood emerged through the interplay of institutions and literature, two systems that seem to operate in quite different ways. Institutions work to provide broad pathways designed to route individuals through programs written to apply to the many. The patterns formed through this repetition make visible narratives already implicit in bureaucratic structures. Benedict Anderson describes this process in terms of fluid dynamics, writing that "the flow of subject populations through the mesh of differential schools, courts, clinics, police stations, and immigration offices created 'traffic-habits' which in time gave real social life to the state's earlier fantasies."[39] By tracing how institutions imagine and implement these "fantasies," we also recover the stories in which they place their subjects and the logics that cross from expert discourse into common culture. The reliance on children to represent the border between individual and collective life makes the act of interpreting childhood a specifically literary task, rooted in figuration and characterization, even when its texts are bureaucratic. Many of the labels I discuss arise in institutional contexts outside of literature, but their force is to make a literary argument that these children are representative beyond themselves. The incorrigible delinquent was created amidst the paperwork of juvenile prisons, but it also provided an interpretative framework for narrating the social body and those who fall outside it. Medicine, likewise, produced the idea of the prodigy as a limit case for legible inheritance, endowing it with its own relationship to genealogy and history. The texts themselves bring a literary hermeneutic to interpret children capable of representing multiplicities outside of themselves.

However, explicitly literary texts are also crucial to the project's archive. As these figures repeat in more conventionally defined literature, their complex implications for the kinship and the social world of the United States are typically explored in greater depth. These implications can then be reabsorbed by the original institutional discourse. Combining institutional discourse's focus on multiplicity with literature's attention to singular subjectivity allows for the clearest attention to the ways that various iterations of childhood shaped the recognition of group identity and of the continuity of a group over time. I therefore make no case for a strong division between the literary and the non-literary, but instead attend to their overlapping languages while respecting that they often prioritize different questions. *Vicious Infants* begins and ends with chapters focused on two of the literary genres most interested in the problems of childhood—the coming-of-age narrative and the sentimental reform novel—bookending chapters that are focused more closely on law and medicine. However, each chapter combines the bureaucratic with the literary in some way, tracing figures of childhood as they pass from one type of language to another.

The recognition of antisocial childhoods gave authors a chance to reshape the form of coming-of-age narratives. I begin with a pair of authors who, having been swept into the categories of antisocial childhood themselves, grappled with writing about lives like their own. The conventions of the bildungsroman present maturation as a gradual accumulation of property and freedom, culminating in an entrance into society. William Apess and Harriet Wilson both survived very different comings-of-age: they survived violent indentures as children to enter into a society in which white supremacy kept them from the privileges of adulthood. Their respective writings in the autobiographical *A Son of the Forest* (1829) and the semi-autobiographical novel *Our Nig* (1859) take up the paradoxical legal theories of apprenticeship indenture as a way of rewriting the bildungsroman. By tracking personal development with markers other than integration into the social world, Apess and Wilson conceptualize what it means to grow up into a society without being accepted or giving acceptance to it.

During this period, the contract law central to apprenticeship gradually began to give way to what remains the most sweeping legal mode of controlling children—the juvenile delinquency and carceral system. The 1820s and 1830s saw the first official classification of child criminals as a distinct group and the earliest institutionalization of these juvenile delinquents in child-only jails known as houses of refuge. I explore the legal theories of child criminality that emerged in communication with popular writings on parenting. At the same time that corporal punishment was condemned for teaching children to lie about their thoughts and feelings, the rhetoric of juvenile prisons created a class of the incorrigible: a name for primarily immigrant children whose thoughts and feelings could never be known by adult authorities and who could therefore only be disciplined by force.

Antebellum medicine, too, produced stories of physically alienated childhood through the figure of the prodigy. The longer history of *prodigy* extends the modern associations with child achievement to label any unexplainable happening, whether miraculous or frightening. Redeployed in the Atlantic world to classify young Black genius together with spectacles of Black disabled bodies, however, the dual nature of the concept of prodigy came to pathologize and exclude African American childhood from historical genealogy. These figures of Black infancy as a site of aberration and failed inheritance took hold in literary fiction, most famously in Herman Melville's *Moby-Dick* (1851), and drew forth rebukes from the African American author Susan Paul. Paul's work provides a further opportunity for examining how Black authors rewrote antisocial childhoods to insist on the humanity of Black children while also using these alternative models to sidestep the inadequacies of sentimental childhood.

Finally, the conventions of childhoods have had a deep connection with how novels have imagined satisfying endings. In my last chapter, I argue that Harriet Beecher Stowe's brush with Malthusian views of children allowed her to rewrite the easy resolutions of sentimental fiction, in which the birth of a new generation often offers utopian escape, into the more crowded world of her novel *Dred* (1856). As scholars such as Elizabeth Povinelli, Lauren Berlant, and Elizabeth Freeman have discussed, the conventional role of children in sentimental reform novels is to promise an easy end to the problems raised by the novel. The birth of children, as signs of pure futurity, banishes the social problems of the plot to a redemptive horizon beyond the end of the book. Reading Stowe's second novel in light of her interactions with Thomas Malthus, however, reveals a vision of white children as indexing histories of settler colonial violence through the specter of an overpopulating United States.

This arc from laws written to subjects reimaging indenture law to criminalized children to pathologized families and the economies of births suggests how broadly and inextricably antebellum visions of childhood were tied to visions of socialization and of the social world itself. Whether a social group is presented as naturally and continuously replenishing itself with children who were legible heirs to its adult members or whether its children were eclipsed and its population imagined as erratic, disjointed, or irregular could determine if that group could be counted as a part of the nation and determine its members' claim to citizenship. The damage that can be done by declaring certain childhoods antisocial occurs both individually and in the aggregate. However, the child deemed antisocial has therefore also been a means of imagining different forms of sociality and new configurations of sociality. The denial of innocence can insist on historical memory. Conversely, the erasure of history can make space for less constraining types of belonging. Most antisocial childhoods proved to be sources of pain or dispossession, and even those authors bent on reinvesting them with other meanings were necessarily engaged with a discourse that held the potential to wound. Rewritings of the child retain an awareness of the category's past and ongoing violence. By insisting that new experiences of childhood and new relationships between generations or within generations all be recognized as such, these authors challenge the inevitability of what "the child" might be.

CHAPTER 1

Bound Children

Sidestepping the Social Contract in Apprenticeship Literature

Cynthia Barns entered the public record in 1822, when she was seven years old. Described as the child of a dead father and a mother "who is poor and exposed to want and distress and has no one to take proper care of her," Cynthia represented a problem to the town of Pomfret, Connecticut.[1] She was understandably considered unable to find a profession on her own, and her mother was considered too poor to act as a guardian. While it was clear that someone had to take care of her, it was an open question as to who in the community would do so. Pomfret lacked the institutions—orphanages, children's homes, or juvenile prisons—that would have stepped in had Cynthia lived in a bigger city or a later decade. Instead, the town deployed an earlier tool for managing unattached children, opting to indenture her to a Samuel Richmond and his wife. In exchange for the promise that Cynthia would serve them "faithfully and dutifully" until the age of eighteen and a one-time sum of twenty-five dollars, the document contracts the Richmonds to care for Cynthia's needs in the present, by "furnish[ing] her in sickness and health with proper food, physic and clothing suitable for every day ware and suitably for Lord's day with suitable Lodging and washing" and to train her for the future in "the business of housewifery & pinning & knitting & sewing." As a precursor of the welfare state, indentures of this kind functioned as an explicit suturing of a subject into social structures from which they were otherwise excluded.

The resulting document looks strange from the perspective of contemporary divisions of public and private. Cynthia is held to be too young to enter into the market herself and so must be placed within a family, yet her physical labor is still presented as a marketable object that can be purchased for the cost of her care. Similarly, the wages that Cynthia receives come in the form of goods and services that are often seen as falling outside of the sphere of employment; she receives no money during her apprenticeship but does have a promise that her physical needs will be met. Cynthia Barns's indenture comes close to a privatized system of welfare, but her status as both a laboring body available for contract and a subject in need of protection from the market creates a more fundamental complication to ideas of private and public. Indenture subsidizes her eventual entry into the workplace through a limited exposure to the same, projecting a future of work that is paid for by the same labor that the text excludes from the public sphere.

Indenture's troubled borders between a subject who is both private and public, consenting and dependent, make it a unique space for challenging a key legal fiction of contract—namely, that the public body of the child inevitably fades into the private body of the adult and the child self must also follow the opposite path from privacy into the public sphere. This rethinking of how the individual is gradually bound into a larger population is, I argue, one of the principal tasks of two narratives of child indenture: William Apess's autobiography, *A Son of the Forest* (1829), and Harriet Wilson's semi-autobiographical novel, *Our Nig* (1859).[2] Both texts turn on a child working in bondage to white families and trace that child's progression into an economically unstable adulthood. While the texts are not usually read together, they both use the forms of indenture to reframe how unfree labor connects child bodies to the public sphere and how it subsequently shapes their relationship to the social world as adults. In her reading of *Our Nig*, Nazera Sadiq Wright has described the centrality of "survival skills" in Wilson's message to her readers.[3] This emphasis on survival as a literary mode operates within this larger network of law and practicality to create an argument about the politics of community. By centering consent to an agreement by children who have no other choices and, under most legal reasoning, no right to consent at all, Wilson and Apess rethink the bildungsroman to make it as much about finding and using basic necessities as about self-expression or finding a place in society.

Because the consent attached to indentures is so explicitly artificial, it is a more effective tool for representing what it means to grow up as a child of color in the antebellum United States than it is as a sign of consent itself. Wilson and Apess respond to having their child selves excluded from sociability by imagining an alternative orientation set against the population at large.

I track Wilson and Apess's use of indenture on two levels: first on the literary level as a subversion of the bildungsroman's traditional use of the social contract and, second, on a more literal level, as a critique of labor contracts' immediate effects on laborers. On both levels, the critique rests on the erasure of the body. For the first, the traditional bildungsroman glorifies the decision to abide in a society as the culmination and proof of personal freedom, neatly excluding the physical needs that might push a person to stay where they can at least have food and shelter. The second turns on the labor contract's exclusion not only of the coercive effects of physical needs but also of the long-term effects that labor can have on the body. Through this erasure, labor contracts make the welfare of the working body into the exclusive concern of the worker. Using apprenticeship as a rare space in which the law does give bodies a momentary presence in the public sphere, *Our Nig* and *A Son of the Forest* make the physical needs of their protagonists an explicit part of the choices they make.

The centrality of indenture in these texts is, in some sense, banal. Indenture was a common feature of the lives of many children, and a document like the indenture of Cynthia Barns would have been commonplace. Its contents are entirely generic, listing the parties involved, then the term, then the duties of the apprentice, the reciprocal duties of the master and mistress, and, finally, a standardized concluding oath. It is a contract written under the conventions of a contract. Two parties have come to a potentially mutually beneficial arrangement, sanctioned and enforceable by law. It takes no special close reading, though, to see that the norms of contract just as absolutely do not apply to the seven-year-old Cynthia. Instead, the indenture offers a contract that takes place around her inability to consent. Her signature does not appear and the introduction lists "Select men" of the town who are making arrangements on Cynthia's behalf. Regardless of these limitations on Cynthia's consent, recognized even in the indenture binding her, the document nevertheless maintains the basic forms of contract and appears *as if* Cynthia's consent can be safely stipulated without its actual inclusion. Cynthia Barns, as we know her through this document, thus appears as a curious inversion of market tendencies to emphasize the will and privatize the body. The indenture can try to anticipate her physical needs, but it avoids saying anything about what she thinks.

The status of the Cynthia Barns indenture as a not-quite contract relies on its connection to another and equally recognizable genre, that of the coming-of-age narrative. Spanning the girl's life from seven to eighteen, the indenture sets out to imagine how she will progress from an impoverished and fatherless child to a skilled worker, equipped with personal property (on turning eighteen, Cynthia will also receive "two good suits of Cloths" and a Bible) and an ability to work for herself in making clothing. The resemblance is more than incidental. As this chapter will argue, the logic of an indenture like Cynthia's relies on its narrative power to imagine this development of a child considered to be outside the social world to an adult with a place in it. By writing a contract around a subject whose consent cannot be registered in the document, indenture performs a quintessentially literary action of stipulating consent—positing that the child who cannot consent to a contract nevertheless has enough intrinsic agency to become an adult who retroactively agrees. Indentures, in other words, create narratives of development in which temporarily non-consenting children become grateful adults.

While I argue that Wilson and Apess draw on this link between legal and literary genres, *Our Nig* and *A Son of the Forest* have not been read exclusively, or even primarily, as bildungsroman. The latter, as a nonfictional account of Apess's indenture with the white Furman family following abuse by his own family and also his eventual conversion to Christianity, is typically read as a synthesis of autobiography and conversion narrative and as a foundational piece of the genre that Arnold Krupat termed "Indian autobiography."[4] Anna Mae Duane has suggested that *A Son of the Forest* be read as a re-writing of captivity narratives and Puritan hagiography, while Laura Mielke notes the importance of sentimentalism to the text.[5] *Our Nig*, meanwhile, focuses on the life of Alfrado, more commonly called Frado, a young Black girl who lives in the nominally free North but works in bondage for a white family until she reaches adulthood. Wilson herself had been indentured as a child due to family poverty in New Hampshire about a decade after Cynthia Barns was bound as an apprentice. Frado's captivity, though, has often been read as a close analogue of slavery rather than as a distinct system in its own right. Similarly, though the autobiographical quality of the text is widely acknowledged, *Our Nig* is more often understood as an intersection between sentimentalism and the slave narrative than as a participant in the coming-of-age narrative itself.[6]

A more basic factor that tends to separate Wilson and Apess from the bildungsroman is the problem of their endings. Frado and William are difficult to slot into the traditional role of a character who has come of age because neither of the novels' conclusions leave a sense of either character becoming reconciled with the social order or having an established place within it. By *Our Nig*'s end, which tracks its protagonist approximately through her twenties, Frado has left the Bellmont family, worked at sewing, learned to manufacture bonnets, returned to the Bellmonts, left again, married, had a child, been abandoned by her husband, and gone into business selling hair serum. As the text closes, Frado begins to write her narrative after having been forced to place her son with the poor house, and she has no prospects of escaping the institution herself except—here, Wilson juggles character and author—through the sale of the novel. William, meanwhile, moves from one apprenticeship to another, escapes, and joins the army and fights in Canada. After leaving the army, he works as a baker, a farmhand, a cook, and an itinerant preacher.[7] The narrative concludes with William leaving the Methodist Episcopalian Church after they deny him a preaching license and setting out with an intention to join the Methodist Society. Belonging and stability exist, at best, on the horizon of these endings. Read through indenture law, *A Son of the Forest* and *Our Nig* give us a way of imagining the bildungsroman stripped of its neat resolution.

This generic restructuring has several implications. At the most fundamental level, it expands the genre to encompass lives lived in poverty or in and out of the edges of poverty. While it is common enough to encounter novels that begin with the young and poor, few end with such heroes. The proof of maturation tends instead toward the accumulation of capital and the stability that this capital can bring. As Jed Esty has written, the coming-of-age narrative has long operated as "the genre of progress" whether in showing that society can change to accommodate a new member or, more often, that young misfits can successfully warp themselves into the shapes demanded by society.[8] Such novels equate growing bodies with growing economic power and use this equation to make a progression to the middle class appear like a natural trajectory. Unstable lives (in which no one profession ever lasts very long and no single home is permanent) along with overly stable lives (in which the same labor lasts from puberty until death and one's hometown remains home) have had less of a place in this canon of upward mobility. Reshaping this narrative trajectory therefore also means ushering in new protagonists and substituting a wary sociability for any happy ending. Frado and William each need the people around them, but they are also not surrounded by safe people. Together, Wilson and Apess theorize the transactions and spaces of privacy needed to rely on social bonds without trusting them.

CHILD BODIES AND THE LAW

Child bodies have an uncanny relationship with the law that even the basic terms of childhood reflect. While antebellum Americans would have used *infant* in everyday speech much the same way that we would now, legal writers used infancy to name a much longer stage of special status under the law. An early alternative for the category of the *minor*, the term *infant* was generally used to classify subjects under the age of either eighteen or twenty-one years old as holding different rights and duties than adult subjects.[9] Yet, by modern categories of age and even by the term's informal use at the time, the legal writing that emerges from this convention—in which phrases such as "infant females, at the age of sixteen"[10] or "if the infant be a farmer" were commonplace[11]—feels like catachresis. The insistence that a twenty-year-old has less in common with a twenty-two-year-old than with a toddler or that notion that an infant might sometimes stand, plow a field, or read Latin likewise seem almost bizarrely disproportionate. The disjuncture of these images arises in part from the implied binary between infant and adult, in which maturity arrives all at once, but it also stems from a more basic break in how the law conceives of age. While *infancy* used informally summons up the deeply physical dependency of a subject unable to walk or perhaps even to sit unsupported, the parameters of legal infancy try to treat the details of the child body as though they were largely irrelevant to its classification. Instead, *infancy* stipulates bodily difference without permitting bodily presence.

Infant draws on the word's origins, *in-fans*, or non-speaking, to name an imposed silence, a declaration that the speech of a minor could not properly be recognized in court as the sign of intention or testimony.[12] As an 1835 analytical dictionary explains, legally, "a child is said to be an Infant as long as it is presumed to be unable to *speak* for itself in a Court of Justice."[13] Thus, within the realm of law, a phase that is more commonly aligned with biological development has come to index a set of absent or cancelled voices. Though practical nuances have always existed and state laws did make provisions for younger marriage or younger criminal responsibility, the speech of a twenty-year-old witness was theoretically grouped first with that of a three-year-old, no matter how physically different their capabilities might be. The uniform silence imposed on these varied bodies, however, also points to the law's refusal to abstract civic identities from child subjects. In this constructed omission of child voices, the law thus traces the outline of a physicality that it was reluctant to acknowledge more directly.

It is the sense that children's bodies do not work like adult bodies that drives the exclusion of children from the public sphere. Although legal infancy is a status apparently uninterested in distinguishing the details of how a newborn's body might differ from that of a post-pubescent, its rationale relies on the idea that the actions done by a child body are not a reliable guide to the child mind. William Blackstone's *Commentaries on the Laws of England*, a 1760s treatise on British common law and the central source text for antebellum law, distinguishes infancy from adulthood in criminal cases by emphasizing the difference between *will* and *act*. A crime must represent both a *vicious will* and a *vicious act*, but infants cannot comprehend their actions well enough to be responsible for them.[14] Blackstone writes, "Where there is no discernment, there is no choice; and where there is no choice, there can be no act of the will, . . . he therefore, that has no understanding, can have no will to guide his conduct."[15] Classifying infancy alongside "idiocy, lunacy, and intoxication," he determines that the physical actions of children cannot be understood as representative of their thoughts. Instead, children were held to be bodies acting without will, or without will that was officially legible, so that the silence prescribed to infancy arises from their excessive embodiment. In these instances when "the will does not join with the act," Blackstone seeks to establish why children should be spared from criminal responsibility and the harshest of criminal punishments.[16] However, this interpretation also provides the logic by which children were excluded from a host of civil actions. As a group, he suggests, children were too bodily for the law to view their actions or their speech as a product of intent.

In a pronouncement that would persist in U.S. law throughout most of the nineteenth century, Blackstone determines that, because children's speech is not correlated with rational will, they may not generally enter into contract. He offers one exception: "It is generally true, than an infant can make no other contract that will bind him: yet he may bind himself to pay for his necessary meat, drink, apparel, physic, and such other necessaries; and, likewise for his good teaching and instruction, whereby he may profit himself, afterwards."[17] Essentially, children are not answerable for the contracts they make, but they are answerable to any apprenticeship contracts they may enter. As such, indenture contracts constitute a space of crossover between the child as a dependent body and as a potentially independent agent, or between infant and subject. While children are considered too irrationally physical for other agreements, they may enter an exchange of their freedom in return for bodily necessities. Though they cannot make decisions about properties or incomes, infants may (in theory, at least) decide who will provide for their bodies. Moreover, they can decide who will provide for their development into adulthood by providing "good teaching and instruction" that would eventually equip them with independent reason; they can provisionally enter into a contract, provided that it promises the training that would make their future selves able to enter contracts.

Blackstone's vision of the indenture as the only contract amenable to childhood thus falls into a form common to literary narrations of childhood, that of prolepsis. Blackstone's infant can consent to an indenture because its end result is an adult able to judge the process as worthwhile and therefore offer consent retrospectively. The maintenance of the child body is similarly able to bear a momentary scrutiny of the law if this maintenance points towards an adulthood with no such bodily encumberments. In other words, an indenture is valid if it offers a trajectory along which the child subject can develop into adulthood and, on the strength of that presumptive adulthood, the child earns a temporary ability to speak in the public sphere.

As several literary critics have argued, just such prolepsis guides the bildungsroman. In his study of the coming-of-age narrative and twentieth-century human rights law, Joseph Slaughter contends that, as a genre, the bildungsroman promises a resolution obvious from its outset, because it is expected that the protagonist will gradually assimilate into the social order of adulthood and thereby naturalize that order as inevitable. Slaughter frames the bildungsroman as striving toward utopian individualism, which provides "an idealistic scenario for the human personality to become the sovereign guarantor of its own development" while also prescribing the form that this individual sovereignty will take.[18] Franco Moretti's *Way of the World* imagines a similarly stacked deck, arguing that the structure of the British bildungsroman relies on an adulthood predestined to reach its fullest individual expression in the social world already surrounding it such that: "Self-development and integration are complementary and convergent trajectories, and at their point of encounter and equilibrium lies that full and double epiphany of meaning that is 'maturity.'"[19] The suspense of the story lies less in the arrival of a pre-determined adulthood than in the resolution of how the peculiarities of the private self will be revealed to have their own niche in the social order.

The faith shown in both indenture and the coming-of-age narratives that the private subject will inevitably reconcile with the social order has long been part of liberal individualism's promise that individual success will be seamlessly integrated into the greater good. However, this presumption that personal trajectories of growth will naturally come into accord with one another also relies on and reinforces a shared reliance on the biological as a guarantor that not only is maturity coming, but that it comes in uniform ways.[20] If Blackstone considers subjects under twenty-one to be too bodily to have a recognizable will, he also treats the physical development of the body as both a marker of development toward adult disembodiment and as proof that this second growth toward citizenship is unavoidable. For instance, the physical changes of puberty, for Blackstone, signal the arrival of a new kind of criminal responsibility but also cast the coming of that responsibility as a natural process.[21] Similarly, the momentum of the bildungsroman is partly borrowed from the biological trajectory toward physical, chronological adulthood. The developing body provides the medium through which a host of less-material changes are captured and expressed, while traces of the body itself are gradually erased and replaced with signs of maturity that are intrinsically bound up in the public sphere, such as marriage or property.

That not all bodies were permitted to mature into transparency, whether because they were marked by race, gender, class, or any other measure of difference, therefore acts as another way of explaining that not all subjects were eligible for a trajectory toward civic maturity. This exclusion has longed been paired with a matching limitation in the protagonists who are eligible for a coming-of-age narrative as it has most conventionally been defined, who may sometimes be female but is rarely a person of color or anyone who begins life as a poor worker and who remains that way.[22] The promise that all measures of development will be in accord—that the growing body subtends a developing mind and that that developing mind, in turn, demands an accordingly increased social standing with an attendant increase in wealth—interprets the child body as only the manifest sign of a longer teleology toward a capitalist and civically capable maturity. By largely avoiding protagonists who are not upwardly mobile or who are denied full rights as adults, coming-of-age narratives are able to preserve this sense of developmental synchronicity.

Though the indenture contract takes the same formal logic as the coming-of-age narrative, they have historically extended to encompass a much wider set of subjects. Apprenticeship was a common enough start in the early and mid-eighteenth century for affluent tradesmen, merchants, and the male bourgeois in general. Through the early nineteenth century, as I will discuss, apprenticeship gradually moved closer to this model and away from any real association with personal or economic development, even as its form continued to rely on that proleptic development. Where the traditions of the coming-of-age narrative largely exclude the subjects who would have been excluded from the rights of full adulthood, the indenture contract came to use closely related forms to imagine the maturation of precisely those subjects who were predominantly left out of literature.

As social historian Viviana Zelizer observes, though, increasing industrialization during the antebellum period created demand for an alternative model of child labor.[23] Unlike the longer term and, at least putatively, more skilled positions available to apprentices, factory owners called for an untrained and relatively mobile workforce of children. Many state courts met this demand by weakening the requirements for parental oversight of contracts and increasingly recognized children as economic agents able to negotiate contracts for themselves. This shift to wage-labor occurred unevenly, with white children moving rapidly into these new positions and apprenticeships disproportionately remaining with poor, Black children—namely, the children who would be less eligible for court protection.[24] It is true that larger-scale industrialists may have found greater profit in a more mobile workforce of white children, whose high turnover made workplace abuses more difficult for the law to restrain. However, for child workers who fell outside of the comparatively sheltered status of whiteness and therefore at a distance from even these meager legal comforts, the more permanent status of apprentice gave employers both stability and a workforce who could not easily protest their conditions, a situation that Xiomara Santamarina has described as the "pernicious ways in which 'free' labor could racially immobilize all black workers."[25] Where white child laborers might have suffered from their new designation as a relatively disposable workforce, African American apprentices were given no illusion of the social mobility that indenture once promised. In lieu of narratives of development, apprenticeship acted in practice as a bare exchange of labor for moment-to-moment sustenance.

CONSENT AS A MATTER OF FORM

Wilson and Apess's work participates in a long legal conversation, but their invocation of the law is creative rather than precisely technical. That is not to say that these authors do not treat the law seriously, rather that they remain agnostic about whether the word of the law will correspond with their realities and, more to the point, they treat the authority of the law as situational or even optional. Their invocations of law focus on the ways that indenture law contains a central fiction itself—that the children bound by indentures consent to them. Playing on this fiction allows Wilson and Apess to recreate legal authority itself as a fiction, one that may be convenient or unavoidable for their protagonists but that holds no inherent truth.

Much of Wilson's novel follows the conventional expectations of apprenticeship indenture. Her hero is abandoned by her parents and in need of a new home. Wilson tracks the excessive violence of the Bellmonts and the unreasonable amounts of labor that they demand as well as complaints more specific to apprenticeship: that her clothing is "poor and scanty" and does not include "Sunday attire,"[26] that her schooling was stopped at the age of nine,[27] and that her lodgings were dark and "unfinished."[28] Similarly, the gifts that Frado receives on her departure from the Bellmonts, in lieu of wages, reflect the traditional set of clothes, cash, and a Bible that indentures had once promised apprentices but in diminished form: she receives a "silver half dollar" and "one decent dress, without any superfluous accompaniments" from the Bellmonts, and a Bible from a more sympathetic Bellmont daughter.[29] Compare these gifts, for instance, with the indenture with which I began this chapter in which Cynthia Barnes is promised "two good suits of Cloths proper and suitable for such person and a Bible."[30] Frado's disappointment hinges on the belief that these items are not charitable gifts but payment she has earned.

Despite the importance of indenture in Frado's life, Wilson avoids writing about it directly. In fact, one reason that indenture has received relatively little attention in *Our Nig* may be that the idea of such an arrangement only enters the text through retrospection and, even then, is presented almost explicitly as fictitious. Late in her time with the Bellmonts, when she is approximately sixteen or seventeen, Frado considers her chances at either escaping from or killing the abusive Mrs. Bellmont, whom she refers to as "Mrs. B." With practical concerns and the intervention of an "overruling Providence" preventing these options, Frado "finally decide[s] to stay contentedly through her period of service, which would expire when she was eighteen years of age."[31] This set "period of service" is mentioned causally, as though it has been an established feature in Frado's life for the entire text. In fact, it is the only reference to any formal constraints on her labor, appearing to reference a contract whose existence Wilson has already made improbable. The moment that this arrangement might have been made—when Frado's mother, Mag, first leaves her at the Bellmonts—Mag lies to both child and family, claiming that she will return for her child after an errand. Frado, for her part, continues to believe that her mother will return for the first full year of her time with the Bellmonts, only gradually realizing that she has been abandoned.[32]

Wilson's exclusion of the indenture when it might be expected to appear and her reference to it when indenture was on the verge of being irrelevant, as I argue, forces readers to pause and retrospectively reconsider what they know about Frado's life. In particular, by presenting Frado as actively choosing to abide under an indenture that remained invisible for most of its duration, Wilson pushes us to rethink how and when Frado's will does appear. While it is never in doubt that Frado has needs and desires, Wilson withholds direct knowledge of her protagonist's thoughts while she is a child. The only point at which a first-person pronoun appears in the body of the text, rather than just in chapter titles, corresponds roughly to Frado's reaching twenty-one and full adulthood.[33] Before that point, Wilson provides no direct knowledge of Frado's desires, stipulating that Frado's willpower exists without making it fully visible.

The determination to live is the clearest and sometimes the only motivation that Wilson offers, as she carefully intertwines Frado's wishes with her physical wellbeing. If her contract to the Bellmonts is unofficial or unfair, she nonetheless seems to have to accept its terms, deciding to remain "contentedly" until she reaches eighteen, in part because she questions her ability to take care of her own basic needs if she does not do so—a decision, in other words, so predicated on indirect physical duress that it is difficult to muster evidence of any definite agency.[34] Priscilla Wald has suggested that Wilson makes it hard to sense agency at all, writing that "Frado is possessed, internalizing a prescripted identity, through which the Bellmont family break the mischievous child in spirit as well as body."[35] In Wald's reading, this overwriting of Frado is so pervasive that "her one gesture toward active resistance is itself authored by Mr. Bellmont,"[36] who worries that she is "looking sick" and "cannot endure beatings" anymore and thereby inspires her to resist Mrs. B.'s attempt at whipping her for sake of her health.[37]

Yet the link between body and mind is not only negative. *Our Nig* is permeated with signs of Frado's individual and inextinguishable will, reframing agency as being as inborn as any of her physical traits. The reader's first glimpse of Frado begins with her beauty but quickly blurs that beauty into mental determination; she is, Wilson writes, "a beautiful mulatto, with long, curly black hair, and handsome roguish eyes, sparkling with an exuberance of spirit almost beyond restraint."[38] Her spirit is not reducible to the sparkle in her eyes, nor is it separate from her physical being. It is also not limited to Frado. The coupling of will and flesh also resonates in the side plot of Jane Bellmont's marriage plans, a strand of the novel that works through the troubles of child agency and contract in a far-removed octave: Pressured to marry her rich suitor over her beloved suitor, Jane registers her fettered will through her bodily illness, until her father "bade her not make herself sick; he would see that she was not compelled to violate her free choice in so important a transaction."[39] With Mr. Bellmont's admission that "a free, voluntary choice was of such importance to one of her health," Wilson makes clear that the link between physical needs and consent is not the product of racialization but rather appears as a property of human will in general.[40]

Harkening back to the physical roots of infancy, this framing of embodied agency permits both a powerful critique of the vision of personhood as economic agency and, perhaps more importantly, a means of preserving Frado's will in the midst of her coercion. Emphasizing that Frado knows what she wants (even if the reader does not) might threaten to mask the coercion of her situation under the veneer of consent, whether because of her teenaged decision to remain "contentedly" already mentioned or even the moment when a much younger Frado "resolved to tarry" with the Bellmonts despite the narrator's promise that she "would not hesitate to wander away should she decide to."[41] In these moments, Wilson seems to be focusing on Frado's ability to make choices, even when Wilson also underlines that Frado has no real alternatives.

Far from suggesting that Frado agrees to her own oppression, Wilson is instead more fundamentally troubling the terms of consent. Though the two do overlap, Wilson's version of a will that must be stipulated but remains opaque exists in imperfect alignment with the encapsulated and knowable moment of consent, as its epistemological standing in the text is carefully kept at the level of private truth. Frado's status as "a wild, frolicky thing," to borrow her mother's half-marveling lament, speaks to a will pointing in multiple directions at once, a quality that cannot be questioned but is so unrestrainable that it refuses to be channeled into a single, instrumentalizable resource.[42] Reiterated later as "the spark of playfulness [that] could remain amid such constant toil" as a result of "her natural temperament," this essential source of self is precisely that which thwarts the Bellmonts' disciplinary efforts to control it or, in other words, is aligned precisely with the public illegibility of legal infancy that cannot be captured by contract.[43]

Similarly, the language describing Frado's first entrance into the Bellmonts's home carefully establishes the existence of Frado's will but refuses to presume that either she or her readers can understand it. We are told that Mag's order to go into the Bellmont home "seemed a novel request, but she consented."[44] Clearly, some type of decision has been made. Yet, as the narrator immediately continues, the act simply cannot be analyzed further, for "why the impetuous child entered the house, we cannot tell."[45] Where, in a true contract, consent would mark a moment of understanding between two parties on the strength of which mutual understanding each is then made accountable to the other, the choice made here is fundamentally inexplicable and, so, signals no possible establishment of a bond. All that is visible is that Frado, even as a small child, possesses a will, but the reader is allowed to feel no insight into it, much less intimacy through it.

Such privacy is perhaps a meager comfort, but, slender as it is, it reserves a type of personhood for Frado outside of the logic of economic agency that is also more than a patronizing indulgence of a child able to be governed and assimilated. Rather than writing a young subject that is transparent to adult scrutiny, a self whose intent may be grasped and interrogated in a reductive opposition between consent and compulsion, Wilson sidesteps the absolutism of either classification by writing a child whose interiority is not on exhibition. By the bracketing of the origin of Frado's will as unknowable and its existence as unquestionable, the agency behind her decisions can be recognized without demanding that those particular decisions be perfectly separate from physical necessity. Frado's childish decisions may not be transparently rational, may not be free of duress or of bodily need, and therefore may not be those of a liberally imagined subject, but they nonetheless demand ethical recognition as being those of a subject. This ability to register a choice made in isolation as an act of will, rather than requiring there to be an agreement between two subjects, is a model that indenture can offer but contract cannot.

In contrast to Frado's largely unspoken apprenticeship, Apess's invocation of indenture is far more explicit but it is equally concerned with the stipulated consent on which indentures rely. When the five-year-old William is bound to the Furman family, Apess provides readers with a full account of his indenture's terms. Despite these details, Apess writes about indenture with an air of unreality:

> According to the spirit of the indentures, if I mistake not, I was to have so much instructions as to be able to read and write, and at the expiration of the term of my apprenticeship they were to furnish me with two suits of clothes. They used me with utmost kindness—I had enough to eat and to wear—and every thing in short to make me comfortable. According to their agreement, when I had reached the sixth year, they sent me to school—this they continued to do for six successive winters, in which time I learned to read and write, so that I might be understood. This was all the instruction of the kind I ever received. But I desire to be truly thankful to God for this—I cannot make you sensible of the amount of benefit I have received from it.[46]

The terms of the document are apparently present but Apess reminds us that the document itself very much is not. At best, we have "the spirit of the indentures," but Apess also tells us that he might also "mistake" that spirit and have nothing correct. His uncertainty is a given since these are the memories of an adult man about what he may or may not have been told at the age of five. Apess, though, underlines also a more basic problem. At the time when the document scripting his life was written and agreed to, William could neither read nor write; part of what he is promised in his apprenticeship is literacy. We are limited to the spirit of the indenture because it is the indenture itself that promises to let him read the text.

What Apess provides in this description of what his indenture might have contained is closer to the silhouette of a legally binding agreement than a description of one. Apess, and therefore his readers, cannot know what was in the agreement, but we can know that there was such an agreement. In one sense, Apess is marking indenture as a space of personal estrangement and failed communication; the indenture is "their agreement" rather than his, and the education that was to make him "be understood" leaves Apess declaring that he "cannot make [us] sensible of the benefit" that education has provided. On the other hand, Apess still cares enough about the logistical details of the indenture to catalogue them, even while he is unable to vouch for the accuracy of those details.

This invocation of the law without precise reference to its content is key to how Apess approaches and uses the law more broadly. When William is around the age of eleven, the Furmans sell his indenture to a judge on the pretext that William is too much trouble. Apess notes that the judge was no great respecter of law and that "he fulfilled only one item of the transferred indentures, and that was work," quickly reselling William when the judge sees him as too much trouble.[47] While William understandably feels abandoned, Apess suggests that the problem is not the lack of adult feeling for the child but a failure of legal forms. He recalls that he absolutely did not want to leave the household, but that "if my consent had been solicited as a matter of form, I should not have felt so bad."[48] The idea of "consent as a matter" of form is deeply strange from the framework of traditional contracts—either one is electing freely and rationally to a choice or one is not consenting at all—but for indenture, the idea is commonplace. Children could and often did sign indentures, but their signatures were rarely required; it was simply seen as a nicety. Similarly, Apess seems to accept that his younger self had no actual influence over the situation but suggests that the illusion of agreement still matters. The holders of his indenture do not need to listen his thoughts, but they should act as if they do. When an apprentice can pretend to consent and the parties to the indenture can pretend to care, Apess suggests that indenture works as a kind of game with rules.

The value of indenture for Apess lies in this fictiveness. Apprenticeship indentures are written around a consent that it postulates but does not include. Because they work by formal rules rather than sincerity, these rules are eligible for him to use. While Wilson emphasizes how much society erases Frado's desires, Apess tells us clearly what his younger self is thinking and feeling in order to emphasize the disconnect between his desires and the dictates of his indentures. Both writers emphasize the gap between the legal documents structuring their social world and the individual wishes of their protagonists. The alienation of children of color is hardly unusual in antebellum literature, or history, but when a coming-of-age narrative marks the guiding trajectory of a protagonist's life as beginning with an unreliable formality, it changes the meaning of maturation. If a child only acts like they condone their place in the world because, as we are reminded, they must in order to survive, that child's growth will not be a growth into society but a development in the midst of and despite society.

DEFINING LIVES BETWEEN PRIVATE AND PUBLIC

The historical archives of indenture also reflect an ambivalence about how much the documents think they know about the children they bind and how much of that knowledge can enter the public sphere. For instance, in 1834 a Pennsylvanian child named Mariah Elizabeth Perry was entered into a labor contract with one Humphrey Dillon, a man whose profession is not named in her indenture but whom contemporary records indicates was an innkeeper in Bedford County.[49] The contract, signed by Dillon and two county officials titled "overseers of the Poor" and witnessed by two justices of the peace, identifies Mariah as a "female of color" and states that she is henceforth bound to work for Dillon, his heirs, and his agents. In exchange, she is promised "sufficient meat, drinks, apparel, lodging, and washing" as well as "the customary freedom dues to the amount of at least twelve dollars" at the time of release. The indenture was set to run from the date of the contract—May 28, 1834—until October 3, 1850, a date the contract text notes will also mark her being eighteen years old. Barring the calculation implicit in these dates and the ambiguous sign that Mariah's own signature is not among the marks on the contract,[50] no other aspect of the contract indicates that the laborer in question is a two-year-old child with all of the productive potential of a two-year-old child.

Instead, the indenture's portrait reveals little about Mariah as she is, using the majority of its some two hundred words to describe who this child will be: an unfree laborer, a consumer of certain resources, and an eventually free woman with twelve dollars to her name.

That this last image of maturity and of Mariah setting off with the twelve dollars of her freedom dues has a stronger presence in the document than Mariah's reality at the time of writing, an unprotected toddler bound into a system that was singularly poor at enforcing its promises, points to the concentrated futurity of the text—a futurity that encompasses both the ongoing future of a growing body in need of regular food and care and the future perfect of the emergent adult Mariah. As a result, it minimizes Mariah's status as a physically dependent child to treat her as a pure agent of labor; the indenture also attempts to manage her bodily integration into adulthood. Her body's future physical needs are explicitly built into the future adult, eligible for freedom from bondage. Although the adult emerging from this contract is framed as a fully independent agent on the market, she retains an explicit history of a much more embodied self.[51]

The difference between an indenture for apprenticeship and the contract ideally imagined by law is thus a difference in how the two agreements register the temporality of the people involved. Contract has historically been understood along two primary axes: first, as a "pure" (i.e., disembodied) exchange between the wills of two rational subjects and, second, as a projection from present intent to future action. As Thomas Hobbes's foundational theory of contract in *Leviathan* (1651) states, it relies accordingly on a syntax of intent:

> Signes of Contract, are either *Expresse*, or *by Inference*. Expresse, are words spoken with understanding of what they signifie: And such words are either of the time *Present*, or *Past;* as, *I Give*, *I Grant*, *I have Given*, *I have Granted*, *I will that this be yours:* Or of the future; as, *I will Give*, *I will Grant:* which words of the future, are called PROMISE.[52]

This "promise" thus rests on a chain beginning with the understanding and will of the contract writer—Hobbes continues on to gloss "signs by inference" as any implication of the text that "sufficiently argues the will of the Contractor"—and extending into an imagined future.[53] The future tense of contract in Hobbes's account, though, carries a stronger weight than the futurity of common speech. While informal statements about a plan bear no obligation or, in Hobbes's terms, transfer no right, setting down a future in contract enshrines it:

> In Contracts, the right passeth, not onely where the words are of the time Present, or Past; but also where they are of the Future: because all Contract is mutuall translation, or change of Right; and therefore he that promiseth onley, because he hath already received the benefit for which he promiseth, is to be understood as if he intended the Right should pass: for unlesse he had been content to have his words so understood, the other would not have performed his part first.[54]

Contract, in this reading, works to stabilize two variables, the difference between two individual wills and the space between present and future. It acts as a "mutuall translation" between two understandings and two sets of interests, as well as guaranteeing that acts will have the agreed-upon consequences. It binds two subjects to a common narrative of benefits to be given and received in a certain order.

Apprenticeship indenture complicates this attempt at a shared projection because, though Hobbes accounts for the instability of time and the need to reconcile two views of the world, he takes for granted that the individuals themselves will be stable. Indenture, on the other hand, sets out to take a subject and transform him or her into a new, or significantly changed, subject. As a result, even though standards differed greatly by state and era whether minors should sign these contracts themselves, the legal standard applied was that the contract would not be binding on the child if it does not benefit their development.[55] Where Hobbes's view of contract assumes that the necessary translation is from one agent of contract to another, indenture takes up the additional task of mediating between infant and adult subject, or between the child that Mariah is and the adult that she will become. If the contract fails to be an agreement that the adult eventually emerging from the indenture *would have* agreed to, then it is potentially void, because it fails to translate between the child who is immediately party to the contract and their adult self who will be capable of sanctioning the contract. A good contract, he argues, is one that makes the child's consent continuous with the adult's will.

To demonstrate their benefit to the child subject, indentures provide their own version of a coming-of-age narrative, setting out a projection of how the child's life will unfold. For example, the 1817 indenture of Isaac Pennell Jr., a boy living in Radnor, Pennsylvania, who was most likely about twelve at the time of signing, explains his apprenticeship in terms of exchange between Isaac's labor and his master Joseph Dunn's investment in Isaac's future life. Isaac, we are told, will "[Dunn's] secrets keep, his lawful commands everywhere readily obey," nor will he travel without permission, marry, or any other way damage Dunn's household. In return, Isaac will be granted professional standing by being "taught or instructed . . . in the trade or mystery of a farmer." Isaac's promised road to adulthood is, like Mariah's, enabled by provisions for food and shelter, but, unlike Mariah, he is also promised schooling in increments of "two months a year." The adult Isaac projected to exit the indenture will be a man with schooling and a trade, as well as "two good suits of Clothes."[56] All in all, this portrait of the adult Pennell is far more complete than the child Isaac's , because as a farmer and property owner, he possesses qualities that can be recognized by the law; the earlier Isaac possessed only infancy.

Yet it is more critical that the indenture manage the continuity of Isaac as a subject even as it promises these changes. While the adult Pennell is given most description in the document, the contract is nonetheless structured around his infant counterpart. While Isaac did leave an official mark of consent on the contract with a slightly lop-sided X, even if he had not, the adults authorizing the contract on his behalf—in this case, his father, Isaac Pennell Sr.—would have been able to do so only by merit of his status as an infant. For the indenture to have purchase and for that X to receive a socially agreed upon meaning, it must mediate between these two stages, tracing the arc of Isacc's physical development into an arc toward consent.

The curve of aging toward a pre-set adulthood also worked to cover greater gaps than that shown between Pennell Jr. and Pennell Sr. As an early function of the welfare state, indentures also imagined continuities from children positioned further outside the social order that the contracts supported. Oliver Gautier, another boy who lived not far from Isaac Pennell, was indentured in 1785 to a local merchant with the proviso that he was "a Minor and a Stranger here."[57] He, too, leaves a mark alongside the signatures of the adult officials, but the consent he musters is clearly under constraint even within the document itself. Gautier's co-signers, two "Justices of the Peace" and six men identified as "Managers of the House of Employment," are identified as the active agents of the indenture; it is they who, according to the text, "have put Oliver Gautier" into his apprenticeship in a convergent policing of poverty and displaced youth. In this context, Oliver's mark does not register as his will, because there is no pretense that he could have refused—particularly because, without the literacy promised by the apprenticeship, his addition to the document reflects nothing about his understanding of the document. Instead, the mark stands in only to testify to Oliver's physical presence. Like Apess's "consent as a matter of form," it tells us that he was there, that he participated in the agreement in some undefined way, and little else.

The coupling work that the indenture does to link this "Minor and Stranger" with an uninterpretable signature to the socialized adult self with full signature is a process of norming a potentially deviant subject. Apprenticeship might give Oliver a place to belong, but it also clearly works to fit him into a preexisting slot. The coercion inscribed in Oliver's contract makes more explicit what was also true of Isaac's indenture to become a farmer. When they appear as pre-printed forms with spaces left for names, gendered pronouns, the details of profession and degree of education, indentures are, quite literally, fill-in-the-blank interpretations of maturity, with little other room for variation in the coming of age. Under indenture, Oliver must work to mature out of his status as an infant "stranger" in a way that Isaac perhaps need not, but the distance between the two indentures is a matter of degree rather than a fundamental difference. Within the archival document, though, the only trace that remains of Oliver is the X that he signed; even as the text tries to script his maturation, the child himself remains outside. Instead, the central subject of the indenture is the projected character whom Oliver is tasked with becoming.

REWRITING ADULTHOOD

The cypher of these lingering Xs provides a framework for thinking about Wilson and Apess's unstable emergences into adulthood and what this adulthood means to these authors' understandings of the social world. Looking at these signatures from the present, we know that a child was present and performed an act that would be interpreted as consent. We know that this performance of agreement was largely irrelevant to the legal force of the indenture and was often excluded entirely. We also know that, even if apprentices' signatures had been required, the children signing frequently did so under circumstances that left them with few or no other options. In that context, the X that we see is a reminder of an obvious absence. A child was present, but none of his or her desires have been captured in the public record beyond a putative desire to not starve. The energy of the indenture as it appears in law and most literary texts is to narrate around this omission into a future assimilation. When Wilson and Apess instead center the omission by underlining that it is purely fictive or purely formal, they are also changing the nature of the bildungsroman. The trajectories of Frado and William's maturation differ, but they share the sense that a stipulated consent to society changes the obligations between a society and an individual.

For Wilson, Frado's indenture provides a framework for demanding reparative care. As *Our Nig* unfolds, Frado leaves the Bellmont family after turning eighteen, but after working through the summer becomes too "thoroughly sick" to continue.[58] Because she has been left unable to afford medicine or even a room for herself, Frado falls back on the only social ties that she has left, the Bellmonts. This claim of intimacy is clearly a matter of last resort for Frado and explicitly outside the bounds of even the most generous indenture. Still, the reasoning that Wilson offers to explain why her former capturers should take in her adult self draws from the notion that employing indentured labor creates a responsibility for physical needs. As Frado puts it, she was reluctant to ask, "yet she felt sure they owed her a shelter and attention, when disabled."[59] The commonsense impulse that the Bellmonts "owed" her and continued to owe her a basic physical welfare, despite her departure from their household, stems from Wilson's ability to invoke indenture, rather than wage labor, as the basis for labor agreements. Frado's impulse is to say that her illness cannot be privatized, which is to say that it cannot be reduced to her own personal burden, because her health had been a part of her projected agreement with the Bellmonts. This argument hinges on the assertion that the employers of children must take on responsibility not just for wages but for food, clothing, and medicine. Wilson sanctions this belief by generalizing it to the town, noting that after a second period of Frado being unable to work, "all felt that the place where her declining health began, should be the place of relief; so they applied once more for a shelter" from the Bellmonts.[60]

Such an assignment of responsibility echoes the basic tendency of apprenticeship to find a family able to bear the otherwise public cost of supporting a community member, but the tendency to narrativize the physical toil of labor also reflects the temporal difference that indenture makes. Contract registers a moment of agreement and flattens the process of labor extraction back to that moment, but indenture evolves in order to narrate a continuity between the child who enters an apprenticeship and the legal adult who emerges. Indenture thus is able to track longer-term physical effects and is able to register when the physical cost of an agreement continues past the end of the agreement itself. Frado's "declining health began" with identifiable agents, and the Bellmonts continue to bear responsibility despite the nominal close of the apprenticeship. It is here that Wilson's use of indenture law to critique the terms of adult labor more broadly begins to emerge. Although Frado sets out in the market after turning eighteen as an apparently free contract laborer, her experience of work is interwoven with an accumulating cost to her health. She repeatedly sets out in new trades, only to repeatedly become disabled in ways that make it impossible to continue in them. With each iteration, Wilson returns to the notion that the Bellmonts are still ultimately the ones to be blamed.

As the rest of Frado's life unfolds, these revisions to the relationship between worker and employer begin to resonate with a reimagination of the proto-welfare system more broadly. As Frado's disabilities leave her intermittently unable to work, she moves from the Bellmonts to the town-subsidized care of two women and then to what the text's appendix—a series of testimonials endorsing the author's virtue—calls the "County House,"[61] and is eventually forced to place her son, George, in the same institution while she sells hair dye.[62] From her own indenture to her need to place George in parallel circumstances, Frado is continually forced to reckon with the public nature of her daily existence. This is not to say that the same is not true for people like the Bellmonts, who just as clearly rely on the labor provided by Frado's indenture. Frado is, in fact, quite cutting about the notion that any of this assistance is selflessly given, describing one family that her adult self stays with as having "principle enough to be willing to earn the money a charitable public disburses."[63] Frado is also upfront about the misery of her needs being so explicitly a part of the public sphere, complaining of "the unpleasant charities of the public" and stating her determination to be self-supporting.[64]

Although Frado sets out in the market with every intention of participating in free contract labor, her experience of work is interwoven with an accumulating cost to her health. The urge to be productive is harmful for Frado, because, as Wilson writes, she so often tried to work *as if* she were the disembodied laborer of liberal theory, so that "many times her hands wrought when her body was in pain; but the hope that she might yet help herself, impelled her on."[65] The damage builds until she is unable to work at all and must rely on the town to pay for her treatment. For Wilson, the source of the harm is work itself, noting that "Frado was anxious to keep up her reputation for efficiency, and often pressed far beyond prudence" until "she entirely gave up work, and confessed herself thoroughly sick."[66] Frado thus experiences labor as fundamentally tied to her experience of her body and as having effects of far longer duration than conventional contract could register. Instead of her contracts operating as a fleeting sale of her labor, Frado's work appears to linger in the pain that she experiences. Wilson takes care to narrate what she terms Frado's "weary sickness" as having a history of its own.[67] Though it intensifies after every job she undertakes, following a particularly acute attack, Mrs. B. tries to blame the whole of Frado's condition on her most recent employer. Responding to a doctor's description of Frado as "all broken down," Mrs. B. responds, "Yes, it was at Mrs. Moore's . . . all this was done," only to be corrected by the physician that "it was commenced longer ago."[68] The status of the Bellmonts as the origin point of Frado's illness, of being what Wilson writes was "the place where her declining health began," anchors Frado's disability as a continuation of her early mistreatment.

The difference made by reading these episodes through indenture is two-fold. First, the narrative force of indenture in its ability to bridge between a present apprentice and an imagined adult emerging from that apprenticeship enables Wilson's understanding of labor as something that shapes a subject and can linger with them far beyond the time of the labor itself. Second, and perhaps more important, the recognition that work could result in such long-term and intimate changes to the worker also resurrects indenture's previous assertions that physical care was a basic tenet of employment. What Frado receives from the town is only what she first demands from the Bellmonts—food, lodging, and medicine—all of which formed the basic expectations of apprentice masters. As Wilson describes it, when the Bellmonts refuse to take in Frado a second time, there is "one only resource; the public must pay the expence."[69] The failing that Frado's town is compensating for, as a result, moves from a presumptive failure on Frado's part to an inadequacy of Frado's employers, a reframing that is even more forceful given that the Bellmonts' indenture was part of this welfare system from the beginning.

The deprivatization of the apprentice's body that is necessary for this shift can be one more way of controlling and dehumanizing subjects like Frado, but a return to Wilson's legal framings changes the significance of physical references. The nature of that indentured body is far from a straightforward object. Recall, for instance, the possibility of the sixteen-year-old infant plowman classed beside the toddler as equally incapacitated. What indenture records of the body is only the most indirect and notional reference; the flesh is recorded as a trace, not as an object eligible for scrutiny. The heft of indenture law is that the actions of the infant body cannot be separated from legal agreements, but that the two also can never be equated. Wilson's point is that Frado is the sole possessor of her body, but since she has been injured while working for her town and more pointedly for the Bellmonts, she does not hold sole responsibility for her bodily wellbeing. Frado's acquiescence to her indenture was always most immediately about her own basic needs, and what she expects of the town and of her readers in return is help meeting those needs.

While Wilson uses indenture to write the body into the public sphere, Apess destabilizes the public sphere by focusing on how little indenture captures of personal interiority. Having had his consent to indenture reduced to an empty form, William stops internalizing any contract. As a result, Apess recasts the social contracts into agreements that are as superficial and fleeting as any labor contract—a tactical mode of survival that undercuts conventional signs of success. As Peter Bayers argues, the culmination of William's personal growth has little to do with "material success or self-aggrandizement."[70] Instead, Apess focuses on how his development gave him the skills to move through an unfriendly world.

Soon after escaping from the abusive household to which he was bound after the Furmans, William enters a new contract when men recruiting for the army ply him with alcohol and cash. On the run from his former master and drunk, Apess writes that he "had a cockade fastened on my hat, and went off in fine spirits for my uniform."[71] In the same moment, though, he writes that he "could not think why [he] should risk [his] life and limbs in fighting for the white man who had cheated my forefathers out of their land."[72] The contradiction between his "fine spirits" upon enlisting and what is, at its mildest, apathy toward U.S. militarism makes it impossible for readers to gauge whether he has truly agreed or if the "fine spirits" are liquor rather than emotion. Either way the outward and only reliable signs of the contract—having the right clothes and properly decorated hat—align with William's willingness to follow the letter of the contract without particular attention to its intent.

Appropriately, when William is pushed into a combat role, he leans on the same technicalities of contract to try to make his way out of the army, inadvertently deserting based on a false belief that the law would allow it. Apess recalls that, "As I had only enlisted for a drummer, I thought that this change by the officer was contrary to law, and as the bond was broken, liberty was granted to me; therefore being heartily tired of a soldier's life, and having a desire to see my father once more, I went off very deliberately."[73] There is some irony in Apess's recollection of his teenaged innocence, but the logic is also fairly reasonable. For his part, William sees himself as bound only by the obligation of drumming, not of any more general service to the army. By contrast, the army's charge of desertion rests on a belief that enlisting is an emotional investment that has purchased William's loyalty and general submission rather than any particular action. William's reading of law does not have much effective power, but it allows him to rethink the terms under which he will accept belonging. Apess's critique of U.S.

imperialism invokes the quid pro quo logic of contract, arguing that "as long as our nation is debarred the privilege of voting for civil officers, . . . the government has no claim on our services"; any feelings come decidedly second to reading nationalism as a fair exchange of actions.[74]

Cynical pragmatism makes immediate sense in context of the U.S. government, but Apess's insistence on legal formality extends into his religious conversion as well. After he is denied a license to preach for the Methodist Episcopal Church, William declares his intention to join the Methodist Society instead and is accused of having lied about his beliefs when he joined the denomination. Apess counters with the distinctively legal reasoning that "as this [[denominational]] law was not continuous in its nature, whenever I ceased to be a member of that church, its binding and distinctive law, touching my person and my conduct became *dead*—it had no farther of future jurisdiction over me."[75] In other words, as long as William abides by church rules as a member, he is a member in good standing, and as soon he decides to leave, those rules have no claim over him.

Invoking legal formalism gives William mobility, because abiding by forms creates no lasting obligation on him as an individual. As an expression of freedom, it is severely constrained. Apess describes the first part of his life as a constant scramble to find new, more bearable ways of living day-to-day, and his assertion that he can come and go based on technicalities does not materially change his circumstances; he can decide he is allowed to leave the army, but the army can do much more to enforce its own perspective. However, the extra space that Apess maintains between himself and the people who hold power over him does preserve him from self-loathing. Compared with the child who had felt at home with the white Furmans but was terrified of Native people, the adult voice to which *A Son of the Forest* arrives is at least free to recognize and to resent racism and to demand better.[76] Financial stability and civic inclusion are not in Apess's future, but that is not the only stability he can reach.

AGE AND ENDINGS

At first reading, Frado and William's early lives appear strikingly singular. Diegetically, both protagonists are intensely isolated, and, extradiegetically, both texts fit uneasily into canonical genres. This, and the fact that my analysis hews relatively closely to Wilson and Apess's texts, could obscure the wider impact of their theorizations. But the idea of contract as an analogy for a child's entrance into the adult world has been a central argument in European and American philosophy since the time of John Locke. Wilson's deployment of indenture in the place of contract does more than document an unusual labor practice in New England; it opens a basic challenge to how we understand social bonds. Social contract theory posits that a nation is made up of a collection of voluntary members. Although both Jean-Jacques Rousseau and John Locke agree that birth into a society does not entail any obligation to that society, they also insist with equal strength that staying in a society indicates full agreement. Rousseau writes that "residence implies consent: to inhabit the territory is to submit to the sovereign."[77] In Locke's model, meanwhile, even "the very being of any one within the Territories of the Government" is enough to register as a "tacit consent" to that social contract.[78] While children are nominally free from public obligations, for adults, the fundamental need to occupy a space is enough to bind one to the local social order. Thus, coming of age stands as an act of endorsement for the world that a subject has aged into.

The model that emerges from Wilson and Apess gives us something closer to social indenture theory, which suggests an alternative relationship between a maturing subject and the people around her. A population shaped by her version of indenture inverts the presumption that involvement in a society reveals something about that person's beliefs while leaving her responsible for her own physical needs. For Wilson and Apess, participation in a community might mean nothing more than that someone was born into it and that they rely on it for survival, but it does not imply approval or even acceptance. Their revision allows for coming of age without assimilation. Social indenture theory speaks to the subjects who grow up with attachments to systems of power that they can never enter and, most importantly, grants these subjects the right to make demands on authority without reaffirming that authority's legitimacy. Indenture provides a language for having needs without having freedom, and these narratives differentiate between acting within the constraints of labor systems and having agreed to them. The common urge to see the coming-of-age narrative as a genre that ends in contentment, conformity, or complacency, or to equate the end of childhood as an emergence into society cannot hold for comings-of-age about subjects alienated by white supremacy. Moving between the markers of age that are social—money, occupation, and even the power to establish and protect one's family—were often practical impossibilities. Wilson and Apess give us endings that are unsettled and perhaps unsatisfying, but they also give us endings that are not entirely foreclosed by the world as it existed at the end of the texts. It is not clear what could happen next for Frado or William, which is terrifying and dangerous, but also leaves open a possibility for change.

CHAPTER 2

The Incorrigible Child

Juvenile Delinquency and the Fearful Rise of the Child Self

Ann has perhaps been one of the most troublesome subjects in the House, now and then evincing however a disposition to do well, but again would break forth in wickedness, the last very bad act was in stealing the matron's sweetmeats, and plotting to burn the female house.

—*Entry from the New York House of Refuge's juvenile prison records on Ann McCollister (Inmate #5), dated August 1, 1828*[1]

One peculiarity of the child's deportment remains yet to be told. The very first thing which she had noticed in her life, was—what?—not the mother's smile, responding to it, as other babies do, by that faint, embryo smile of the little mouth, remembered so doubtfully afterwards, and with such fond discussion whether it were indeed a smile. By no means! But that first object of which Pearl seemed to become aware was—shall we say it?—the scarlet letter on Hester's bosom!

—*Nathaniel Hawthorne,* The Scarlet Letter, *1850*[2]

Popular fears about ungovernable children in the early nineteenth century were unsurprisingly paired with demands that children be governed far more closely, the most immediate example of which is the development of juvenile delinquency as a category of discipline. The case of juvenile incarceration can appear unique or estranged from less obviously violent models of childhood. This exceptionalism—which holds the supposed wickedness of a child such as Ann McCollister as extreme or the isolation of the fictional Pearl as fundamental—is inseparable from the rhetoric that some children need imprisonment in the first place. However, it is also interwoven with popular theories of how the most privileged children were assimilated into society. Pearl's isolation—Hawthorne describes as her as possessing a "depth" that "lacked reference and adaption to the world into which she was born"—appears to have been cemented by a primal scene gone desperately wrong. In place of an emotional connection with her mother, in which Pearl might have echoed, "as other babies do," Hester's smiles, and so learn to share affect, Pearl's first social encounter occurs under the emblem of punishment. As Hawthorne describes, the spark of Pearl's affective life is the scarlet letter itself. It was a combination of layperson psychology and carceral thinking that banished Ann McCollister from free society and, at the same time, assured more affluent white parents that such a thing would never happen to their children.

During this time, an unlikely pair of genres—domestic parenting manuals and the records of newly founded juvenile prisons—joined in a project of re-imagining the child self to allow for this possibility of child criminality. The dual formation of the child self with the child criminal, however, is more than a quirk of antebellum child history. This newly independent conception of child character, when applied to affluent white children, worked to manage the contradictions between U.S. individualism and the dependency of childhood. By promising authority beyond physical force, it reassured the parents of these children that their parenting was enlightened and kind, rather than tyrannical. However, the same ideas insist that other childhoods can only be ruled by force. Such writing theorized the limits of whiteness and whether it could be molded into the body or stripped from it. These proto-psychological theories of child character help to define the reproductive limits of antebellum citizenship, estranging poor and immigrant children from child socialization and instead institutionalizing them indefinitely.

Specifically, I want to suggest that a legal construct from the early days of delinquency discourse, that of "the incorrigible child," frames this isolation as a problem of bodily interpretation. By the turn of the nineteenth century, incorrigibility marked a penal category tied to those people held to be the more fundamentally criminal. In William Blackstone's *Commentaries on the Laws of England*, the "incorrigible" criminal can be recognized either through "repetition of minuter offences" or "some one crime of deep malignity" and must be imprisoned without delay or clemency to prevent their "repeating perhaps the worst of villainies."[3] For antebellum juvenile law in particular, incorrigibility came to be an offense deemed in itself, labeling those children as existing beyond correction and, paradoxically, giving them over to unchecked state discipline.[4] In its wider meaning, however, the status of the incorrigible takes on a certain ambiguity from being declared beyond correction. The *Yale Literary Magazine* in 1847, for example, deploys "incorrigible" to describe not a recalcitrant child, but a geometric principle that cannot be disputed.[5] In this sense, the "incorrigible" takes on a specific epistemological standing based on the idea that some statements must be accepted as true. Grounded in the phenomenological experience of the body—scents, tastes, pains—the incorrigible assertion is one that, whether true or not, exists beyond interrogation by any other parties.[6] Under this model, criminalized children defy scrutiny because their bodies have been marked unreadable. Paired with growing anxiety over juvenile delinquency, incorrigibility maps a child self beyond adult comprehension.

This discursive investment in ungovernable children was accompanied by a demographic wave of children in northeastern cities. In the 1820s and 1830s, industrialization had increased urban populations of all ages, and child workers, useful in factories for hands able to fit the tight spaces of factory machines, were no exception. A boom in immigration also brought around three hundred thousand new arrivals to New York every year.[7] The immigrants who remained were, in the words of Walter Kamphoefner, disproportionately "young, single, and mobile."[8] Moreover, because states had responded to the need for short-term child labor in factories by allowing juvenile workers to make their own contracts without requiring parental oversight, many of the children in these cities were operating with an unprecedented degree of independence and mobility.[9] In New York, one of the most affected cities, the chief of police estimated in 1849 that ten thousand children lived in the streets.[10] While a fraction of these subjects were funneled into the public orphanages that proliferated between the 1830s and

1860s, a parallel discourse emerged from the penal system to define the social standing of these urban youth as criminal, justifying their confinement in prisons called "Houses of Refuge."[11]

Labelled with the newly popular term "juvenile delinquent," children in the city could be criminalized for having unstable housing or a home that was deemed unsuitable by authorities, or for participating in informal economies ranging from sex work to petty theft to picking up chips of dried horse manure to sell as fuel. Because time served in the House was regarded as rehabilitation rather than punishment, inmates were not given sentences of a specific length.[12] Instead, if inmates' behavior was deemed suitable and an opportunity was available, they left the institution by indenture into an apprenticeship or, more rarely, they were released to familial care. Otherwise, Houses had authority over their charges until they reached the age of majority, which was typically twenty-one for male subjects and eighteen for female. Prison advocates generally saw such confinement as a replacement for parental authority that they deemed inadequate or inappropriate, and so they directed prison discipline toward the reformation of individual character.[13] Immigrant children and the children of immigrant parents were particularly targeted by these early juvenile prisons. By some counts, children born outside the United States represented more than half of inmates in 1830 and, by 1850, Irish American children alone represented slightly more than half of the prison's population, while only twenty-eight percent of inmates had been born in the United States.[14]

The development of the special category of the criminal child required a reworking of both labels, reconciling the guilt attached to the former with the innocence attached to the latter. On one hand, the version of criminality that could encompass childhood's diminished agency called for a focus not on personal morality but rather on subjects formed by environmental determinism. On the other hand, to criminalize juvenile subjects is to imagine a child without attachment to the social order whose future they represent. Thus, instead of framing children as the natural property of the state, delinquency presents a set of young subjects who must be forced to belong and, in doing so, projects a set of eventual citizens explicitly coerced into their civic roles. Delinquency discourse instead abandons judgment of the personal character of the delinquent by imaging that character as being wholly inaccessible to others and therefore to disciplinary surveillance as well. Sovereignty under such a regime becomes an explicit assertion of power operating without fictions of consent and, in turn, generates a trajectory to adulthood for these subjects that is not a growth into the social contract but a static exclusion. Delinquency discourse, in other words, naturalizes the position of poor or immigrant children who have no legal adult roles available to grow into, categorizing them as subjects who can never be incorporated into the social order in order to justify their exclusion.

I approach the category of the incorrigible child by bringing together two distinct archives written from either side of the question, one that assumes deviance and the other that assumes its absence: records from the early years of New York's juvenile delinquency facilities and the popular genre of domestic manuals on child rearing. Despite the differences between their intents and venues, both discourses converge on the same question: by what means can one assert authority over an unformed subject and, more difficult still, from that foundational assertion, what paths exist to a socialized, adult citizenship? By reading these two archives in parallel, we find a conjunction of state sovereignty and everyday domestic life that moves beyond the common metaphors of paternalism and into the messy details of ushering a subject, often an unwilling one, from the bare life of infancy and into the possibility of civic life. In each set of texts, the attachment of sovereignty to the child subject relies on managing a balance between the projected interiority of the individual and the physical body born into a system of power. The uncertain civic status of children highlights this tension between narratives of sovereignty by bringing together fictions of citizenship by blood or birthplace and citizenship freely chosen. That the domestic manual and the legal institutions of delinquency, on the whole, deploy divergent strategies for imposing belonging upon their charges points to a process of differentiation between the types of citizens that they can become. Middle-class children, disciplined by appeals to sentiment and inner feeling, are raised to internalize sovereignty while poorer children are raised into adult roles that never escape the reassertion of power by force. Incorrigibility comes to describe this latter form of subjectivity, inscrutable to power and thus left to remain under its full power.

In framing how antebellum U.S. Americans attempted to frame interactions with children, I read from five popular domestic manuals discussing the methods of correct parenting. Four of these are products of roughly contemporary American writers and were originally published in either Massachusetts or New York: Amos Bronson Alcott's *Observations on the Principles and Methods of Infant Instruction* (1830), Lydia Maria Child's *The Mother's Book* (1831), Heman Humphrey's *Domestic Education* (1840), and John A. Gere's *The Government of Children* (1851). The fifth, John Locke's *Some Thoughts Concerning Education*, is an obvious outlier geographically and temporally, but despite its English origin and 1693 publication, Locke's work had a considerable afterlife shaping American attitudes about childhood. Its most prominent antebellum publication was in an 1830 volume, *The Library of Education*, edited by prominent educational writer and the editor of the *American Journal of Education*, William Russell. Moreover, in her work on the coevolution of child rights and American independence, Gillian Brown also reminds readers that Locke's *Thoughts on Education* was broadly consumed, even more so than his most popular work on political theory, *Two Treatises on Government*.[15] Nor was Locke's advice taken merely as abstract philosophy. As the *American Annals of Education* describes Russell's edition, Locke's work is "not mere speculative essays,—but the most simple and direct discussions of subjects in the highest degree practical."[16] Thus, while Locke's historical role in forming the foundational ideas of U.S. childhood was considerable, I here group him with U.S. manuals to preserve the ongoing use of Locke to address immediate questions of child rearing.

These texts were prominent either for their famed authors or for their popularity with readers. Locke's importance to the genre, as I have discussed, is clear. Lydia Maria Child had gained fame for her earlier historical fiction as well as for another household guide, *The American Frugal Housewife* (1829), and her work in the juvenile periodical press. Her *The Mother's Book* met with such success that it was republished not only in England, but also in Germany. A. Bronson Alcott was another emerging, if polarizing, celebrity in the field of education for his pedagogical experiments, particularly at the Temple School in Boston, and for his ties to the Transcendentalists, ties that also helped his ideas receive repeated coverage in the *Dial*. John A. Gere, a leader in the Methodist church, was lesser known, but his guide found very high, if not entirely surprising, praise from *the Methodist Quarterly Review*, which declared a wish that his book might "[find] its way into every Christian family in the land."[17] Finally, Heman Humphrey, though no longer well-known, was a widely published Congregationalist minister and early president of Amherst College who was discussed and published in a range of periodicals including *the North American Review*, *the Christian Observer*, *the Christian Secretary*, and *the New-York Monthly Magazine*.

From these manuals, I turn to a survey of the inmate profiles written during the first five years of the juvenile delinquency institution of New York, beginning with its first entry on December 25, 1824.[18] As I interpret them, the records of the New York House of Refuge work as an ad hoc attempt to reconcile the methods put forward by such domestic manuals with a group of delinquent children to whom they can claim no genealogical connection and whom House officials were preparing for lives in a different class than their own. Because they did not see these children as versions of themselves, House officials turned instead to environment as a key to understanding delinquent children and to violence for molding them. In selecting the physical as the sole object of scrutiny, however, House officials lost their claim on the inner lives of delinquents, declaring them to be a mixture of inaccessible and unchangeable that I classify under the term incorrigible. These delinquency records were functionally bureaucratic documents, but when read as formal experiments in characterization, they reveal the strange place of incorrigible subjectivity between the environmental and the individual, between the physical body and the projection of a mind within. Rather than arguing that this log offers a well thought-out framework, I emphasize the moments of rupture when the observer can make nothing of the child observed. Faced with a child self whose interiority cannot be fully gauged either in the terms of agential consent or physical duress, the authors of these records came to see young bodies with a menacing degree of social illegibility.

Despite the differences between their intents and venues, both prison records and parenting advice converges on the same questions: by what means can one assert authority over an unformed subject and how does one work to transition that disciplined subject into a socialized, adult citizenship? By reading these two archives in parallel, a larger pattern of thinking emerges in which children's inner selves are not necessarily connected to their outer affect; the connection between inner self and outer expression may be stabilized by genealogical bonds, linking parent-child bonds to their physical similarities, but it can also be broken by physical punishment that, supposedly, drives children to act in a way that they do not feel. The social pressure to eliminate corporal punishment, though, relies on a perceived physical continuity from which most of the children entering Houses of Refuge were excluded. The same logic that saved affluent, non-immigrant children from violent treatment declared that it might be the only path available for disciplining poor and immigrant children. The divergent archives of domestic manuals and juvenile prisons give us access to this model of the incorrigible child, deemed inscrutable to authority and thus left under its full power. Through these writings, child criminality was constructed by a problem of reading and, specifically, of child bodies that could not be read to reveal their inner thoughts.

SOCIALIZING THE CHILD BODY

For all his famous interest in educating the mind, John Locke was also absorbed by the problem of disciplining the body. Even in Locke's writing, where one might most expect a disembodied subject, the foundational principle of disciplining children is physical. While the bulk of his *Thoughts on Education* is devoted to developing faculties such as reason, judgment, and virtue, Locke begins his text by noting the impossibility of rational improvement without physical management: "I imagine the minds of children as easily turned this or that way as water itself: and though this be the principle part, and our main care should be about the inside, yet the clay cottage is not to be neglected."[19] Unlike the easily swayed mind, the physical conditions of the child could only be managed, not scripted wholesale. Locke's famous treatise on the training of human reason accordingly begins with an exhaustive regime for addressing the child body. Cold, wet feet are recommended to strengthen character.[20] Melons, peaches, and plums must be banned, but gooseberries are acceptable—provided they are eaten ripe, with bread, and only before meals.[21] Beer is allowable but only at "Blood-hot" temperatures,[22] and bowel movements must be carefully monitored and kept to a strict schedule.[23] Locke's digressions on the body seem to balloon, unable to leave any aspect of physical life as a variable in his curriculum. Attempting to control the bodily condition of the child at every turn, Locke suggests that the physical must be corralled by constant and painstaking discipline to give access to the mental. In other words, the unruliness of the child's body is threateningly contiguous with the limits of adult authority.

This problem of socializing the corporeal was at the heart of one of the driving tensions of the antebellum domestic novel as a genre: the need to incorporate children into liberal democratic society while preserving the decidedly non-liberal dependency of childhood. In his history of the concept of character in U.S. reform literature, James Salazar argues that such writing struggles with the paradox of being simultaneously a nationalist project in training children in American behavior and a project in asserting that an independent American character had existed all along. He writes that because they acted "as guides as well to the formation of self-governing and independent citizens, these character-building manuals imagined the child not simply as the 'plastic' material . . . but also as the kind of self-founding, antigenealogical national subject."[24] As Salazar observes, the drive to naturalize national identity required the projection of an innate personality, where an innate Americanness might reside. Moreover, the idea of a child who could be perfectly conditioned into obedience conflicted with the need to understand adults as individuals capable of autonomous thought and, therefore, properly democratic voting practices. The child of these manuals' rhetoric must retain a measure of selfhood that remains asocial in order to imagine them growing and having the personal freedom necessary to be a socially functional adult.

The difficulty of imaging even the model childhood as continuous with the disembodiment of rights-bearing adulthood was most pointed in such manuals when they attempted to address the determined corporeality of the child—the awkward predicament of severing physical growth from rational development and, subsequently, of preserving a fantasy of the pristinely disembodied citizen. Much as the officials of the House would do, these domestic advisors relied upon the body as an index to understanding and asserting authority in the form of corporal punishment over child subjects who seemed too little socialized for other appeals. In this reliance on the body as a failsafe to accessing a selfhood posited as elsewhere, however, there is a lurking threat of disconnection between bodily comportment and interior state. Too much attention to the body could produce a deceitful subject who learns to conform only outwardly. These manuals collectively reveal, then, a crisis over the child body as the simultaneous grounds and obstacle to socialization.

Locke's emphasis on the physical management of childhood as the underpinning for moral adulthood permeates guides written during the antebellum period as well. Humphrey, in fact, very nearly paraphrases Locke's metaphor of water and clay cottage, declaring in one passage, that "although the young *mind* is that priceless gem which it should be a guardian's supreme care to polish, the *casket* must not be overlooked, nor neglected."[25] Alcott similarly believed that the primary force in infancy was the "claims of animal nature" and insisted that a session of active play was the necessary preparation for a child to be able to engage intellectually, claiming that bodily energy must be dealt with for intellect to be invoked.[26] Child, in fact, goes so far as to trace the national characters of the Dutch and the French back to the manner in which they are physically handled as infants. Dutch "heaviness," she ponders, must spring from Dutch infants being kept in "repose" for too long, while French "vivacity" originates from the parental tendency to be "perpetually tossing them about."[27] An American body, too, was not simply born but had to be handled into being. If the ideal subject of the early United States was the disembodied subject of liberalism, these manuals make clear that the training of that eventual adult was nonetheless a process rooted in corporeal connection.

This method of infant training through bodily response, however, had its more brutal extensions. Gere agrees that there is no reason to delay training a child until they are capable of either speech or reason because they can instead be made to respond to physical stimuli. He therefore promises a technique for teaching crying children to calm themselves on command before the age of six months. Instead of maternal empathy, though, Gere advises that "in general, it will be indispensable to make an appeal to fear."[28] His advice is that a guardian faced with a crying child should first attempt to distract them with a few words but, as this will often fail, recommends that he or she escalate to violence:

> It may be necessary to add, on the same principle on which physicians apply counter-irritants, suddenly but gently, a *slap*, or a *shake*, just sufficient to render fear the predominant passion . . . But some rare instances will occur, in which these means will not only

> not answer the purpose, but serve only to increase the passionate excitement which obtains in the midst of a fit of squalling, or of obstinate, silent resistance to parental authority. In such instances, imitate the practice of physicians, who order blisters to establish upon the surface a centre of sympathy, and repeat the slap, or ply the rod . . . with an intention to *smart*, but never to bruise or injure, until it is obvious that the sensation upon the surface becomes the centre of interest, and no longer.[29]

Given the excess of the advice itself—that if slapping an infant once fails, then the answer is to strike again, more sharply—it does possess a strange kind of internal logic, offering a theory of interaction with what is still held to be a largely asocial being. If the child is crying, Gere reasons, the adult can distract it out of a tantrum by inspiring a new "predominant passion" of fear or pain. In his choice of medicine as the arena for a training that could as easily have been made a matter of etiquette or religion, Gere asserts that the route to a child's thoughts and feelings is fundamentally a physical one. Sympathy, as it appears in this interaction between parent and child, is hardly the product of abstract affinity but rather the physiological impulse that can spur feeling; the "centre of sympathy" is the site of an instructive pain, coupling physical sensation and mental attention in an immediate proximity.

Gere's suggestion would have been thoroughly controversial and he himself acknowledges that some of his methods have been condemned as "oppressive and cruel,"[30] but Gere's theoretical basis, if not his conclusions, follows directly from Locke, for whom corporal punishment threatened to disqualify children from democratic citizenship. While Locke's extrapolation between child liberty and the political rights of adults springs from a considerable tradition of paternalist analogies—his *Two Treatises of Government* famously rebuts Robert Filmer's own conflation of royal and paternal authority—his discussion moves beyond analogy and into an analysis of how corporal punishment shapes the development of child subjectivity itself. He critiques whipping, therefore, as making the child into an adult unfit for political participation:

> Such a sort of *slavish Discipline* [as whipping] makes a *slavish Temper*. The Child submits, and dissembles Obedience, whilst the fear of the Rod hangs over him; but when that is removed, and by being out of sight, he can promise himself impunity, he gives the

> greater scope to his natural Inclination; which by this way is not at all altered, but on the contrary heightened and increased in him; and after such restraint, breaks out usually with the more violence.[31]

The prospect at least of physical discipline seems inevitable, because for all his reluctance, Locke still admits that when faced with what he interchangeably terms "obstinacy" and "rebellion," physical checks are the only assertion of control.[32] Counterintuitively, the failure of corporal punishment is the submissiveness it first seems, for the child's "natural Inclination" is not subdued but "heightened and increased" until it is capable of all the more violence. Whipping is ineffective, in other words, because it isolates the body and thereby teaches the child that outward appearance can be used as a shield between its inner self—and any illicit desires lurking there—and disciplinary surveillance.

Locke's warning against corporal punishment links questions of the child body and civic identity by suggesting a bifurcated theory of the self. To some extent, treatment of the child body matters because it molds the character of the adult. Yet it cannot do so entirely. Locke's model of the self in this passage instead distinguishes between the social presentation of the self and an asocial, private self, labeling them "temper" and "natural Inclination," respectively. Temper, as the aspect of character that can be made "slavish," is socially determined and determines, in turn, how the self is expressed to others. Natural inclination, meanwhile, is the innate element of the character that does not seem to depend on nurture and that may be hidden or revealed to others according to the individual's temper. Corporal punishment intervenes in this dynamic by strengthening the asocial tendencies of the self; as Locke concludes, a beating leaves the child's natural Inclination "heightened and increased," but better concealed. To grow into a proper citizen, children must be trained with a temper that can moderate between their desires and the external social world. Essentially, it must undergo the process I have been referring to as socialization. For Locke and his antebellum readers, this socialization appears as a directly racialized process. As Richard Brodhead has argued, there was a general shift in discourse around corporal punishment, particularly the language of whipping, that made it inextricable from the violence of plantation slavery.[33] Locke's imagined child begins with whiteness, only to be threatened with the category of enslavement in an especially pointed instruction for how to preserve the democratic mindset, and tacit whiteness, of a potential citizen.

The aversion to corporal punishment in Child's manual is similarly not concerned with an abstract dislike for violence or even a wish to avoid causing the children pain, but rather with the fear that it would teach children how to put on a deceptive face of obedience. They might learn to act as if they were members of the social world without being so. Unlike Gere, Child finds intimidation to be an inadequate source of authority, on the grounds that "mere fear of suffering never makes a person really better. It makes them *conceal* what is evil, but it does not make them *conquer* it."[34] As she continues to explore the division between children that "conceal" and those that "conquer" their vices, Child outlines the dangerous possibility that a man may grow up having learned by force to "regulate his outward behaviour" and to project "outward goodness" all without having "cleanse[d] his heart," avoiding punishment through "hypocrisy" or "concealment."[35] In this worst case scenario, the child disciplined by force matures into an adult who lives deceptively, functioning socially yet never revealing a true self to the rest of the world. Indeed, Child's feelings about the dangers of corporal punishment were so strong, or the social pressure to condemn it compelling enough, that she added a "Concluding Chapter" to her 1844 republication of the *Mother's Book* that recants her original edition's stance that physical discipline might be acceptable in some very rare instances and instead insists that force could never be used without sparking "rebellion" even when "its outward manifestations might be restrained by fear."[36]

For both Humphrey and Alcott, too, corporal punishment comes to be associated with an antisocial inner life. Rather than restricting the practice as Locke and Child do, they reshape corporal punishment to make the body into a conduit between individual and social feeling. For Humphrey, this attempt to reconnect the child's mental and physical response is a fairly conventional suggestion that guardians themselves perform the emotional effect that corporal punishment is intended to have upon the child. "Let him see," Humphrey advises, "from your countenance and from the tones of your voice, that every stroke costs you more pain than it does him; and he must be perverse indeed, if he does not yield and reform."[37] Though beatings should be rare, when they happen, parents must actively present that beating as an act of emotional transference, suppressing the role of physical suffering so much that the apparent chief injury should be parental grief. What Humphrey's recommended ritual assumes is that the physical punishment will not naturally have an affective impact or will have an impact that is unpredictable. Much as his advice pivots syntactically from one meaning of pain to another, the suggestion is a pedagogical exercise in teaching children to translate from violence to sentiment and to understand corporal punishment as focused on that latter intangibility rather than on physical threat. To put it differently, Humphrey implicitly argues that if parents want to discipline children through the body, they must also socialize the way that children connect interiority to flesh.

Alcott extended this idea further still. In an even more unusual stance on corporal punishment, instead of advising guardians to convey their own pain with every blow, Alcott entirely redirects the physical pain to the adult. Although he does not directly discuss the practice in his own writings, Elizabeth Palmer Peabody's *Record of a School* (1833) describes him inverting the scene of punishment and requiring that disobedient students strike Alcott for penance.[38] As Peabody describes it, this reversal was the "most complete punishment that a master ever invented," because it produces a pain that can "touch the heart to love."[39] Likewise, in Alcott's explicit advice on governing infants, interiority is a learned trait. He writes: "The reflection of [the teacher's] character will open the deeper fountains of their nature, and prepare them for the knowledge of themselves. Taught to look within for the dictates of duty, they will be led to the exercise of self-knowledge."[40] This elaborate pattern of reflection and substitution—children must observe adults so that the children can observe their own desires and learn to live without external guidance—follows a similar pattern to his insistence that a child strike an adult to see adult suffering in order to teach a self-inflicted pain born of remorse.[41]

Alcott's reversal of disciplinary roles appears bizarre, if not somewhat sexualized, from modern perspectives, but, though it was always controversial, there is also evidence that his methods struck a popular chord in its own time. When his daughter, Louisa May Alcott, fictionalized his pedagogy and included approving scenes of his unique proxy approach of punishment in her 1871 novel *Little Men*, public interest was enough to spur Peabody to republish her own account of Bronson Alcott's teaching. Indeed, read in the context of these other domestic manuals, Alcott's inverted approach to pedagogical force responds to the same problem of how to understand and discipline an asocial subject as his generic contemporaries, even if his answer is a more extreme one. Set alongside Humphrey, especially, the scene of suffering adulthood takes on a different light and becomes an exercise of teaching intersubjective relationships. Humphrey's lesson that internal and external must correspond recurs in Alcott's underlying premise that when a guardian feels grief at the behavior of a child, its corollary is that the child should cause the corresponding physical pain as well. Rather than teaching children to mimic the grief of their parents, Alcott assigns physical pain to adults in order to make the punishment a pristinely emotional exchange. In thus forcing children to inhabit the place of the striking adult while also in the place of the chastised child, Alcott expands a child's misbehavior into a communal injury in which physical pain cannot mark an incorrigible child self because even that pain is attached to the parental authority. Alcott transforms the isolating effect of corporal punishment into a way to make children embody discipline themselves and thereby submit to it.

The risk of such an oppositional childhood, however, is higher for some children than others. Much like Locke's warnings of children made "slavish" precluded any protection for children who were enslaved, these manuals turned to genealogical proximity to white adults as an anchor for socialization. From their perspective, the danger of the body barring access to the child's character was far less with one's own, biological children than with the children of strangers. In fact, according U.S. manuals, the supposed bond between a mother's and child's bodies offer the first means for socialization. Recall, for instance, Humphrey's belief that a mother's face was innately legible to her child. Similarly, Child extrapolates from this theory of face that a version of the child body must remain connected to its mother even after birth. Claiming that infants will cry at the sight of their mothers looking unhappy, Child frames the situation as an instinctive physical bond that links their emotional states, explaining that such a young child "cannot possibly *know* what that expression means, but he *feels* that it is something painful."[42] The extent of this corporeal connection to the family is so intense that Child returns to an already rather outdated theory that a mother's emotions could be transmitted to a child through milk, declaring that "children have died in convulsions, in consequence of nursing a mother, while under the influence of violent passion or emotion."[43] This connection, so visceral that it almost exceeds the category of communication, stages the child as always already socialized by merit of belonging to the body of the mother. She imagines infants as, in a very literal but temporary way, being a part of a social body through the intensity of the maternal bond.

Where a biological relationship could stabilize this fear that the body would prevent true socialization, then, no such privilege existed for the children of strangers. In a passage that she later recanted, even Child, the otherwise staunch opponent of corporal punishment, made an exception for the children who might join the family as adoptees, servants, or apprentices. She explains that while she "[does] not believe that most children, properly brought up from the very cradle, would need whipping," she also cautions that "children are not often thus brought up; and you may have those placed under your care in whom evil feelings have become very strong."[44] Violence, for Child, is reserved for children brought from outside the household, as a means of compensating for the affective gap between a guardian and a child estranged by the "evil feeling" of an improper background. It might evoke incorrigibility, but it seems the only bond possible when a child has been raised so outside an adult's experience. For House officials, too, the paranoia that their charges harbored secret inner rebellion marked a sense of wider disconnection. The institutions had brought them in contact with the types of childhood they had never lived, from classes and ethnic groups to whom they felt no affiliation. To see a child as incorrigible, then, was to see him or her as a break in the social order, living at a remove from any life that persons in authority could imagine. The use of the body as that source of social grounding is not identical to race, but it draws on the raw materials of racial logic suggesting that emotional continuity is only truly possible where there is a pre-existing physical continuity.

DELINQUENT CHARACTERS IN PROFILE

The first prison intended specifically for juvenile criminals in the United States was built in New York City in 1824. Known as Houses of

Refuge or, less frequently, as Houses of Reformation, such institutions were part of a larger transatlantic fascination with juvenile delinquency, explicitly borrowing their design from similar establishments in London and Dublin.[45] Though the United States was slower than Britain to adopt separate penal systems for minors, the idea caught on quickly enough that within thirty years, as the *Pennsylvania Journal of Prison Discipline and Philanthropy* from 1854 reports, Houses of Refuge had since been founded in Philadelphia; Boston; Portland, Maine; Providence, Rhode Island; Westborough, Massachusetts; Rochester, New York; Pittsburgh; Cincinnati; and Chicago.[46] While the details of the schools differed, the typical program for inmates consisted of a full workday meant to train the children in a profession while also allowing the institution a source of financial support. An 1827 report by the New York House of Refuge, for instance, reported that inmates attended two two-hour school lessons and labored for another eight hours with its one hundred and twenty-two boys working at "chair-making, shoe-making, tailoring, brass nail manufacturing, and silver plating" and its twenty-seven girls working at "baking, tailoring, sewing, and washing."[47] As this schedule comes from an official report on the institution's benevolence, real work hours may have been longer in practice, particularly because the income from inmate labor was both a source of direct funding and evidence of sustainability used to argue for future support from external patrons. Moreover, the report itself notes that the in-house work done by female inmates "engrosses almost the whole of their time" as those twenty-some children were responsible for clothing the whole of the institution's population.

The common arguments for building Houses of Refuge, rather than age-integrated prisons, relied on bringing together two contradictory halves of the discourse on juvenile criminality. On one side, the pathos of a popularized vision of childhood innocence suffering in prison permeated many sentimental appeals for the construction and funding of institutions of delinquency. The chief justice of Massachusetts in the 1820s, for instance, wrote a much-quoted endorsement of South Boston's House that declares prison unfit for minors, because "these unhappy little victims of neglect, or shameful abuse of authority, are hardly proper subjects of punishment—their offences are not their own" for, as he continues, "what more terrible than to immure in the physically and morally foul apartments of a jail, a child of eight or ten years of age, without means of instruction or information, and then to turn him into the world with an atmosphere about him, which will repel every thing fitted to purify his body or his soul!"[48] Children, such advocates argued, erred through ignorance of the law brought about by bad upbringing rather than individual malice. Putting minors in prison, therefore, was merely to educate them in the ways of adult criminality, corrupting their remaining purity by contact with convicts.

In contrast, texts such as Gustave de Beaumont and Alexis de Tocqueville's *On the Penitentiary System in the United States* (1833) complained that because of the pathos inherent in the child prisoner, juries would refuse to convict even repeat offenders when the only option for sentencing seemed so harsh.[49] As advocates for the Philadelphia House of Refuge put it in an 1840 pamphlet entitled *The Design and Advantages of the House of Refuge*, this pity itself can breed further criminality in its young objects: "If such delinquents are liable to be treated, when pursued, in the same manner as older and hardened ones, it is almost impossible to arrest their progress in depravity and mischief. Most men shrink, with repugnance, from harshness to youth. The prospect of making them convicted felons is repulsive; and thousands have been permitted to continue unmolested, in preference to hurrying them to the Penitentiary. Thus our most natural sensibilities become panders to public wrong, and contribute to keep up the juvenile gangs so necessary to the schemes of old culprits."[50] For these reformers, too much sympathy is actually an act of unkindness instead of mercy because it leaves children on the street, where they may be preyed upon by gang leaders. Keeping child criminals away from adult convicts, in other words, returns them to the hands of the adult criminals still outside of prisons, so that the only way to keep the two groups reliably apart is to found an alternative institution. In separating these two classes of bodies, the pamphlet also seeks to guard a rhetorical gulf between the social standing accorded to criminals and the standing accorded to children. To juxtapose the treatment of the former onto the putative precious body of the latter produces the "repulsive" chimera of social positions; it is to imagine into being the hardened criminal child known as the incorrigible.

Translating the mechanisms of the adult criminal code into a penal code for juveniles, however, also required developing a system for gauging the character of subjects liable to be seen as blank slates. Thus, along with this new form of criminality came a need to recalibrate the alignment between individual and environment as commentators were forced to reckon with just how responsible delinquents could be held for their actions. A few reports of juvenile crime did frame it, explicitly or tacitly, as a matter of individual moral choice. The discussion of a young thief in an 1835 New York newspaper shifts immediately into a repetitive apostrophe of the "Young Man!" reader, warning that he avoid the same fate.[51] More famously, Charles Dickens, an otherwise strong proponent on behalf of criminalized youth, formed his 1839 *Oliver Twist* around the notion that his protagonist's innate goodness saves him time after time from attempts to drag him into crime and so disinherit him; Oliver's continued innocence offers proof of upper-class moral strength and condemnation of all those lower-class characters around him who do not themselves resist delinquency. More generally, too, the basis of nearly all reform movements, Houses of Refuge included, was that of moral education, with the accompanying notion that a "good" child could not be a criminal child and, conversely, that criminal child could not be a good one.

As a general rule, though, the discourse of delinquency was less likely to ascribe bad character to a delinquent than it was to ascribe an absence of any character. That is, the discussion of child crime was far less interested in inner motivation or intention than in inventorying the external causes that had produced child subjects as criminal. The suspects were many. For example, when the board of managers of the Philadelphia House of Refuge offered a prize for the best essays on juvenile delinquents, they introduced the winners with a list typical for the period, including "the rapid natural increase of our population," "the influx of ignorance, sottishness and crime from foreign lands," and "the corrupt influences which grow with the growth of our cities, and extend with the prosperity and enterprise of the country."[52] For such commentators, delinquents act as a social barometer, absorbing and reflecting whatever set of social evils are preoccupying the writer, such that their share of childhood "innocence" lies in their lack of personal will. The 1850 New York sermon *Juvenile Depravity and Crime in Our City* by revivalist and eventual utopian Thomas Lake Harris presents delinquency as a product of overwhelming influence rather than personal failing, writing that, "A man can conquer circumstances of evil provided his spiritual will be quickened . . . *But the Child is passive.* Circumstances exercise over it a forming and influencing power. Poison may be mingled with its food and with its drink that shall disease and madden its young life in body and mind. It may drink vice from its mother's bosom and imbibe contagion from its father's touch."[53] Child subjects in this framework were distinct from adults in their unusual openness to the influence of their environment. They were able, as Harris writes, to "drink vice" and "imbibe contagion" because they lack the clear boundaries between internal and external worlds that would allow for anything like a private self in the liberal sense. They are reflective, not agential figures.

The importance of the environment in anchoring adult understanding of the child was not a model exclusive to delinquency. While the juvenile delinquency system was fixated on urban childhoods most immediately because the system targeted urban immigrant communities, the system took its justification from an older but related coupling of children and nature. Observing the period's preference for meadows as the site of "true" childhood rather than factories or even classrooms, Alan Richardson has observed that the prototypical child of early Romanticism is "Edenic, natural, and asocial," in that the child's singular connection to the idyllic natural world marks its innocence of human vice, even as the child's innocence acts as guarantor that the natural world really must be idyllic.[54] The use of the pastoral to link ideas of childhood with pristine nature carried over into the U.S. context as well. As Ralph Waldo Emerson described childhood in his 1836 essay "Nature," the natural world surrounding a child is so constitutive of the child's character that there is no clear boundary between the one and the other. While "the sun illuminates only the eye of the man," he writes, it "shines into the eye and heart of the child" such that "the inward and outward senses" perfectly correspond.[55] The idea of innocence relies, in part, on a natural setting, because the child's singular connection to the idyllic natural world marks its innocence of human vice, even as the child's innocence acts as guarantor of the natural world's idyllic character

From this perspective, for a child to be born and reared in a bustling city bordered on perversion. Where a child in open exchange with nature signified purity, a child whose sense of self fused instead with the artificial space of the city verged upon an equally unnatural character. Children of the city might have been objects of pity, but they were not to be trusted. An 1856 self-help manual from Boston titled *How to Be a Man: A Book for Boys* put the matter directly, declaring that "cities abound with boys who are old in mischief and crime. They take great delight in leading astray the simple-hearted; and if boys from the country come within reach of their influence, they are almost sure to be ruined."[56] Rural boys are "simple-hearted" and untainted, but city boys become "old" beyond their age. City children are equally corrupted and corrupting to others, acting at once as victim and perpetrator. This rhetoric also draws on an implicit nativism in which connection or non-connection to land shapes character in a way that is fundamental and irrevocable.

The inmate profiles written by the House superintendent mirror this divide between delinquent as a victim of environment and as criminal agent. As institutional texts, these case histories are reasonably consistent and systematic in their structure. As each new inmate entered, he or she was assigned an identifying number and would have an interview with the current superintendent, who would ask for a brief version of their early biography (age, birthplace, ethnicity, status of parents, with whom the child had lived) and then press them for an account of all past crimes, however minor, the inventory of which would be recorded in full. This biographical background forms an introduction to the second half of the document, which records the child's time after they had become an inmate of the House. This portion, entitled "Remarks," consists of dated entries that could vary in frequency from every few days to an annual update and featured brief character sketches or recorded significant events in the child's reformation, or non-reformation, such as indentures, escape attempts, or persistent rule-breaking. Nearly all remarks sections include at least one entry made after the delinquent had left the House recording relapses, professional standing, or merely a lack of further information.

The disciplinary history of Ann McCollister, the fifth inmate to enter the House and one of its early failures, suggests the frustrated attempts at communicating with a delinquent subject. Her biography prior to entering the House includes more criminal activity than the average entering child, but their accusations of petty theft and sex work was nothing unusual. Born in New York to an enlisted and subsequently absentee father and a working mother, Ann bounced between informal employments, roaming the streets, the almshouse, and, after being taken up for theft, Bridewell prison. On January 5, 1825, Ann was transferred from Bridewell into the House of Refuge. She was, at that point, twelve years old. She remained at the House until 1830, when she aged out of the program and was moved back into the almshouse as a "hopeless subject." In the interim, she escaped or attempted escape from the House continually, stole, injured a teacher with a knife, and was almost consistently defiant. At last record, she had left the almshouse, collected several other women who had been delinquents with her in the House, and, together with these House veterans, started her own brothel. In sum, Ann McCollister was not reformed.

The process of Ann's non-reformation as it was recorded by superintendents Joseph Curtis and N. C. Hart was a process of trying and failing to find a medium of communication.[57] Most pressingly, the records come as an attempt to make Ann's body into the point of contact for her subjectivity, against her considerable resistance. The unusually lengthy first entry of the superintendent's remarks written twelve days after her entry to the house in the log portion of her profile offers a miniature drama of refusal on Ann's part to be involved in the House's discipline. The superintendent describes the event:

> She is the most refractory of all the girls she appeared to treat the repeated admonitions with indifference, and as if to [[illegible]] whether she could receive any but pleasant words her conduct during most of the day bespoke a total indifference to all that was said to her; in private (before tea) she would not give the least appearance that she was disposed to do better, [[I]] found it necessary to chastise her as a child which she received with a display of stubbornness to me surprising though she must have suffered much yet after she was seated there was no appearance of a tear or any irregularity in breathing Her reply to my first question was as clearly spoken, as full of temper as before she was corrected, after a few moments reflection, I found myself considerably exhausted I then found it necessary to give her solitary confinement. She went to Prison at 6 o'clock PM with much firmness of manner Shortly after I carried her 3 Blankets and made her bed not a word was spoken.[58]

This interaction comes in three waves. The first is purely discursive. At stake are "repeated admonitions," "pleasant words," and Ann's "total indifference to all that was said to her," whether praise or criticism. Ann does reciprocate, though, in her meeting with the superintendent through her entirely clear and forthright refusal to change her behavior; she is honest about her intention to remain unruly. After talking fails, the superintendent turns from words to action—asserting his authority over her body by "chastis[ing] her as a child," a euphemism for corporal punishment that emphasizes the body as a source of influence for subjects seen as underdeveloped in reason. Finally, the corporal punishment having failed to subdue Ann's speech, all attempts at verbal communication are cut off ("not a word was spoken"), and the superintendent reduces the demonstration of his authority to his control over her physical experience in its entirety by isolating her in prison; his personal delivery of blankets to her appears then as a performance of Ann's material dependence on his good will.

I want to pause at the specific moment of failed corporal punishment in this anecdote, and suggest that its ability to leave the superintendent "considerably exhausted"—and thereby to turn the record's scrutiny fleetingly back on its author—represents a crucial moment of disjuncture in the attempted socialization of Ann. As I have mentioned, under Foucauldian models, the disciplined body acts as a means of inventing an inner self or soul, with materiality acting as the immanent medium on and through which power can operate. What the author encounters in Ann, though, seems to be a body that itself has not been socialized to respond to discipline. Though the superintendent imagines from his experience of bodies that Ann "must have suffered much," she shows none of the bodily signs that would have let him interpret her pain, for, as he marvels, "there was no appearance of a tear or any irregularity in breathing." Unsurprisingly, without Ann's body as a point of contact, her posture toward the House, and her "temper" at the superintendent, remain unchanged. Instead, it is the superintendent who is left apparently shaken and in need, as he writes, of "a few moments reflection" by the paradox of corporal punishment's effect on a subject whose physical body appears unruly. The regularity of Ann's breath has itself become an element of her moral deviance, not because it reflects any specific vice, but because it marks the superintendent's utter failure to engage anything other than the body.

The lessons that Ann learns in her time at the House and the height of her improvement lies, in fact, in constructing a wall between her intentions and her outward comportment. At her best, Ann's profile presents her as having tricked her observers into optimism. Only two notes of more than two dozen show approval of Ann, one noting that she has "recently made profession of a religious nature which gave us much encouragement" and the other, more ambivalently, observes she "now and then evince[s] . . . a disposition to do well."[59] The case history, however, describes both her religious awaking and more general wish to improve as diversions and false signs that prove utterly useless in predicting Ann's future behavior. In each case, the entry that signals hope also includes its disappointment. Her religion is quickly submerged in "her strong propensity to evil" such that "she again becomes ugly and troublesome," and the entry that observes her occasional improvement in disposition declares that she would always "again break forth in wickedness," and comments, almost passingly, that her "last very bad act was in stealing the matron's sweetmeats, and plotting to burn the female house."[60] Where, in most cases, arson plots alone are enough to justify an entry in the log (which is not to suggest that they were especially rare), for Ann, the case is extreme enough that they become merely anecdotal evidence of an incorrigibility that is much broader than any set of acts alone. After this latter entry, the record stops for two years, resuming only to recount the aftermath of Ann's departure from the House, as if stymied entirely by her recalcitrance. In fact, Ann's education lies entirely in this improved ability to perform a mode of sociability that she does not feel, moving from an unrepentance that permeated speech, body, and putatively mind into an unrepentance that could be kept temporarily apart from her external behaviors and sheltered in a version of selfhood that remained illegible.

Perhaps an even more pointed example of the anxiety surrounding the unstable signification of child bodies comes in the profile of Samuel Slowly, who was admitted in 1826 at the age of fourteen. Unlike Ann, Samuel Slowly was criminalized without having committed criminal acts of any kind, entering the House solely because his father took him to be committed to avoid supporting him.[61] The first portion of his stay in the House is accordingly low-profile. The initial note made under "Remarks" records Samuel's indenture away a little less than five months after his arrival, suggesting that he was found to be in no need of major reform. The profile takes a sharp turn, however, after it records Samuel's escape from his indenture and his eventual recapture by police, because the child who returns is markedly different than the one who had left. The superintendent marvels at the scenes caused by Samuel's arrival:

> His appearance was very excentric—his hair long—his movement much like a female &c.—He states that he left his Master Mr. Mappa in Girl's clothing to avoid detection—served better than a year in the country in the capacity of a Girl—came to the City in the same habelement—some however judged that he was a Morphredite—and whenever he appeared in the Streets, let his apparel be what it might, he was mobbed by boys &c. so strong was the impression that he was neither male nor female by the remarks of the boys in the Yard—that means was taken to ascertain the fact,—when lo, he was a man—but had practiced to put on female airs in walk &c.—so much that he still in walk &. carries the appearance to this day[62]

Samuel returns to the House physically changed, but the superintendent is hard-pressed to locate the precise nature of the change. The most he can do is to list attributes—"hair," "movement," "walk"—but his frequent refrain of the catchall "&c." in this short paragraph suggests his difficulty in finding exactly what it is that signifies Samuel's gender as female. Foiled by appearance, he turns to anatomy as the ultimate arbiter of identity, recasting the mob assaults of Samuel, which he also reports as incessantly repeated, into a singular moment of discovery building to a dramatic apostrophe, "lo, he was a man." Of course, the physical conclusion itself was a foregone one. As a former inmate, Samuel's anatomy would have almost certainly already been known to House officials. However, the insistence on returning to the body to settle what had already been an officially settled question, whether Samuel was to be treated as male or female, appears as an attempt to manage the fact that Samuel's body had learned to be female so thoroughly that, even after a seemingly definitive conclusion, the superintendent circles back to the femininity that continues to mystify him.

Whether Samuel saw their assumed disguise as an opportunity to express a gender identity that had to be otherwise hidden or strictly as a role that they had be forced into situationally in order to avoid arrest is beside the point, because what is threatening about the incident from the superintendent's vantage is the impossibility of resolving that question. One way or another, Samuel's body has ceased to be a stable expression of their identity. Even the noun provided to name this gender indeterminacy, "Morphredite" (a colloquial variant on "morphodite," itself a variant of "hermaphrodite"), is a hazy assignment of an already unstable signifier, rather than any stable pathology or a taxonomy. Etymologically, too, the label is apt. "Morphredite" sheds its ties to the classical namesake suggested by "hermaphrodite" and instead takes up a closer association to the Greek "-morph," a suffix that would normally indicate a formal similarity to the thing named by the first portion of the word. Without this first element to anchor the suffix to a particular thing, however, "morphredite" signals the purely formal, suggesting the recognition that a structure or order exists, while giving no sign as to what that organizing principle might be. To mark Samuel as a morphredite, then, is to record a form of subjectivity that eludes other understanding; the Samuel of House records is coherent but not recognizable.

The superintendent's greatest frustration, though, comes not in spectacular failures like Ann McCollister's recidivism or Samuel Slowly's femininity, where there is at least a narrative to the failed reformation, but in those cases where he realizes his inability to describe the problem at all. A persistent rhetoric emerges across the first five years of the House's records in which, rather than characterizing the most difficult children, the superintendent collapses into tautology. Entries declaring, often in full, that "John is John still," "Wesley is Wesley still," and "Alfred is Alfred still" are less description than they are an abdication of description: when past entries struggle to set down just what John, Wesley, and Alfred were like, such notes add nothing but temporal duration to the portrait.[63] Similarly, to move from a portrait of Sarah Doxey that describes her as having "a curious combination in conduct and disposition" in that "sometimes she is as good a girl as can be wished" but "at other times she is disagreeable and stubborn and but little dependence can be placed upon her" into the plain declaration that "Sarah is about Sarah still" is an abbreviation, not a change in meaning.[64] The latter is the only reliable thing to be said about a girl who is sometimes one way and sometimes entirely different. Where external signs promised to be symbols of an inner self, these tautologies suggest a collapse of this relay. To "be Sarah" has a particular meaning, but the superintendent has no insight into the content of that meaning beyond that particularity. Her behavior can be documented endlessly, but nothing like the portrait of her private self can be gleaned from that data. From this perspective, the superintendent cannot have the slightest assurance that a moment's good behavior is an internalized improvement rather than either a calculated ploy or just a fluke. Because the House cannot construct a knowable version of Sarah's self, it certainly cannot hope to reform that self into a lawful citizen.

As a result, the language of individual progress, that ideal bildungsroman of growth into conformity that would signal institutional success, instead lapses into stasis. Tautology, by definition, cannot develop into anything but itself, and bureaucracy takes on something very near despair as it struggles to manage such records like those for Peter McKeaman, a boy sent to the House in early 1828 at the age of ten for petty theft and vagrancy, for whom sequential entries read:

> March 31, 1831—Peter is about Peter still
>
> October 27, 1831—I hardly know what to say about Peter—he affords but little hope,—no confidence can be placed in his word, gets clear of all the labour he can by dishonesty—restless in his disposition, forward in his manners—and on the whole we have to hold him with a curb bit as to government to keep him any way tolerable
>
> Sep. 10, 1833—Peter is about Peter still[65]

The imposition of dates seeks to corral the profile into an appropriate temporality, dutifully insisting that two and a half years have elapsed, but the contents of those remarks suggest strongly that something other than the linear time of calendars is at work. Peter at sixteen is indistinguishable from Peter at thirteen, and at thirteen equally seems alike to the eight-, nine-, and ten-year-old described in his biography as having denied his "roguery so innocently" to the judge that he was twice let off from jail. Peter seems at once to be a fixed point in the history of the House, but also, to be a figure who defies any stable description; the superintendent has "but little hope" for the future, while also "hardly know[ing] what to say" about the present. Peter cannot grow up because he cannot be known well enough for officials to notice a change, and, severed from the potential for an eventual maturity, he loses his claim to childishness as well. Paradoxically, the categories of delinquency present him as a subject removed from age itself, stranded in a persistent exclusion.

TRAJECTORIES OF INCORRIGIBLE LIVES

> Having then so publicly declared himself incorrigible, he is become dead in law.
>
> —*Alexander Pope*, The Dunciad, *1743*

If delinquency can have a freezing effect on individual development, eclipsing biological age by excluding its subjects from the privileges of adulthood, the status of delinquency also threatens to expand beyond any discrete period in a subject's life. It is a preemptive dismissal of a life in its whole. In this light, the trouble that inmates like Peter McKeaman and his associates represented to the House was not a problem of a few exceptionally "hard" cases, but rather the exposure of an underlying complication to disciplinary methods in general, one that the cultural standing of childhood at the time brings into particular relief. Delinquency discourse thus reproduces domestic manuals' fears of how corporeal punishment alienates rather than integrates the child. Beginning as it does from a position of alienation, it reaches a more extreme conclusion. That is to say, domestic manuals, whether they support or oppose corporal punishment, identify the consequences of focusing attention on the body as losing the chance to control interiority—a program that, thus far, is quintessentially Foucauldian. The difficulty the House encountered was that it claimed no stable handle on the body either. This illegibility of incorrigible delinquents gives the superintendent's records an air of paranoia, as they struggle to attach meaning to signs given by inmate behavior while also doubting the reliability of those signs. But, of course, that paranoia coincides with even closer scrutiny, as well as the sense that escape from the carceral system (or "reform") is impossible at any age with any behavior.

In these records, bad behavior is understood as a faithful reflection of the child's wishes; good behavior, however, can equally signal reformation or manipulation. For instance, when fifteen-year-old John Beekman was sent to prison for three days following an escape attempt, his promises to improve were read only as further symptoms of his depravity. The superintendent records: "He is this evening taken out of Prison, he appears penitent, as could be expected; we think him capable of acting the Hypocrite to an uncommon extent, shall not restore him to full privileges at present."[66] By forcing John to submit to authority, the punishment would seem to have had exactly the desired effect, but as the superintendent presents it, the effort was a failure. The promise offered by John's penitence is reversed by the qualifier that it is only what "could be expected" and thereby reframes it as a confirmation of his skills in "acting the Hypocrite." This socialization into acceptable behavior is as much a liability as it is progress because it is shown transparently as a product of force. John's penitence is to be "expected" from his circumstances and therefore is discredited as evidence of personal inclination. Delinquent motivation is thus caught in a curious bind. Though it must be legible to the superintendent for him to trust it as a stable sign of character, for it to be too legible as that stemming from convenience, necessity, or coercion risks leaving the child's projected truer desires more inaccessible to the House than ever.

This sense of inaccessibility breeds in turn a feeling that incorrigible delinquents are entirely unpredictable in their actions. If good behavior might be calculated to deceive, then past action is no sign of the future. Thus, the superintendent often returns to his fears that inmates who reform do so only when an authority is watching. Of James Bennett, for instance, he writes that "perhaps we never had a much more hopeless case but by preserving with strict discipline of every variety, that appeared rational for several months, he begins to be afraid, however of nothing but punishment."[67] Charles Wright, too, an inmate repeatedly beaten for trying to climb over the House walls, is damningly set down for good behavior so strategic that it cannot be believed, for, as the superintendent frets, "the whole of his conduct appears to be governed by policy." The improvement in Charles' behavior is no sign of an increased willingness to follow House rules, for the superintendent speculates that in fact "he has never lost sight of his former propensity for escaping."[68] The practical effect of guarding subjects like Charles and James who were "governed by policy" or "afraid . . . of nothing but punishment" is to mandate the keeping of policy and punishment constantly present, so that the like-reformed behavior, however insincere, also remains present. Hypersurveillance is the only response to a prisoner who always needs watching. The apparent common sense of this policy stems from incorrigibility's particular production of an unknowable subject; by failing to provide a deeper self for the House to monitor, incorrigible delinquents are excluded from the more common narrative of internalizing and reproducing an external force and remain instead in the stage of needing a constant monitor.

If incorrigibility sounds like a frustration of power on any level higher than the personal temper of the superintendent, its longer term effects suggest that any temporary victory came at a high price. Most obviously, incorrigible children tended to be incarcerated at the House for far longer because officials had no legal recourse for expelling unredeemable inmates. They were allowed to send inmates deemed physically unable to work away to the almshouse, and there are hints that the House used this outlet to expel at least a few troublesome children.[69] Given the number of successful escapes from indenture as well, it is tempting to suspect that some of the runaway apprentices were pursued harder than others. In general, though they were without set sentences, inmates had to be held until they were no longer delinquent, whether because they had reformed enough to be indentured or because they had aged out of the category. When they did leave, the category of incorrigibility channeled inmates' lives along tracts that were deeply gendered but joined by their marginal statuses and their persistent vulnerability to the type of absolute power represented by the House.

Male prisoners had the most defined path for leaving the House. The labeling of male inmates as incorrigible may have kept them from entering many of the more skilled professions, but as a group believed to be in need of constant force, they were primed to enter into the whaling industry's system of coerced labor. Whaling became a place of last resort to warehouse delinquent boys who were held to be unfit for other professions. A sampling of these dismissals gives a sense of how common and how unvaryingly boys were written off from the House as well as from the general freedoms that life on land provided:

> Isaac is an unstable and wickedly disposed Boy and I think will never do for anything out of the House but a Whaling Voyage[70]
>
> He's a smart boy, but deep—little can be said as to his state of mind, we fear that he will not stay anywhere, except on board a 3 year voyage[71]
>
> In the Boy there is nothing special he is rather inclined to vagrancy than otherwise. We hope that the advantage of a good long voyage will help him[72]
>
> We fear James will ruin himself. Nothing more can be done for him if returned, except sending him a Whaling voyage[73]
>
> Edward became unmanageable by his Master, who in consequence sent him a whaling voyage[74]

The most popular destination for troublesome male inmates, whaling in many ways offered a close approximation of House conditions for incorrigible subjects believed never to have matured into a larger scope of freedom.[75] With open ocean substituting for the walls of the House, shipboard indentures prevented the escapes frequent in the countryside, while the beatings that had forced submission from inmates continued as floggings onboard. The concordance, however, reads both ways. The whaling industry suited the beliefs of House officials that incorrigible delinquents could not be self-controlled agents, but the House's production of a set of young men eligible for unfree labor also fueled whaling with a body of men that it could justify coercing into work. Whipping a negligent sailor might have been seen at best as an unfortunate necessity, but whipping an incorrigible delinquent into productive citizenship was a public service—an early and casual privatization of penal reform enabled by incorrigibility's pathologies.

For incorrigible girls, adulthood held still fewer options. Without a profession available to women that held equivalent recourse to the bare force and strictures as whaling, they were largely left to struggle haphazardly to find a place outside the House. The records of women who left unreformed are thus slipshod and patchy. The assumed fate for those who did age out was that, one way or another, they would eventually end up in institutions that were the adult equivalent of the House. Hence one inmate, Sally Ann Kingsland, is sent off with the note that "We fear the Refuge has done her no good—and that she will fetch up at Bridewell or the penitentiary."[76] Many women's case histories did end with a last record in an institution, but many more slipped out of the archive altogether. Euphemisms such as having "returned to her former habits" or being "back on the Town" obscure the precise fate of women who might be surviving off hidden economies such as sex work and theft or be engaged in an illicit relationship or be living in a way not legible to House officials. Precise fates seemed to matter less when subjects neither qualified for legal positions in the market nor fell back into the reach of record-keeping institutions. For women, then, the legacy of incorrigibility was the permission for official legers to leave their lives in disapproving silence, under the assurance that they were incapable of more productive lives and undeserving of happier ones.

The final blow of incorrigibility is thus to isolate those lives it has touched and cut them out of history. The judgment that a person was fundamentally sealed off from the other lives around them was also a judgment that to be incorrigible was to be external, exceptional, and forgettable as minor flukes of a system that bears no responsibility for their condition. This erasure is already at play in the archives dedicated to amassing delinquent histories. Even a cursory reading of House records can feel like an exercise in superlatives: each bad case contends to be the worst, wickedest, and most hopeless case that the House has ever had the misfortune of seeing. Where this hyperbole at first individuates its objects by making them at least remarkable in their shortcomings, by the fourth, fifth, or tenth extreme, these worsts of the worst begin to blur together. The rhetoric of each individual profile argues that that the case is too unusual to represent any larger whole, but the repetition of singularities builds its own collective.

CODA: INCORRIGIBLE AFTERLIVES

In 1925, Sigmund Freud wrote a brief foreword to a colleague's book, *Verwahrloste Jugend* (*Wayward Youth*) by August Aichhorn. The choice of Freud to write an introduction seems as though it should have been a natural fit: Aichhorn's text consisted of a series of case histories of delinquent youths in Vienna, detailing in classical psychoanalytic terms the drives behind acts of deviance and advising how these drives could be redirected in appropriately social ways. Yet, within the space of his three-page foreword, Freud falters as he tries to lay out the relationship between psychoanalysis as he understood it and the analysis of troubled children. "The child," he writes, "has become the main object of psychoanalytic research," supplanting even its original object, the "neurotic" because "analysis has revealed that the child lives on almost unchanged in the sick patient."[77] Thus the child, even as it supplants, is subsumed and remade into a diagnostic tool for the neurotic, worth understanding as the reference point for a neurotic patient's development that, by evidence of a deviant adulthood, must have gone awry. Childhood is important because it produces the symptoms of adulthood, and thus as the chief tool for analysis becomes more important than present symptoms as the way to understand neurosis.

That positioning, however, simply does not fit children who display deviant symptoms in their own right, and Freud seems ill at ease in characterizing these patients who seem to be precocious in their neuroses. In what is already a relatively brief introduction for a lengthy monograph, Freud strikes a tone that is stranded between self-deprecation and dismissal as he distinguishes the "healing" process of analysis and the "education" of child analysis and then distances himself from the latter, explaining that he has only a "slight" role in this new child-centered model. Yet the relationship between adult and child subject shifts again, as Freud attempts to distinguish his work in treatment—as he calls it, re-education—from the pedagogical work that he introduced:

> The child, even the wayward and delinquent child, should not be compared to the adult neurotic, and re-education is something quite different from the education of the immature. The possibility of exerting influence through psychoanalysis depends on quite definite conditions, which may be described as the "analytic situation"; it requires the formation of certain psychic structures and a special attitude towards the analyst. When these factors are lacking, as in the case of children and young delinquents and, as a rule, in criminals dominated by their instincts, the psychoanalytic method must be adapted to meet the need.[78]

While the neurotic as victim of delayed development *may* be usefully compared to the child, the child *must not* be compared with the neurotic because their development is too early even to be delayed. The psyche to be analyzed, those "certain psychic structures" that separate the child from the child-like neurotic, does not yet exist fully enough to be treated. As Freud seems to understand childhood, even in the case of delinquency, the problem takes the form of a dearth to be filled, a need for education to install those apparatuses that would then allow the analyst to confront a recognizable subject.[79] For Freud, the neurotic adult is treatable or even commonplace, but "young delinquents" and the adults they become are too animalistically "dominated by their instincts" to undergo regular psychoanalysis. Neurosis, seemingly, is far more normative than delinquency.

Freud turns instead to an alternative pairing, that of the child and the criminal, through the idea that both possess unformed interiorities and must be educated into developing "psychic structures" before they can be disciplined into psychological normalcy. This leap from one form of asociality to another, as Freud likens the child too underdeveloped for therapy with the equally unresponsive criminal, hints at the ways that incorrigibility and its offshoots are coded into the models still in use for imagining the psyche. Just as the linking term of "young delinquents" emerges in Freud's passage to bridge between the categories of child and criminal while existing in an unsteady combination of contrast and overlap with each of those two, incorrigibility provides a language of alienation to describe criminality through unlikely analogy with the child. Childhood deviance provides evidence of adult individuality, registering interiority as an accumulation of memory and private development. The possibility of delay or rerouting in child development promises a tool for observing, understanding, and normalizing adults behaving outside of social constraints. The delinquents themselves remain inscrutable; absent the socialization into psychoanalytic constructs, they have no inner landscape that Freud can recognize. Freud's inclusion of the criminal "dominated by . . . instincts" further underscores that the delinquents of Aichhorn's study are largely ineligible to grow into the neurotics of his work. The projections of anti-sociality that leave children more likely to be labeled delinquent can therefore disqualify them from the very concept of a psychoanalytic adult self.

CHAPTER 3

Prodigious Births

Black Infancy, Antebellum Medicine, and the Racialization of Heredity

> "I have heard," murmured Starbuck, gazing down the scuttle, "that in violent fevers, men, all ignorance, have talked in ancient tongues; and that when the mystery is probed, it turns out always that in their wholly forgotten childhood those ancient tongues had been really spoken in their hearing by some lofty scholars. So, to my fond faith, poor Pip, in this strange sweetness of his lunacy, brings heavenly vouchers of all our heavenly homes. Where learned he that, but there?"
>
> —*Herman Melville,* Moby-Dick, *1851*

Prodigy has historically been a double-edged term that joins the marvelous and the monstrous together to name a category of the unpredictable and unprecedented.[1] This coupling of mental and physical difference with a separation from earthly constraints and temporalities drives the basic terms of Starbuck's analogy in the epigraph from *Moby-Dick* above. Pip's so-called lunacy after he has been stranded on the ocean grants him divine revelation, much like a fever could reportedly spark the chanting of an ancient language. Yet Melville's analogy also draws on another specifically racialized legacy of the prodigious as a disruption of genealogy that is concentrated in figures of African American infancy but is by no means confined to them.[2] Prodigy, as I discuss it here, is the white tendency to treat Blackness as unpredictable and, more pointedly, as existing outside of genealogy. Prior to genetic understandings of inheritance, antebellum medical discourse turned to African American infants to construct their theories of heritability by treating them as markers of failed inheritance who are estranged from the normal course of time. This practice in turn contributed to a persistent association of Black infancy in the antebellum United States with medical abnormality and genealogical unpredictability. However, the logic of prodigy expanded outward to treat Black subjects in general as always unexpected arrivals, stripped of chronology.[3] As a character whose age is impossible to determine and whose stated origin ranges from Alabama to Connecticut, Pip is one particularly canonical example of a much broader cultural figuration that mystified the age of Black people and worked to erase their genealogical continuity.[4] Prodigy, in short, racializes by refusing heredity.

As it was deployed during the Atlantic World, the presentation of Black births and Black people as prodigies came to pathologize and exclude Black childhood from genealogy and assert the instability of African American populations. In my analysis, inheritance, or rather the exclusion from inheritance, therefore takes two primary meanings. First, in the early days of race science and shortly before the rise of genetic theory, the burgeoning science of inheritance sought to define how traits were passed from parent to child and to create racial boundaries based on these heritable traits. [5] As it moves into literature, though, inheritance has a less clinical role in historical imagination, determining who can claim what history and what future.[6] As Habiba Ibrahim's work has shown, Black women have been made into spectacles of "impossible age" as a way for white audiences to imagine national history on a scale beyond human lifespans.[7] Conversely, the effect of prodigy discourse on the Black infant operates on the dimension of family rather than nation, imposing a perpetual newness that erases the temporal depth of Black kinship and gives white kinship its defining borders.

Starbuck's confusion about Pip's relationship to past and future alike echoes throughout *Moby-Dick*, reflecting the larger dislocation of a character who has neither a certain age nor origin. For Melville, the terms of biological childhood and social infantilization are identical, and though Pip is repeatedly called small, dubbed "Black Little Pip" and "poor little Pip," [8] Melville gives him more pathos than definite standing as adult or child. Likewise, his being called "boy" relentlessly throughout the novel could as easily signal the racist address of a grown man or the status given to workers low on the ship's hierarchy. As Melville writes in *Redburn* (1849), "boy" is also a class demarcation onboard a ship: "You must not think . . . that persons called *boys* aboard merchant-ships are all youngsters. . . . In merchant-ships, a *boy* means a green-hand, a landsman on his first voyage. And never mind if he is old enough to be a grandfather, he is still called a *boy;* and boys' work is put upon him."[9] Because it has been so implicated as a language of power to demarcate who should and should not be accorded authority, age cannot be isolated to any simple biological or chronological absolute. His personal history is similarly muddled. As an "Alabama boy"[10] from Connecticut,[11] Pip defies any simple categorization as enslaved, free, or fugitive, but he also troubles the conventions of backstory; Pip presumably had a life before he boarded the *Pequod*, but not one that we are allowed to see.

Pip, in other words, has an uncanny relationship to historical genealogy, one that I term prodigious. In its common contemporary meaning, only one aspect of prodigy's definition has truly survived, the idea of a child who is precocious beyond her years. In the antebellum period, however, the word indexes a deeper history of collision between science and religion, as the term that had once meant "miracle" moved into medical journals to name the unpredictable form and behavior of unruly bodies and to call for their great scrutiny from the medical profession. The kernel of religious wonder at the root of prodigy became a way of naming something that seemed to fall outside of scientific explanation and therefore to urge the need for closer scrutiny by medicine. As such, the term *prodigy* was used to name the body whose difference emerges from outside of medicine's understanding of causality, and therefore seemingly from nowhere. The prodigy names the moment created where science looks from child back to parent and recognizes no link, or when science examines the child and cannot recognize the possibility of the parent. It is, in part, the stripping of kinship that Hortense Spillers describes when the medical solicitation for Black test subjects and cadavers denies the subjectivity within and kinship between these bodies, rendering, as she writes, "the entire captive community . . . a living laboratory" for dissection.[12] But more particularly, it is the child left as an apparently spontaneous life after the genealogy that created her had been erased, illegitimated, and ignored.

When analyzing the racism in antebellum narratives of Black childhood, scholars most often frame their analysis through the figure of the *picaninny*, the dehumanizing term most popular in white descriptions of children with African or indigenous ancestry. The two figures certainly have overlap, but studying their cultural presence brings a different set of questions into view. In my reading, the prodigy represents an inverse of the picaninny, which racializes Black childhood as a site of utter fungibility. As Jayna Brown shows, the word itself encodes the economics of slavery into Black childhood by equating the name of a coin, the *picayune*, with Black children themselves, presenting those children as a "living currency."[13] To frame a child as a picaninny, then, is not merely to dehumanize her, but also to homogenize her value as one commodity among a pool of many.

As Brown notes, this lateral mobility encodes an alienation in temporality similar to the prodigy's, citing Topsy's famous declaration in *Uncle Tom's Cabin* that she'd had no parents but had "grow'd" as a sign of her displacement in time.[14] However, the fungibility associated with representations of the picaninny shapes discourses of the Black child body quite distinctly from those of prodigy. To take an example from *Uncle Tom's Cabin*, on his first introduction, Eliza's son Harry is made to perform in the role of picaninny, singing and doing a series of imitations. At the heart of the performance is the frenetic mobility of Harry's body, which allows him to match his song with "many comic evolutions of the hands, feet, and whole body" and enables his parody of old age with a transformation of "the flexible limbs of the child" into an "appearance of deformity and distortion."[15] The ease with which Harry's body shifts from one role to another on command hints at the more literal ways in which he cannot possess his own body and harkens back to the liquidity of a body circulating on the market, which Brown observes. The prodigy, on the other hand, particularly as it emerges from medical discourse, brings to the fore a white supremacy focused on seclusion rather than equivalence and imagines a very different corporeal life. The prodigy is described as having too unique a body and is thus estranged from others. Further, it names the child left as an apparently spontaneous life after the genealogy that created her had been erased, illegitimated, and ignored.

To track the use of prodigious childhood as a means of denying Black futurity, I turn first to medical discourses presenting Black childhood as a site of aberrant bodies and disrupted genealogy. These increasingly technical discourses surrounding infancy seize on the body of the Black child as a spectacle of frighteningly unpredictable inheritance that threatens to overwrite categories of whiteness. From this broader survey of medical journals, I consider two texts that exist in both the literary and medical spheres: Sir Jonah Barrington's "Skinning a Black Child" (1827) and Henry Clay Lewis's "Stealing a Baby" (1843). As these authors draw from medical discourse and ideas to construct their fictional worlds, they provide a clear fossil record of the prodigy's transformation into a literary figure and its role in the narration of racial kinship. Thus, I argue, the prodigy offered a way to capture and contain challenges to white paternity by exiling Blackness outside of genealogy.

By contrast, I then turn to a foundational work of African American biography, Susan Paul's *The Memoir of James Jackson, the Attentive and Obedient Scholar, Who Died in Boston, October 31, 1833, Aged Six Years and Eleven Months*, arguing that this early portrait of African American childhood as a positive experience draws on the elements of the prodigy in order to challenge that erasure of prodigy but also to expand recognition of kinship beyond the nuclear family. An attempt to rewrite the figure of the Black child denied futurity into a hagiography, *The Memoir of James Jackson* transforms the atemporality imposed on Blackness into a saintly transcendence. Paul's portrait of her brilliant and doomed pupil thus acts as a means of harnessing Black prodigy into a form of practical utopianism, in which James' early potential and untimely death unify readers in a call for their own self-perfection. This under-read narrative, labeled by its editor Lois Brown as the first biography by an African American author and likely the first nonfiction biography of an African American child, also challenges the most basic conventions of sentimental child death.[16] By redefining the child martyr as a Black boy, Paul transforms the exclusion of the prodigy from history into a transcendent overcoming of history that eschews linear genealogy for a network of communal pedagogy and care.

Finally, I return to Pip to show how reframing him as one among a company of comparable prodigies reveals a network of intersecting models of racial kinship already present in *Moby-Dick*. While the isolating logic of the prodigy pushes us to see Pip as a singular, exceptional figure, the fuller reading of the figure's history allows us to see him as a part of a larger system in which children of color are made exceptional in order to exclude them. Recognizing this pattern allows us to see not only the persistent cancelation of African American kinship, but also how dependent antebellum understandings of white kinship were on that cancelation—namely, that the cultural work of prodigy provides the necessary backdrop for white genealogy to take shape at all.

MEDICAL LITERATURE AND THE ELABORATION OF THE PRODIGY

In 1808, more than a dozen physicians were summoned to a New York court to give their expert testimony on the race of an eighteen-month-old girl. The case at hand was a paternity suit brought against Alexander Whistelo, a Black coachman in the city, by the municipal almshouse housing the child and her mother, Lucy Williams, a woman who described herself as the daughter of a "Scotchman" and a "black sambo."[17] Williams had identified Whistelo as the father because, as she testified, he had kept her prisoner and repeatedly raped her in the time leading up to the pregnancy. Whistelo, in turn, claimed that a white man who had broken into his home and had also assaulted Williams was the father, while Williams maintained that she had successfully fought off her white attacker before he could rape her.[18] The role of this panel of medical experts, then, was to determine whether her daughter, a child apparently with phenotypically white features, could have been fathered by an African American man.

Medical expertise, however, could arrive at no consensus about the infant. The majority of the physicians agreed the child's appearance appeared too white for her to have a Black father. A few, however, were not so sure. Most notably, a witness for the almshouse introduced as Dr. Mitchill argued—in testimony ranging from albinism to vitiligo to his past treatment of a woman so startled during pregnancy by the butchering of a favorite cow that it purportedly reshaped her child's feet into hooves—that parentage did not have such a stable effect on racial presentation.[19] The immediate reason for the difference of opinion was that Mitchill drew his conclusion from a much broader mixture of sources than that of the other physicians testifying, including three case studies from contemporary medical journals, references to Buffon's natural history encyclopedia, a personal anecdote, an appeal to Scottish poetry, and a story told by early modern philosopher Nicolas Malebranche.

In other words, the crux of the case rested simultaneously on the definition of racial heritability and on the consolidation of medicine as an expert discourse. This confrontation between the exceptional case and more everyday medical experience is best defined by another witness, Dr. Williamson, who argued that "if this was the child of that woman [Williams] by that man [Whistelo], it is a prodigy; and he did not believe prodigies happened, though daily experience unfortunately proved that perjuries did."[20] Drawing on older definitions of *prodigy* as a religiously tinged wonder, Williamson's quip, which was repeated in the defense's closing statement, outlines a boundary to the data that is intelligible to science. To understand the child in question as being the phenotypically white daughter of a Black man would make her appearance unexplainable by modern medicine and therefore place her outside of medical experience. Unable to reconcile Williams's account of her pregnancy with his understanding of science, Williamson discounts the former. Thus, in contrast to Mitchill's openness to considering reports of nearly any genre, his testimony evokes and then banishes the older scientific tradition of marvels and hearsay.

Williamson's point of view proved to be the more persuasive. The judge eventually found in favor of Whistelo, and Williamson's sense of a more carefully controlled set of scientific data matched the larger trends of the medical field as the century progresses.[21] Yet, if the prodigy represented cases too extreme, unexplainable, or arcane to be treated as medicine, that term would have a surprisingly resilient life in antebellum discourse. The new centrality of childhood to popular culture helped to put its most popular modern meaning—a precociously talented child—into heavy circulation, as part of the discussion around the "natural" potential and limits of youth, but this was only one type of many. When the *Boston Medical and Surgical Journal* describes the conjoined twins Chang and Eng Bunker as "prodigies" in 1829 or comments on the "prodigious muscular power" of J. A. J. Bihin, who was known as "The Belgian Giant" in his act for P. T. Barnum, the word retains Williamson's broader sense of bodies that do not fit medicine's narratives and therefore become spectacles of that narration.[22] Returning to the context of Lucy Williams's daughter, a child who was scrutinized by a dozen doctors to determine whether she had three Black grandparents or only one, *prodigy* emphasizes how medical discourse relies on cases of Blackness to construct narratives of heritability and on infant bodies as a touchstone for essentialist models of identity.

Accounts of Black infancy as a limit case for the inheritance of parental traits stem in large parts from the continued influence of Enlightenment authors on antebellum medicine. A passage republished repeatedly in the antebellum U.S. from *Natural History* by Georges-Louis Leclerc, Comte de Buffon, for instance, lingers on the cases of albino children born to Black African parents as a potential threat to theories of innate, heritable Blackness, only to dismiss these children as "accidental" and "barren" flukes not broadly reflective of race.[23] Similarly, Immanuel Kant's "On the Different Races of Man" (1775) uses the heritability of Blackness to children in order to define the concept of race, arguing that the children of one white and one Black parent are "necessarily hybrid, or blendlings," rather than proper continuations of either parent's genealogy.[24] Unlike the case of the child of a blond and a brunette parent, in which the infant might have the physical traits of either one of her parents, the child of a Black and a white parent would, Kant contends, resemble neither parent. In these ventures into scientific inheritance, the infant born Black became a key sign of congenital difference, promising through the evidence of complexion to be an empirical metric for the relationship between parent and child as well as for racial categorization. In other words, because Blackness was seen as a hypervisual and distinctly bounded trait, it became one of the key phenotypes used to represent both racial and familial inheritance.

In this pursuit for a scientific measure of race, the Black infant was significant not as a symbol of racial stability, but as a point of apparent systemic breakdown. Specifically, much as these early iterations of racial science were drawn to discussing Black infants as signs of intrinsic difference, they were also faced with what was for them an uncomfortable fact: like white infants, Black infants can be born with a range of complexions, including some of the same complexions as white infants. As a 1797 translation of Buffon explains, the "children [of African descent] are born white, or rather red, like those of other men. But two or three days after birth their color changes to a yellowish tawny, which grows gradually darker till the seventh or eighth day, when they are totally black."[25] An 1865 English translation of Johann Friedrich Blumenbach's anthropological treatise similarly declared that infants were born all with the same complexion and that it is only "in progress of time [that] the skin of Ethiopian infants turns to black."[26] For some, including Blumenbach, this shift in skin tone was evidence that whiteness and Blackness were environmental effects only gradually inscribed on the body, but for others, the existence of light-skinned African children remained an unexplained oddity—Kant's "Physical Geography," for instance, lists it as one of several "curiosities" of Blackness[27]—paralleling the figure of the "albino negro" as a limit case for complexion's ability to function as the marker of race. As environmental theories of race declined, infant complexion fit uneasily into models of race centered on an emergent biological essentialism.

The white confusion and sometimes consternation surrounding the complexion of Black infants thus lasted far beyond Enlightenment science, lingering in white medical discourse produced throughout the nineteenth century. As late as 1898, the New York-based *Medical News* ran a column declaring its total ignorance about the complexion of the Black newborn. The impetus of the column was an international debate on the subject; the *Medical News* piece mocks the London-based *Lancet* for its uncertainty about a French doctor's claim that "negro babies up to the age of seven days are similar in every respect to white babies" and ridicules the *Lancet*'s call for physicians in South Africa to settle the question. The anonymous New York columnist suggests that American doctors might be able to answer the question more conveniently, but, strangely, the American doctors whom it cites are equally contradictory: "An Alabama medical man says negro babies are black from the beginning, a Missourian says they are sallow or creamy-white."[28] While apparently mocking the general confusion over the question, the *Medical News* itself is absurdly unable to answer it, concluding with a general call to readers "with a newly-born picaninny or two on hand" to write back with an answer. If the sarcasm of the author seems directed at English doctors' ignorance of something commonplace for U.S. doctors, the piece illustrates its own equal ignorance. The variability of infant complexion that was well-known a hundred years earlier, if in an exaggerated or distorted form, has by the point of this publication been so erased from official knowledge that to ask the question itself appears as a joke.

Before this officially sanctioned ignorance of the late nineteenth century, antebellum medical discourse more readily discussed the obstacle that a newborn's complexion offered to the racialization of infancy. New Orleans physician and race scientist Samuel Cartwright contends in his 1857 essay "Natural History of the Prognathous Species of Mankind" that races constitute different species, going so far as to assert a fundamental difference in the number of skeletal plates in the skulls of white and Black infants. Absolute as Cartwright attempts to make this divide, he stumbles over what he terms "one remarkable particular," the question of infant complexion: the children of white and Black parents "are both born *white*, and so much alike as far as color is concerned, as scarcely to be distinguished from each other [emphasis in original]." Cartwright quickly promises that, however white at birth, the child of African American parents "begins to darken and continues to grow darker" after an unspecified "very short time." The emphasis that he places on both how dark the child will eventually become—a healthy child will age into a "shining black color"—and the care with which he underlines the inevitability of this differentiation, which will happen "whether exposed to air and light or not," signal the potential danger of such an instability and Cartwright's desire to contain it.[29] For infancy to have a changeable complexion, particularly in a period when the very notion of heritability was under heavy debate, was to suggest a permeability in racial boundaries in serious need of management.

Thus, as color solidified as the primary marker and metonymy of race, the Black infant (or rather, the Black infant who might not yet be discernably "black") existed in a state of strange suspension. Infancy could appear to prove that race was congenital and essential to the individual body, but the actual bodies of Black infants did not fit such a convenient model for medical discourses of race. Instead, as I have suggested, the material circumstances of birth fed into a more oblique but no less destructive ideology of race: the construction of Black infancy as a chaotic site of freakishness on which history and genealogy alike have no purchase. As disability studies scholar Ellen

Samuels defines it, the discourse of freakishness was used in the antebellum period to racialize disability. In her discussion of Millie and Christine McKoy, Samuels explains the racialization of disability in this way: "Enfreakment describes the process by which individual difference becomes stylized as cultural otherness."[30] But the enfreakment of Black childhood, to borrow Samuels's term, runs in both directions. The figure of the Black infant "born white" conflates the categories of racial difference by making individual variation into a trait of racial variation. Thus the Black child "born white" is racialized not only by the color of her eventual complexion or that of her parents', but also by the perceived unpredictability of her body.

In the early nineteenth century, this association of Black infancy with physicians' attempts to study heritability on an empirical basis was further intensified by new interest in superfoetation. Now more commonly referred to as *superfetation*, the phenomenon refers to the purported possibility of an additional fertilization occurring in an already pregnant woman, producing two fetuses gestating simultaneously without being twins. Eager to find instances of this rare occurrence, doctors had essentially two ways to recognize a pregnancy involving superfetation. The first was to look for cases in which a woman either had a miscarriage and then, shortly after, delivered a child, or had two miscarriages within a short period of time—the presumption being that twins would have miscarried or been born together and that such events must represent two distinct pregnancies. Such scenarios were reported, but they could be hard to substantiate, given the difficulty of diagnosing a miscarriage and the hazy sense that doctors still had of normal conception times.[31]

A more supposedly definitive method of demonstrating superfetation, and one certainly more salacious to readers, was to report women who seemed to have fathered twins by two different, racially distinct men. For example, a letter written in *the Medical Repository*, a New York medical journal (incidentally, edited by Dr. Mitchill of the Whistelo case), supported claims of superfetation with two cases of women giving birth to twins who appeared to have different racial identities. In a brief anecdote, mentioned as an aside, the author recounts that a "negro woman brought a black child and a mulatto at a birth," after purported sexual encounters with her Black husband and, later, with a white man.[32] His focus, however, is given to a longer tale of a white woman who delivered twins with differing complexions, leading the physician to conclude that she had been impregnated by both her white husband and an unnamed Black man. He teases out the mechanics of this situation in some detail, reasoning that "the one [egg] was accidentally impregnated with semen of the white man, and the other impregnated with semen of the black man, and therefore one [child] was white and the other a mulatto."[33] By this account, race (or, more precisely, the phenotypes associated with race) is made to act as an early guarantor of parentage, promising to differentiate between the "semen of the white man" and the "semen of the black man." Paternity can, the author suggests, be indisputably inscribed on the body.

Much as these reports seem to promise to stabilize genealogy, they also reiterate the constant threat of a broken genealogy, summoning up visions of women who cross the color line to have multiple sexual partners and threats of African American men lurking to ruin white marriages. This is a familiar set of tropes invoking fears of miscegenation, female desire, and Black masculinity.[34] Collectively projected onto the symbol of the Black infant, however, they take on the more particular form of the prodigy, marking the limits of what can be recognized as kinship. The ability to project racial identity onto infants—effectively, to diagnose a child as Black—provided physicians a seemingly unquestionable way to trace inheritance, but in a way that could only negate genealogy; racial phenotype could not confirm paternity, but it did seem to offer a way to definitively negate it.

The signification of the prodigy as a life outside genealogy could even emerge in more extreme cases in which Black childhood might have no literal presence. One 1808 letter written by a Dr. Chris C. Yates and published in the journal *the Philadelphia Medical Museum* entitled "Account of a Monster" opens with the promise of presenting "a very extraordinary animal . . . produced by a three year old heifer."[35] The details of this origin are quickly thrown into doubt, however, by his tale of a heifer that showed "symptoms of great distress" and is locked in a barn on the farmer's quoted presumption that "she was getting mad." On his return, the farmer finds the heifer "licking what he supposed was her calf," though he had not believed that she was pregnant. In a strange turn, Yates reports that "on a nearer approach [the farmer] discovered its form different from what he expected, and attempted to take it up by the legs, when the heifer darted at him with violence, struck her hoof against the monster's head and broke it," after which the cadaver was promptly sold, preserved, and put on display, where Yates first encountered it.

From this gothic beginning of a disturbed animal that may or may not have given birth to a strange "monster" whom she seems to instinctively fear, the report shifts abruptly into a more conventionally technical description of the body's anatomy, which the examiner presents as the uncanny double of a Black child:

> From the forehead over the back of the neck, it very much resembles a child; indeed the head from a back view would be mistaken for that of a child. The nose resembles about as much that of a negro as of a calf, I think rather more. . . . . The arms or fore legs resemble the human; there is one joint more; it measures from the shoulder to the elbow about four inches; from the elbow to the next joint (which is half way between the elbow and hoofs) three inches; . . . from here the hoofs or webbed fingers begin to extend themselves, dividing into five parts, distinguishing thumb and fingers, having at the extremity small marks or spots where the nails should have been, the substance of the hand or hoof the same as of the calf. From below the under jaw or chin down to the pubes, human; breast broad, abdomen *full* [emphasis in original].[36]

It is hard to pinpoint the ethical standing of the body that Yates describes. It is most likely nothing more than a cow fetus that had developed in an uncommon way and whose owners had packaged in extra mystery for the sake of business. But it is impossible to miss, in the constant refrain of how very much like a Black child it is, the possibility that this was a human life that Yates has reduced past the level of even the animal. Note, too, how careful the farmer is to avoid stipulating that his heifer actually gave birth to the body he sold; absent for the birth and unsuspecting of the pregnancy, he can only say that he "supposed" the body to be a calf.

Rather than trying to tag some certain status to the body described, then, it is more critical to notice how easily the Black child becomes the form through which uncertain genealogy is attached to a body. In reports of superfetation, the Black infant signaled a transgression across racial boundaries, but her complexion also promised to allow an accounting for genealogy. For "Account of a Monster," the transgression is more stigmatized and relies on the conflation of Blackness with animality. Bestiality, rather than miscegenation, is the threat underlying this report, an explanation that Yates manages both to suggest and to distance himself from with his conclusion that "at first glance every one is impressed with its resemblance to a negro child, and many suppose it the issue of a man with the heifer." The accusation would follow antebellum associations of Black masculinity with hypersexuality, yet this is not precisely the scenario that Yates offers. Rather than attributing Blackness to the putative father, race emerges only in the child, acting not as a sign of membership in a group identity but as an additional symptom of its confused status between human and animal.

There is a further material factor to this rhetoric only hinted at in Yates's mention of the infant body sold and displayed. Because enslaved people were often sold, or just given, to physicians as objects to be manipulated for research, they became a central source of subjects for reports on physical deformity and disease. As Todd Savitt's work on antebellum medicine establishes, the bodies of enslaved people of all ages were routinely made test subjects for experimentation, dissection, and exhibition.[37] In addition, the greed of plantation owners who were eager to raise birthrates left pregnant women and their children especially vulnerable to physicians attempting new procedures. This worked to the advantage of medical students as well as to established practitioners. In Southern medical schools, students learning obstetrics routinely used the childbirths of enslaved women as opportunities for practice until their skills were deemed polished enough for white clients.[38] For many doctors working in that area, the first infant they delivered would have been Black and born enslaved, while enslaved women were forced to endure the mistakes caused by their inexperience. For established physicians, too, access to enslaved women significantly enabled the early and violent research into reproductive health. Among other examples, J. Marion Sims, the so-called father of gynecology and inventor of the modern speculum, claimed his title through prolonged sequences of experimental vaginal surgeries performed on three enslaved women named Anarcha, Betsey, and Lucy, all of which were done without anesthetic and frequently in the presence of spectators.[39]

The living bodies of enslaved women and their children provided the foundation for the new field of reproductive science.[40]

While physicians framed their work on adult enslaved women largely in terms of their reproductive potential, Black infancy came to be particularly associated with the commercial and medical display of congenital disability. In her history of childbirth under slavery, Marie Jenkins Schwartz demonstrates the informal but competitive marketplace for the bodies of Black fetuses and infants as medical samples, particularly when they commanded the extra medical "interest" of disability.[41] She notes, for instance, one southern doctor named Charles A. Hentz whose journal revels in receiving one infant cadaver that had been taken from an enslaved woman and swathed in newspaper as a "present" for his collection and another, an only partially developed fetus, which he kept for himself after treating an enslaved woman who had miscarried.[42] As Schwartz demonstrates, attending the birth of a child with unusual, congenital disability was a source of publication and prestige for physicians, who in turn were ruthless in obtaining the bodies of such children from enslaved parents unable to protest. Schwartz records at least one formerly enslaved woman, Ellen Betts, who recalled a child who had been born with two faces being bought from its owner by a physician, who then murdered the child and preserved its body.[43] Through such practices, Black infants became one of the key populations through which physicians discussed disability and therefore were often used as spectacles of disability to be presented to the wider public.

Because of the conditions of medical practice, Blackness became doubly associated with unpredictable bodies, first because non-white skin was represented as a physical abnormality in itself but also because the most prominent examples of disability drew on the bodies of enslaved people and were recirculated from plantations into the market of medical specimens. While antebellum discourses of Blackness and disability converge on a very broad level as categories of bodies pushed outside of normativity, through the filter of infancy they took on a far more particular and overlapping symbolic weight. The "unruly" complexion of Black infants appears already in such discourse as a body that defies management, its categorization suspended or made provisionally as an act of faith in the heritability of racial markers. Its association with congenital disability mirrors and reinforces this fixation on the body that seems to break from its genealogy. If normative reproduction imagines the birth of each generation as a uniform extension of the present into the future, through medical discourses of abnormality the figure of the Black child came to represent a perceived threat to these continuities.

As mentioned, Spillers identifies the medical gaze as having an unbinding effect on enslaved bodies' relationship to social structures because medicine's objectification acknowledges no possibility for Black kinship.[44] Yet, paradoxically, the Black infant, perhaps precisely because her origin has been so mystified by this refusal to see kinship, provides the key figure for medicine to consider how bodies are inherited between generations and the limits to that inheritance. At the same time that medical portrayals of Black infants as prodigies erase Black kinship, they provide the technical framework through which white kinship is allowed to exist. When these images of the prodigy moved into the realm of the literary, they took on still greater and more explicit power in defining white genealogy, such that the ejection of Blackness from history became the precondition for consolidating white genealogy.

LITERATURES OF MEDICINE

Accustomed as we currently are to a sharp division between the prose of the medical report and the prose of literature, the two appear side-by-side in antebellum journals, making the drift of medical notions of race into literature, at times, a very short journey. Also at this time, the growing preference for medical schools over individual internships was contributing to the establishment of medicine as an expert discipline with an emerging system of credentialization and technical discourse. Still, this shift was in its early days, and even professionally trained physicians routinely drew on information from other medical traditions, such as female midwifery and folk knowledge of herbs.[45] Medical discourse could thus be quite wide-ranging in scope. For example, in *Almshouse v. Whistelo*, the paternity suit I discussed previously, the expert witness Dr. Mitchill draws one of his references from poetry and treats the authority of that case as comparable to his other evidence.[46]

Literature and medicine certainly represented different fields, but they were fields with significant crossover.

Medical journals at the time tend to take a protective view of their authority, frequently publishing columns decrying "quacks" or making uncomplimentary asides about midwives, but even they can be decidedly esoteric in their contents. Discussions of disease often run alongside commentary on medical ethics or the health concerns of marrying young or long epistolary debates on academic scandals; *the London Medical and Surgical Journal* includes in an 1830 issue, with no context, a recipe for dandelion coffee taken from a gardening manual.[47] Likewise, a blurb it published in the following year considers new regulations concerning beer brewing.[48] Even articles that are conventionally medical in content also often take the form of literary genres. Reports on the state of medicine abroad are often upfront about presenting the author's memories of a trip and thus strongly echo the form of contemporary travel literature.[49] Similarly, first-person narration was the common model for case studies, which recounted how the doctor encountered a patient, how treatment unfolded, and, at times, the dialogue exchanged between doctor and patient. Published in another venue, some antebellum case study could be taken for memoir or short story rather than rarefied science.

As the often-sensationalist language of the above case studies may have suggested, medical writing drew on sometimes capacious topics and borrowed literary techniques to capture practitioners' emotions.[50] Barrington's "Skinning a Black Child" and Lewis's "Stealing a Baby" emerge in this overlap from either side of the Atlantic, with both using a pseudo-medical discourse to depict white physicians stymied by the unexpected arrival of a Black infant. These texts reveal that when the prodigy migrates into literature more explicitly interested in social structures, it figures most immediately in a crisis over the status of white paternity. Where the social structures of kinship had served as the sole guarantors of fatherhood, the medical trappings of the prodigy threaten to overturn the authority of these structures. The possibility of using race to define biological inheritance and kinship—to proclaim with confidence, as the superfetation cases studies do, that this twin is the child of a white man and that twin the child of a Black man, regardless of whom their mother had married or of what their mother might say—threatened the traditional authority of white genealogy. If a medical examination could assign children from one race to another and therefore from one father to another, it could also throw any other signifier of kinship into doubt. The ability to expel the Black child from narratives of white family and to disqualify them from genealogy as spontaneous and isolated flukes is a reiteration of the imposed kinlessness which, as Nancy Bentley argues, "extract[s] the sheer materiality of a human population . . . from the sphere of the familial."[51] It is also, though, an attempt to stabilize white genealogy by contrast.

The earlier of these texts, Barrington's "Skinning a Black Child," seems to have migrated into the medical world partly by merit of the already literary qualities of case studies. The story, a comic account of Irish country doctors first published as a part of Barrington's memoir, was republished fairly predictably into *the Athenæum*, a London literary journal. Then, and perhaps less predictably, it reemerged in the *London Medical and Surgical Journal*, where it was presented between a report on blood chemistry and a report on cholera treatment and given the headline "State of Medicine in Ireland." The format of all three of these articles is the same, with only an editor's foreword to warn that the story's report should not be read seriously. Nor was the inclusion of conventional literature (fiction, drama, or poetry) a recurring feature of the journal, which suggests that the journal's editors saw "Skinning" as some combination of a satire of a medical case study and commentary on colonial medicine, a topic that was often covered in the journal.[52] When the excerpt was republished in the United States, it appeared mainly in generalist magazines or literary gazettes.[53] The medical jargon that forms a central portion of the prose echoes the other conventional medical articles often republished by mainstream papers and might persuade an unwary reader that it is a scientific, rather than fictional, account.

The scene that opens "Skinning a Black Child" is a hopeful one. A white George Washington is hosting a banquet to celebrate the birth of his first child as his white wife is in labor upstairs. The revelry is interrupted, however, by the midwife's stammering announcement that, while mother and child are both healthy and resting, there is something unusual about the newborn son. First, she exclaims of the infant, "It's—not so—so *white* as it should be [all emphasis in original]," and, to the contrary, "the dear little boy is—is—is—quite *black*."[54] As a chorus of "'*Black! black!*' echoed from every quarter of the apartment," the women of the party quickly decide that, as Mrs. Washington's virtue is beyond question, the child must be Satanic, a quite literal offspring of the devil. Meanwhile, Mr. Washington and his wife's brother seek a more empirical reassurance in the form of a physician who convinces them that the coloring of the child's skin is actually a rather large birthmark. Though acknowledging that the mark is unusually expansive, covering the entire body of the child, he argues that it might still be removed like other birthmarks, through a gradual removal of the affected skin. Thus, they settle on the titular strategy—skinning a Black child in order to find the white child within. The plan fails in an unsurprisingly ghastly fashion, as deeper and deeper gashes reveal only deeper and deeper levels of blood, flesh, and finally bone that is itself revealed to be black. The physicians declare the boy to be a hopeless case and refuse to attend further to "a thing that was so clearly supernatural." The family exiles the boy to live with a dry-nurse and to die an early death after being gored by his father's cattle.

Readers of its day seem to have encountered "Skinning a Black Child" as a relatively light comic tale about rural Ireland. Although it is introduced in its Philadelphia and New York republications with little comment, "Skinning a Black Child" was printed in London's *the Athenaeum* with the description of being a tale "too good to pass up" and is recommended for "those who love a hearty laugh."[55] The *London Medical and Surgical Journal* very carefully and somewhat stodgily outlines the reasons why the story should not be taken as documentary truth, but eventually settles on the surprising endorsement of it as a "precious narrative."[56] These short paratexts are, of course, nowhere close to a satisfying reception history, and presumably not even all white readers, much less Black readers, would have taken the violence quite so in stride. Still, the dramatic irony of a narrator announcing an obscure, Latinate condition to explain a white woman's giving birth to a Black child in almost the same breath that he mentions a Black man also being in the household makes it clear that the story was structured to be humorous. The ease with which laughter and Black children—or, more particularly, laughter and the medical torture of

Black children—go hand-in-hand points to the particular short-circuit that Black children represented to white supremacy between thinking of family as a social structure and family as a biological unit.

This insistence that marriages (not sex) produce children forms the basic premise of Barrington's joke. Polite society is so eager to preserve Mrs. Washington's honor that they overlook the Black valet living nearby in her brother's household, revert to antiquated and absurd medical theories, and eventually attempt to physically hack away the evidence of an indiscretion from the newborn's body, all in order to avoid doubting her loyalty. However, rather than simply being a misogynist parody about the faithlessness of women, though it certainly is that as well, "Skinning" reveals fundamental anxiety about whether patriarchal genealogies have ever been reliable.[57] From the outset, the father figure's own identity is as much a matter of dispute as his son's. Mr. George Washington is not *the* George Washington but "Mr. George Washington, of Dureen, in Ireland," and is only "supposed" by local rumor to be "some distant blood relation" to his more famous counterpart.[58] The basis of this belief, which Barrington frames as laughable, is the town's absurdly strong faith that social genealogy (the stuff of marriage, pedigree, and surnames) is the equivalent of biological genealogy and blood relation. The same logic that makes his wife's son unquestionably his son drives Washington's assurance that two men of the same name must inevitably share a lineage.

Through this blurring between the social and the biological, the specific crisis of inheritance represented by the unexpectedly Black child is a crisis of inherited property. A large part of the obsession with his child's racial presentation lies with Washington's attempt to reinforce his own claim to a vaguely imagined, but strongly held belief that "his Excellency [President Washington], when dying, would leave a capital legacy in America to his blood relation, Mr. George Washington."[59] This more distant and more explicitly property-minded tie thus ultimately becomes most important goal in the bloody attempts to re-race the infant: "the mode [the physician] pursued was very *scientific;* he made two parallel slashes as deep as he could in reason, about three inches down the upper part of the arm, and a cross one, to introduce the forceps and strip the loose Black skin off, when he could snip it away at the bottom, and leave the white or rather red flesh underneath to generate a new skin and show the proper colouring for a god-child of General Washington."[60] The fantasy of manipulating and remaking the infant's body suggests a desire to take over the role of the mother's body in forming the child with a "new skin" in the husband's image, a pre-*Frankenstein* attempt to replace maternity with masculine science. In this substitution of father for mother, though, Barrington also overleaps the immediate father for the abstract approval of the putative godfather, General Washington. The Irish Washington needs confirmation that biological reproduction follows the forms of social kinship and that marriage in particular secures paternity, in order to make a shared surname into a blood tie and affirm his own fantasized genealogy.

The persistence of Blackness, which lasts down onto the very bones of the child, points to a more existential problem than extramarital sexuality. The doctor's search for the "white or rather red" to be found within young Washington echoes and brutally redefines Buffon's assertion, discussed earlier, that all children are born "white, or rather red," substituting the red skin of a newborn for the red of a wound. However, while Buffon's original assertion would make all newborns racially ambiguous, Barrington's interpretation rests on a notion of Blackness as fundamental and immutable. Thus, after his final cut into the child, the doctor announces a difference that permeates the body, declaring that "he could see the very bone, Black also . . . actually dyed in the grain."[61] The child's difference runs so deep that it cannot be effaced. Yet what is interesting here is not that the child is banished from the putative line of Washingtons but that his Blackness banishes him from genealogies in general. While the reader is meant to understand that the biological father is the Black valet from America, the medical conclusion is that the child is "either the devil or a *lusus Naturæ*" (a "freak of nature").[62] He does not become the son of a Black man; he becomes an imp whose origin is spontaneous and beyond human knowledge and yet whose body, as a sign of those origins, acts as a site of obsessive and brutal investigation.

As the text describes it, then, the child's Blackness upsets established notions of genealogy as a whole. If a child of Washington would inherit property as well as whiteness, the child of a practically or tacitly enslaved "servant" paradoxically inherits the inability to inherit. Not only is the young Washington denied full entry into the Washington family, the identity of his probable father is erased and denied. His Blackness prevents him from being seen as a true son of Washington, but Washington's pride prevents him from admitting that his son might have another father. The child and his probable biological father are thus ironically aligned only by the social refusal to grant either of them family ties. The newborn George Washington, as the product of a relationship that cannot be socially acknowledged, becomes a monstrous object that seems to be emerge from nowhere.

Much like the grotesque humor of "Skinning a Black Child," "Stealing a Baby" is something like white supremacy's take on slapstick. "Stealing a Baby" is a first-person narration by Lewis's semi-autobiographical character, Madison Tensas, or "the Louisiana Swamp Doctor," who recalls being an overly earnest and slightly disreputable medical student, and his courtship of the wealthy Lucy.[63] Obsessed with dissection, Madison steals a Black infant cadaver in hopes of studying its anatomy in the comforts of his own home. The plan misfires, however, when his would-be fiancée, Lucy, involves him in an unexpected tryst that is then interrupted by her father. The hijinks culminate in the untimely emergence of the dead child, who falls out the student's coat in the moment when the couple tumbles to the ground in front of the sweetheart's protective father in a parody of childbirth that ruins Madison's chances at marriage, family life, and access to Lucy's wealth. The punchline is a vile one, even in the context of an unabashedly vile story, hinging on the comic misattachment of childhood and family to a Black body, when, by the reasoning of the story, they should belong only to a white one. The latter promises lineal futurity while the other suspends the narrator in a state of perpetual bachelorhood.

The intimacies around this prodigious birth of a Black cadaver from the pocket of a white man bring an end to Madison's attempt to become a patriarch in his own right. Barred from a relationship with Lucy and disgraced among genteel society, Madison, as his older narrating self explains, fails to marry or have the legitimate children who could carry on his family line.[64] Instead, in his theft of a dead child and its apparently spontaneous reemergence, he enters a distorted version of that kinship, in which the physicality of bodies forms the explicit basis for connection, rather than something to be repressed or denied. Accordingly, the narrator recounts his theft as the moment in which the infant places some hold upon him, rather than the opposite; Lewis writes, "I strove to depart, but something formed a bond of association between that dead nigger baby and myself, which held me to my place with my gaze riveted upon it."[65] This is not a scene of ethical recognition, and dehumanizes the dead child as an object of study and dissection. Yet when Lewis's narrator imagines himself in possession of the child body, the language presents it as a grotesque inversion of family. The medical student's interest in the body causes him to treat it as "tenderly as if alive," and his assertion of ownership remakes the corpse into an entity that he calls "my baby."[66]

In his parody of a family, Lewis also places white domesticity in opposition to corporeality and death, which are instead associated with Blackness. Following this logic, his protagonist loses his right to the former by his connection to the latter. By introducing a particularly material version of the body as admissible into domestic bonds of feeling, the child/corpse transforms Madison's desire for the white Lucy into a similarly ghoulish interest in bodies. In light of his morbid tenderness to the child, Madison's earlier confession that, mid-kiss with his lover, he would sometimes examine her lips and wonder "whether, even in death, electricity by some peculiar adaptation might not be able to continue their bewitching suction" moves from the realm of awkward bookishness into horror.[67] Because he can enter something mirroring the forms of kinship with a body that is politically barred from such elevation, the effect is to recast his romantic relationship as possessing a dangerously similar physical element. By displacing the biological elements of kinship onto a Black child excluded from family, Lewis asserts a white family structure that remains above bodily entanglement.

This unbinding effect that juvenile flesh can have on the social configurations comes through most clearly in F. O. C. Darley's illustration of the moment when the child tumbles into the street in front of Madison's would-be fiancée, her jealous father, and the city marshal, entitled "Stealing a Nigger Baby." The image offers a caricature of an impossible birth; the medical student lies rocked onto his back with his feet up and askew while staring at the child that has appeared beside him. His hat, fallen back to his shoulders, creates the appearance of a feminine bonnet while a peculiar roundness to his chest hints at a bosom. Meanwhile, in the long, thin object trailing out from between

Madison's legs, perhaps a fold of clothing or a riding crop, there is also the suggestion of an umbilical cord forgotten in the afterbirth. It is as if, because his unacceptable selection of child has cut him off from the projected role of the patriarchal head of a household, Madison has slipped into a monstrous form of femininity instead—a stance that, judging from his facial expression, horrifies no one so much as himself.

Moreover, the fleshiness that is the prevailing quality of the dead child sprawled in the foreground—its body is the only skin revealed in the image other than the uncovered faces of the other figures, and the details of its collapsed and chubby limbs, with its tiny detailed hands and dimpled elbows bent at delicate angles, are presented with a more careful realism than the rest of the group—seems to have also carried the female love-interest. Though she is entirely covered by clothing, dark gloves give Lucy the appearance of hands the same shade as the child. Her broken parasol, snapped at the shaft, suggests a complexion whose fairness is no longer protected, while the shared posture of the two (head turned away from the viewer, one arm up, and one down, with cocked wrists) further aligns the pair. Even the symmetry of their two bodies in relation to the sprawled male figure suggests a paralleling of their respective roles in relation to him. The child's undermining effect on a sentimental reading of the couple, which emerges in the text largely as a retrospective reevaluation, appears in the picture as a synchronous realignment of ties. The unplanned arrival of a Black infant not only distracts the protagonist from his white potential wife, at the same time it also puts the values that she represents to the story in doubt. In both the text and illustration, the Black infant, divided by race and death from its potential parent-figures, proves to be an ultimately unassimilable self and one whose inclusion becomes the undoing of the structures that seek to absorb it.

PIP: AN ASIDE

The second half of this chapter moves to Susan Paul's attempt to rewrite the prodigy as a viable life and even a source of liberation, but before leaving the medicalized prodigy, I want to pause and tease out a little more of what it means to be a figure who is pushed outside of genealogy and yet is used to define it. It is not obvious how or why social death, particularly such a complete social death as the all-but-stillborn prodigy, could construct the temporality of the social. Nor is it easy to shift from Lewis's and Barrington's deathly infants into fully living beings who nonetheless remain pushed out of history, because to be labeled a prodigy by medical discourse is to be excluded from subjectivity. The prodigy is presented as a body to be examined, tested, or manipulated, but it is not a person, nor is it a character in any straightforward sense. This projection of blank flesh dovetails easily with the passive dependence of infancy, but can the prodigy outlive this infant exclusion? How does the framing of Black childhood, or, even more particularly, of Black infancy or Black birth, extend to shape the broader depictions of Black lives?

To circle back to Pip, the character with whom I began, Melville seems to offer a case of prodigy attained later in life. Pip's age is never established, but Ishmael believes that there is an acute cause for his separation from the crew and status as a medical oddity: his abandonment at sea. There is no diegetic evidence of a change in Pip's actual behavior, but certainly after the crew decides that he is an incurable "idiot," Pip knows that a part of himself has been lost. Wandering the deck, he reminds the crew over and over that he is not a part of the ship, but has been banished to someplace elsewhere, repeatedly imploring the sailors with cries of "who's seen Pip? . . . Monsieurs, have ye seen one Pip?" and demanding they recognize that "Pip's missing."[68] The social alienation and self-alienation of his position thus become a symptom of delusional speech and further confirmation for the crew that Pip's behavior reflects the pathological, rather than the personal.

However, to present a before and after of Pip's estrangement fails to capture how this social alienation also distances Pip from linear time. Part of his distance from his shipmates is that he must survive with a different kind of history than they do. Introduced as being "prelusive of eternal time," a Melvillian translation of the always already, Pip lives not just in the proleptic time of a novel that continually foreshadows its tragedy, but also in a paradoxical preemption of those warnings.[69] The narrator warns that the *Pequod*'s crew would go "to lay the world's grievances before that bar from which not very many of them ever come back," but, as for "Black Little Pip," "he never did—oh, no! he went before."[70] The syntax is slippery, allowing "he never did" to refer to the journey as much as to the return, such that Pip either does not join the crew in their voyage to death because he will have already drowned on the way, or does not return from that encounter because he will have died and therefore preceded the surviving portion of the crew in their still-eventual death. That both are true, because Pip both does and does not die before the rest of the *Pequod*, indicates how difficult it is to map a timeline of even Pip's personal history, for in either case the contradiction of one who "never did" because he did so "before" loops back to the subject who precedes time. Pip provides us with the negative construction of the always already, the already never, to a subject who is born into social cancelation.

SANCTIFYING THE PRODIGY

The cluster of associations that I am tracing under the term *prodigy* are perhaps especially pernicious because they also work to translate individual achievements that could have undermined white supremacist rhetorics into signs of aberration. Like Ishmael's conclusion that when Pip speaks "heaven's sense" it must be thanks to his "insanity" rather than his wisdom, prodigious thinking trades on a skewed logic of exceptionality.[71] The more extraordinary a Black subject is, the less representative she is of any larger potential, except the potential to be abnormal.[72] Because history was and is often written as a series of famous men, in the style of Thomas Carlyle's heroes, the tendency to pathologize remarkable lives as flukes or oddities not only worked to dismiss those subjects but also dismissed the idea of African Americans having a broader connection to the past. Confronting and transforming the figure of the prodigy was therefore also an important means for Black authors to rescript notions of collectivity and a collective past outside of racial essentialism.[73] Extracting the prodigy from the realm of science or medicine offered an opportunity to reimagine the structure of social kinship at the same time that it allowed a humanizing of individual subjects.

One text that undertakes this project is Susan Paul's *The Memoir of James Jackson*. Paul, an abolitionist activist and teacher, is often considered one of the first African American biographers to be published, yet her work places very little weight on the qualities that conventionally distinguish a historical figure. Indeed, one of the most conspicuous features of Paul's 1835 text *The Memoir of James Jackson* is how little value the text places on fame, public accomplishment, or even narrative suspense. A glance at the full subtitle—"The Attentive and Obedient Scholar who Died in Boston, October 31, 1833, Aged Six Years and Eleven Months"—gives as good a summary of Paul's hagiography as one could ask.[74] This disregard for the trappings of plot or narrative development suits its subject: a brilliant and deeply Christian boy who died before he could *do* much of anything. Yet, in telling the story of such an apparently ahistorical subject as James Jackson, marginalized by his race, his age, and his illness, Susan Paul rescripts the role of the Black prodigy to remake its historical discontinuity into an opportunity. By lingering not on the ways that James's prodigy falls beneath the historical record, but rather how it exceeds the historical record, Paul reconfigures what types of genealogies are worth recording. *The Memoir*, instead, allows for a means of removing genealogy from the domains of both historical time and biology, and redefines it as a spiritual relationship. Paul's prodigy, in other words, emphasizes James's elevation through the active efforts of his community in order to show how the bonds of teaching and faith create a utopian practice capable of giving reprieve, if not full escape, from history.

Harkening back to Puritan stories of saintly child deaths, such as James Janeway's *A Token for Children* (1671) or Cotton Mather's appendix "A Token for Children of New England" (1700), the child hagiography was a tremendously popular and rigidly formulaic genre when *The Memoir* was first published. From the 1820s through the 1840s, the New York-based American Tract Society alone released a series of more than a dozen such accounts of child deaths, at times reaching printing runs of more than ten thousand copies per year.[75] Paul's biography draws from an accordingly well-defined set of religious conventions to mark its subject as one of the elect. James is commended for his devotion to authority, as his "constant desire to please" his teacher makes James "an assistant, by his example" in "the government of other children"; his unusually retentive memory for hymns and scripture; and his love to hear the Bible read, even when his siblings grow restless.[76] Peppered with scriptural excerpts and lyrics from hymns, the text also creates an authorial persona who is far more interested in continuing tradition rather than personal originality. Furthermore, while James is exemplary for his intellect—Paul's narrator reports that "during the first year which James attended school, he learned more than many children do in three"[77]—this scholastic genius is carefully funneled into the norms of childish goodness that is James's true distinction. His memory regarding the rules serves his obedience, his curiosity fuels his questions about God, and his eloquence allows him to play "little *preacher*" to the other children.[78] As Paul explains, James's precociousness registers not as an early advance into adulthood but as a concentration of the virtues prescribed for childhood, declaring, for instance, that "we must be indulged in saying, we never saw a child who seemed so much like innocence itself."[79] James is remarkable precisely because he fulfills the role of the conventional, implicitly white child-saint so perfectly.

As the publication history of *The Memoir* reflects, Paul's placement of an individual and genuinely historical Black child into these standardized forms of white childhood resonates with a radical effect. As Lois Brown, the scholar who recovered *The Memoir* and verified its history, explains, Paul originally sought distribution through the relatively apolitical channels of the American Sunday School Union. Only after the Union refused, presumably for fear of controversy, did Paul agree to have the biography published through abolitionist channels. If, as Max Cavitch suggests, such literary rituals of mourning act as a moment of unification by "bolster[ing] the threatened family ties for which the dead child is also the symbol," then Paul's addition of James to this genre canon therefore acts as a tacit insistence that the death of a Black child should equally serve as a touchstone for bolstering a cross-racial U.S. community.[80] Thus, while the preface names two audiences, its white and Black readers, the opening of the *Memoir* itself combines them into a single body, addressing them familially as "My dear children."[81] By its form alone, the *Memoir* encourages this consolidation into a single family by presenting James's legacy as a collective loss and a shared experience of grief.

Paul's deployment of the child saint to describe a Black child also aligns him with the prodigy narratives I have discussed, threatening to reduce his genius to peculiarity and transform his final illness into a confirmation of his abnormality rather than his holiness. In order to prevent such narratives from isolating James, Paul proceeds with a thorough replacement of the corporeal with the spiritual. For James, himself, this means a total silence regarding his physical body except for three moments in the text: first, an aside mentioning his "dark skin" when he is bullied for his race; second, a brief mention that "sometimes, he was attacked by . . . very wicked boys, and badly hurt"; and, finally, his death scene, which is the only occasion when his body receives prolonged discussion.[82] By contrast to the rest of text, the description of James's failing body, finally dying after convulsions and pain, is both more prominent and more detailed:

> James still looked as if his heart was full of joy; but his eyes began to grow dim, his hands were cold, and in a few minutes all was calm; the glazed eyes of the dear child once more beamed forth with unspeakable delight, and he exclaimed, 'This is God my Saviour; O Lord, this is Jesus.'—His eyes closed, his heart ceased to beat, and all was still. James was dead. Nothing remained but a cold and lifeless lump of clay. But his spirit, with which he used to love God, was carried away by angels to heaven.[83]

James's heart, his hands, and his eyes provide the action in their alternating fading and revival, but their integration into a body, much less into James himself, appears only on the very threshold of death, and still only in the oblique summations that "all was calm" and "all was still." Even this vague collective of "all" is revealed to be a full body only after the departure of James to heaven—when "nothing remained but a cold and lifeless lump of clay"—and even in that moment Paul replaces the physical body with a symbol, proffering a symbol of materiality rather than materiality itself. James's body, then, appears precisely in order to mark its inability to represent James himself.

Such a division between soul and flesh is hardly unusual, but in Paul's hands, the division becomes a sharply pointed rebuke of the expert authority that physicians normally held over Black children. That, at the first sign of illness, Mrs. Jackson "immediately" sends for a doctor announces a degree of respectability and wealth as well as affection.[84] Upon his arrival, however, the doctor is examined by James regarding his spiritual health, rather than the reverse. Asking the physician if "you *love God*, *my Saviour?* [Paul's emphasis]" and if "you know God my Saviour?," the child shifts the encounter to a realm in which he holds the authority and thereby changes the tenor of the doctor's thinking. The physician's response that James is "*a happy child*" proves to be the only diagnosis he makes.[85] Similarly, when physical disability appears in the text, in the form of a concluding poem, "The Little Blind Boy," about a Black child who is refused entrance to an all-white institution for the blind, it quickly transforms from a physical condition affecting him to a spiritual condition affecting white authorities. As the child speaker complains, school officials "cannot see / My soul through my skin." His mother consoles him at the poem's close, saying "many with eyes are far blinder than you."[86] Paul retains a language of stigma for disability, but she makes clear that that stigma should attach to a spiritual quality rather than a physical one.

This careful devaluation of the biological subject in preference for the spiritual subject further gives Paul the framework to make James the impetus for a qualitatively different kind of kinship, one removed from reproductive lines and focused on religious concordance. For instance, the affection and devotion of James's relationship to his teacher, Paul's own persona in the text, rivals and sometimes surpasses the strength of his relationship with his mother. When his mother commands James to grind coffee on the Sabbath, he refuses because his teacher has taught him otherwise, and after this only conflict between mother and child, James persuades his mother to agree. This remaking of attachments follows an antiracist mission as well. Warning her young readers from disliking people for being Black, Paul invokes the nuclear family in order to expand it: "*God* has made them all, and loves all that are good, and so should *we* always have courage enough to love any body who is good. Would you love your sister or brother less because they had black or brown hair? or your father or mother because one had black eyes and the other blue eyes? No, I am sure you would not love them any the less."[87] Anchoring humanity in a mutual relationship with God, Paul begins an experiment of physical substitution with more immediate relatives—swapping one hair color for another, turning one set of eyes black and the other blue—in a transformation that changes her readers' families, piece by piece, into new bodies, and challenges her readers to name the moment when they become strangers. This gradual transmutation separates the sentimental affection of family from not just family resemblance but from any factor other than internal merit, for we are told to "love any body who is good." That is to say, James Jackson is not simply the ultimate Christian for children to emulate. As a culmination of goodness, he deserves to be the pinnacle, Paul suggests, of the reader's family attachment.

This sense that readers should feel closer to James because of his exceptional merit, rather than distanced from him, structures the larger relationship Paul builds between James's genius and his social world. As Brown notes, the *Memoir* directs away from such individual struggles as conversion or doubt and emphasizes instead how much James's wisdom is the result of collective support: "Paul credits James's 'great many friends' in that community for encouraging his Christian faith and his educational progress. . . . This exemplary child is a product of a virtuous community: region, class, and race both define and produce James Jackson's identity."[88] James, for instance, is able to attend school early because unnamed "friends" persuade his mother to make a special application.[89] What is perhaps even more remarkable about the kinship system that supports James, however, is that these friends have no clear status outside of friendship. They are not identified as either relatives or as belonging to a profession that would encourage this mentorship, such as teaching or religious ministry. Instead, their connection to James appears solely as the product of their benevolence and James's own merit. Any determinedly realist reading of the *Memoir* would recognize that these friendships must have relied on existing systems or institutions, as factors like James's relatively comfortable class standing and his family's church membership must have been the conditions of possibility for these advocates to take interest in a then three- or four-year-old child. However, Paul's presentation of them as arriving both seemingly from nowhere and as the natural consequence of "the good behavior of James" allows the young reader the space to imagine kinship not as a predetermined or rigid genealogy, but as a safe and malleable environment that they themselves can shape.[90]

This is absolutely not to say that Paul had no interest in practical policy for reform. Indeed, the very fact that there was a school in Boston willing to instruct James at all was partly the product of ongoing activism by Paul outside of the *Memoir*, as well as by means of the text itself.[91] However, her focus lies in fostering the social networks that enable practical change. As her preface frames it, the *Memoir* should spur readers to correct the neglect of African American children, declaring that "these children of our brethren have too long been neglected. There is among them many a gem, and whose is the guilt that they are not brought out from among the rubbish and polished?"[92] In other words, because James's uniqueness stems from the attention that teachers and other adult role models have given him, his accomplishments establish the potential of other African American children, elevating rather than eclipsing them. For Paul, prodigy thus is the result of collective effort and social connection; far from being a freak or a fluke in the system, the prodigy is the best representative of the group as whole, because he or she is the sum of their assistance.

As such, the story of James Jackson opens out from the individualist conventions of most biographies to a sense of textuality as a source of connection instead of isolation. Paul manages this shift in part through an emphasis of literature as shared scripture, inserting a history of the Bible that also becomes a lesson for her readers in their shared history. Beginning with Adam and Eve, she recounts Christian history as a history of writing and preserving texts:

> God directed a man by the name of Moses, to write these things down in a book, so that the people could see how he had punished the disobedient men who lived in that age of the world. So Moses wrote all these things in a book, and the people whom we call Jews, kept this book in their temple. After this, other men wrote what God directed them to. The people had all the writings collected. This made what we call the Old Testament.
>
> There was no more writing for a long time, until our blessed Saviour came into the world. Then God commanded those men who were with *him* to write what the Saviour said, and what he did; so four of them wrote an account of these things.[93]

Scripture, in this account, exists to connect a present generation to one of the past, stretching across geography, race, and time based on the idea that one age should learn of and from another. Likewise, history pauses in the intermission between the testaments because, for Paul, history and text cannot be extracted from one another. Moving immediately into a portrait of James's devotion to the Bible and an exhortation that her own readers should listen and read it with equal care, Paul tracks a continuity of texts from these Biblical origins through the life of James and into the lives of the readers meeting him and, through his story, also consuming this version of scripture.

Paul's emphasis on James's story as a means of connecting lives resonates in her formal choices as well. Nested in the account of the exceptional James Jackson are anecdotes of multiple other, more ordinary children whose narratives only intersect with James's in the loosest thematic sense. Nancy, a "little girl . . . only four years" conquers her fear of the dark through her faith in God.[94] Henry, a "poor little fellow," is taught by his sister to fear Black people.[95] Nameless children, too, populate the short narrative, providing educational anecdotes in their failures to learn their lessons,[96] their attempts to convert family members,[97] and their attention-seeking.[98] Some echo James as models to be imitated, and others are examples to be avoided, but the cumulative effect is to surround his life with a cloud of parallel lives. His narrative, Paul suggests, can only be understood as part of a network of others, so that while his may be the central story, it remains fundamentally interwoven with and shaped by those around him and those reading about him.

Through such reconfigurations of history, the alternative genealogy around James Jackson also transforms his exclusion from national futurity into spiritual futurity. James's family ties are, from the outset of the text, fixed in a cyclical emergence from and return to the eternal time of heaven, rather than a linear inheritance. Named for his late father, whose death when James was less than two years old spurred his early interest in Christianity, the boy imagines heaven as "*his home in the skies*," locating his future destiny in his origin.[99] Likewise when Paul's preface advocates that the adults responsible for Black children should "store the minds of the children committed to them with religious truth," the return she promises is partly the earthly promise that, "in this life," they will be "respected in society."[100] The main benefit, however, is that "in the world to come, they shall be acknowledged as the heirs to life eternal."[101] By learning what James learned, they can join him as heirs in this inheritance, that in defiance of the legal and social erasure they endure in the antebellum U.S., they can form a family in a utopian pedagogy. This spiritual futurity thus remains a bleak comfort and, arguably, an escapist one, premised on the reminder that even excluded children will eventually die and that the precocious child will do so sooner.

Despite this, to dismiss Paul's vision as quietism is to miss the way that her relative mistrust of either reproductive or national futurity—that is, her unwillingness to distinguish genealogy as the only meaningful connection or historical progress as the only meaningful victory—opens new possibilities for activism in her present. By largely dismissing the types of political futurity put forward by liberal narratives of progress, Paul outlines a system of care for children that does not value them for their potential as future citizens or parents or national saviors, but as the people they already are. James's death does not mean that his teacher's or mother's efforts were wasted. Rather, the *Memoir*'s recognition that his life is a history worth knowing confirms the need to educate and care for Black children as being implicitly worthy in the present, rather than basing their worth on some future promise. Almost precisely a century after Paul's *Memoir*, Langston Hughes published an echo of the prodigy's joint association with exclusion and escape in his 1937 poem "Genius Child."[102] The close of the poem asks the reader whether she can "love a monster / Of a frightening name?" only to conclude that "*Nobody loves a genius child. / Kill him*—and let his soul run wild." Like James, Hughes's child is tragic, because his potential is so great that he cannot fit into his world and therefore appears as a threat to it. Yet in both of their deaths there is something more than simple tragedy: there is a radical refusal to see growing up into an active member of society as an unambiguous victory.

The chance that death offers for these figures of the prodigy to "run wild" is thus a more particular form of the many freedom-in-death tropes of the nineteenth century, because it so thoroughly decouples individual progress from social progress. If the fundamental marginalization of the prodigy is the removal from historical genealogies, Paul gives us a way to see that removal as a utopia on a small scale, insisting on the value in a life that might not otherwise register in history. Indeed, without Paul's text, the only other archival trace of James Jackson is a brief mention in a local newspaper that correctly records the date and location of his death but provides him with the wrong first name, calling him "George Jackson."[103] Yet to the extent that she also shapes James's life into a repetition of the dead children of color that fill the world of medicine, Paul allows us to recognize in those populations of bodies something beyond their abjection and disconnection. If we have lost the way to access the memory of these prodigies, Paul reminds us that historical legacy is not the best measure of a life, nor is a connection to the present the only connectedness that matters.

PIP, AGAIN: REPRODUCING PRODIGIES

In the end, then, is there any use left for Pip? If he is a repetition on a well-worn theme, the takeaway may not be to dismiss Pip as stereotype, but rather to avoid taking his apparent isolation in *Moby-Dick* at Ishmael's word. Once we know that Pip is not such a singular figure in antebellum culture, others like him emerge throughout the narrative as well. Indeed, children of color pervade Melville's novel in figurative and literal forms, and they do so at some of the most critical moments of kinship formation. The queer bond between Ishmael and Queequeg has, for instance, long been something of a critical commonplace for Melville's description of the two lying in bed as a "cosy, loving pair" and of Queequeg embracing Ishmael as if he were "his wife."[104] Less remarked on is that Ishmael's bond with Queequeg is cemented by the symbol of a dead and disabled Black child, in the form of Queequeg's idol Yojo.

When first confronted by the statue, Ishmael interprets it as something very like antebellum medicine's idea of the prodigy. Seeing Queequeg take Yojo from his bag, Ishmael describes it as "a curious little deformed image with a hunch on its back, and exactly the color of a three days' old Congo baby" and, having heard that Queequeg sold taxidermic human heads, believes at first that the statue is "a real baby preserved in some similar manner."[105] This initial image seems deliberately grotesque, reflecting Ishmael's early fear of Queequeg's racial difference, but elements of this first vision echo in descriptions of Yojo, after Ishmael realizes it is wooden and even after Ishmael and Queequeg become close. Thus, Yojo remains oddly childish as Queequeg's "little negro" or his "innocent little idol," resting "cross[ed between] his arms on his breast."[106] Perhaps most importantly, Yojo plays the part of an uncanny child, allowing Queequeg and Ishmael to bond over caring for him during the rituals of feeding and kissing before bed.[107] Yojo thus becomes child-like enough for Ishmael's participation to register not just as the religious syncretism that is explicit in the text but also as a form of alternative family feeling—one able to register the "heart's honeymoon" that follows the shared attention to Yojo as a meaningful relationship, even without the possibility of other reproduction.[108]

If the deathly child of color is used as a supplement for genealogical reproduction in Queequeg and Ishmael's relationship, it also proves to be the point of departure for Melville's vision of an environment outside of historical genealogies of imperial conquest. Nantucket, the center of the U.S. whaling industry and proxy home for Melville's characters, appears as a heterotopian space paralleling white empire in a less devastating form. It has "conquered the watery world like so many Alexanders" and yet seems to occupy a territory outside the dominion of Anglo-American empire. Melville declares, "Let America add Mexico to Texas, and pile Cuba upon Canada; let the English overswarm all India . . . . ; two thirds of this terraqueous globe are the Nantucket's."[109] This apparent escape from imperialist expansion, however, in the history that Ishmael provides, exists only through the tragedy of its Native American discoverers:

> Look now at the wondrous traditional story of how this island was settled by red-men. . . . In olden times an eagle swooped down upon the New England coast, and carried off an infant Indian in his talons. With loud lament the parents saw their child borne out of sight over the wide waters. They resolved to follow the same direction. Setting out in their canoes, after a perilous passage they discovered the island, and there they found an empty ivory casket,—the poor little Indian's skeleton.[110]

This christening of the island through the death of an indigenous child makes way for the silent substitution in Ishmael's explanations: the people of the supposedly extra-imperial Nantucket are no longer Native Americans. Somewhere in the history, but unmarked in Ishmael's telling, these original inhabitants are replaced by its current Anglo-American residents. Instead, Nantucket's origin story does the work, fairly heavy-handedly, of naturalizing this dispossession by founding what would have been the Wampanoag claim to the island on the end of a genealogy. The death of the heir who would have carried the Indian claim into the future allows Ishmael a fantasy of Nantucket as a space in which territory works differently and where an Anglo-American presence does not represent the same imperial expansion as elsewhere, even though it is enabled by Indian death just the same.

Pip's presence on the ship thus stands in to remind us of the lives that have been left out of the narrative, but he is not merely a passive symbol. Pip also hints at his own bitter awareness that, much as the corpse-like Yojo provides the catalyst for Ishmael's bond with Queequeg, the ship's sense of kinship is directly figured by the image of Black kinship under erasure. In one of his most famous experiments with perspective, Melville assigns each of the chief officers a different reading of the doubloon that Ahab hammers to the mast as the reward for the man who spots the white whale, and that "one and all the mariners revered . . . as the White Whale's talisman," binding them together in their quest.[111] Each analysis is revealing of the viewer—Starbuck sees God, Ahab finds ego, and so on—but Pip, encompassing all of these interpretations in his chant that "I look, you look, he looks; we look, ye look, they look,'" offers the final reading of the doubloon as marking a form of canceled genealogy. After renaming the doubloon as "the ship's navel" and complaining that the whole crew was determined to "unscrew" that navel, he shifts his attention to the mast supporting it. Pip, alone in his focus on the structure behind the doubloon, recalls a memory of his childhood: "My father, in old Tolland county, cut down a pine tree once and found a silver ring grown over in it; some old darkey's wedding ring. How did it get there?'"[112] For him, it is a reminder of kinships forgotten.

Pip's initial vision of the doubloon as navel and therefore as the place of primal incubation recasts the oath that the crew swore over it from nihilistic vengeance into a birth. Yet, if the crew has been born as a new social body, they seem equally bent on dissolving that fellowship and "unscrew[ing that] navel," because their unity is based on the shared desire to kill Moby Dick and claim the doubloon for themselves. This birth, then, is a strongly anti-reproductive one, seated not only in homosociality but also in what almost must be called a pre-Freudian death drive. Pip's shift to marriage, the most conventional vehicle for reproduction, hinges on the shared exclusion of racialized marriage from genealogy. The token of "some old darkey's wedding ring," overgrown in a tree trunk with all its meaning lost, is the ultimate symbol of the relationship that will not enter history. So little history attaches to that marriage that the only way that Pip has to identify the wedding ring as having belonged to a person of color is that the ring and the marriage it represented have been abandoned and forgotten.

Unlike the rest of the crew, Pip has some access to the traces left of this kinship, but it is at the cost of his only exclusion and abjection, for, even among the *Pequod*'s crew of isolates, the prodigy remains on the outside. If the vision of Black infancy as an exception from reproductive history and futurity allows Melville to make it a means to rendering other types of non-normative kinship legible, these broadened horizons reinforce the abjection and exclusion of those bodies. By the novel's logic, to have written Yojo as a living child, rather than as a block of wood in the form of a child's corpse, would have driven Ishmael and Queequeg apart, because caring for him would require a reinvestment in future-oriented family that, for Melville, is inextricable from straightness. Similarly, while Melville's crew are made free by abandoning futurity for the present, Pip has no such chance. Trapped with a living body and drowned soul, Pip remains the sign of—not a participant in—the crew's refused future.

Tempting as it is, then, to seize on children as the way to reject kinship that is dependent on its historicity and with it the genealogical fixations of white patriarchy, José Muñoz's rejoinder that not all children are "the sovereign princes of futurity" argues that any viable counter to genealogy must remember that those figures used to prop up genealogy can also be those who suffer from its exclusions.[113] Recognizing the character Pip as both part of an ongoing mode of alienation for Black subjects and as an inroads into recalling lost histories and the alternative possibilities they offered provides a way to think about how the attempts to break out of normative kinship can sometimes reiterate the very kind of exclusions that they seek to escape. In this way, though, Paul's writing is all the more important: by remaking prodigy to center Black children, she also remakes what it means to be in kinship with others.

CHAPTER 4

Too Many Children

U.S. Malthusianism, Harriet Beecher Stowe, and Novel-Ending Births

> In the state of Ohio, the traveler is forcibly struck with the indications which are every where presented of an anti-malthusian tendency. No state in the union can surpass this in flaxen-headed, chubby-faced younkers. In passing down the river on a steamboat, the noise of the steam unavoidably draws the inmates from their abodes, and in front of almost every cabin you soon see a swarm of children.
>
> —Cincinnati Mirror and Western Gazette of Literature, Science, and the Arts, *February 14, 1835*[1]

When the *Cincinnati Mirror and Western Gazette* announced the death of Thomas Malthus, it chose the odd strategy of doing so with an ode to the children of its state. An unnamed author recommends Malthus as "the ablest expounder" of political economy and is confident that his ideas will already be familiar to the newspaper's readers, declaring that "everybody knows something of his peculiar doctrines in regard to population."[2] The substance of that something, however, is also quickly put in doubt, because for the author, the heart of Malthus's argument was neither poverty, nor misery, but children and the freedom to have them. The summary of Malthus's work—that "the rearing up of children was about the worst sort of business which could be pursued; and that their increase would at some day call upon government to interpose checks"—provokes a tangent that occupies the rest of the column, which returns to Malthus only in its final sentence. With the bulk of the obituary instead dedicated to bragging that Ohio is unbeatable for its number of "flaxen-headed, chubby-faced yonkers," the column turns from a more standard biography to a rhapsodic image of sailing down the river and seeing that "in front of almost every cabin . . . a swarm of children" radiates "contentment and affection."[3] For the columnist, these children evidentially mark the true, titular "Death of Malthus" by supposedly demonstrating the ultimate failure of his ideas.

The article offers some fairly obvious misunderstandings—such as the author's notion that Malthus's nine children are a damning sign of hypocrisy—but these misreadings point to a larger history of ambivalence between United States and Malthusian ideas of reproduction. The legacy of Malthusianism has especially targeted and harmed marginalized peoples, but it could sometimes take an unexpected turn in the context of the United States in that the traits it fears in children are the very ones that many Americans revere. The hordes of "chubby-faced younkers" seem like the most perfectly sociable children. They are charming, implicitly white, and numerous, with each one indistinguishable from the last. While the author describing them embraces this indistinguishability, the scene retains trace of doubleness, flashing between the author's enthusiastic adoration and the more sinisterly Malthusian version of this "swarm." This duality between beloved and monstrous exists because the rhetoric and reality of white childhood were themselves positioned as a bridge between the happiness of a private family and the ongoing violence of the United States. I argue that Harriet Beecher Stowe—an author famously interested in the lines between politics, private feeling, and racist violence—took up this particular doubleness as an opportunity to reexamine the threat that white childhood represented.

Harriet Beecher Stowe was not a likely candidate for either the doctrines of Malthus or for any serious criticism of white childhood. *Uncle Tom's Cabin* casts feeling and sympathy as an antidote to the cruelty of economics and also creates a white supremacist binary in its pairing of the angelic, white Little Eva and the hardened and dehumanized Black Topsy.[4] Stowe's second novel, though, the 1856 *Dred: A Tale of the Great Dismal Swamp*, has very different perspectives on the role of white childhood, particularly white girlhood, in the system of U.S. slavery.[5] Whereas Little Eva dies for the cause of freedom, the white girls of *Dred* perpetuate the violence around them by their very birth. Central to this shift is Stowe's new and ambivalent investment in what Malthusian versions of life in general and childhood in specific had suggested about U.S. politics. Although *Dred* has seen a surge of critical interest due to its relative comfort with violent resistance, the novel's fundamental investments in population and in particularly Malthusian ideas of reproduction have been overlooked. By attending to the influence of Thomas Robert Malthus's 1798 *An Essay on the Principle of Population* in the text, we can recognize *Dred* as a collision between Stowe's sentimentalism and her increasing belief that Malthusian theories of population had begun to apply in North America.[6] More specifically, we can see in the archetypical creator of perfect white child characters a rumbling resentment of their relationship with systems of violence.

One major focus of the critical interpretation of childhood in U.S. literature, particularly nineteenth-century literature, has been representations of white children as a touchstone for an extreme version of innocence.[7] The conventional literary role of such children in sentimental reform novels is to promise a simple end to the problems raised by the novel by being so innocent that they are excluded from these worldly concerns. This next generation, the end of such texts promise, could never fall into the same mistakes as their protagonist parents. Stowe, too, appears fascinated in the role that children have traditionally played in providing narrative resolution by reassuring readers that this new generation would do what was right and repair whatever harms the plot had unfolded. However, her forays into her own version of Malthusianism provide an alternative model. As territorial expansion came to look more and more finite in the mid-century, the colonial settler myth that each family could move to new, supposedly unoccupied land—thus escaping politics and history for a private utopia—became strained for Stowe, whose second novel challenges this narrative of reproductive futurity and its centrality in reform novels. *Dred* offers an experiment in representing populations that have run out of colonies to which to escape and families that are not an escape from political violence but rather its vehicle. When read through the lens of Malthus, *Dred*'s infants represent a critique of the tidy resolutions that were conventional in reform novels. In place of the usual ending, the novel offers a prescient look at a rapidly overpopulating world in which new children in positions of privilege only represent a multiplication of social problems, thus reimagining resolution beyond reproduction.

CHILDREN, POPULATION, AND THE MARRIAGE PLOT

At first glance, the relationship between literary children and the marriage plot seems so obvious that it is hardly worth stating—the marriage plot channels the sexuality that produces the children—but one effect of the conventional marriage plot has been to regulate when children crop up in the narrative, usually pushing them from the main body of the novel to either end of the text. Children appear more frequently at the beginning, when the protagonist is a child herself, or at the end, as proof and epilogue of a successfully established marriage. The point itself is an old one. Henry James's 1888 "The Art of Fiction" defines the basic cliché of the "happy ending" as a parceling out of "prizes, pensions, husbands, wives, babies, . . . and cheerful remarks."[8] Progeny, alongside property, has been one of the most popular currencies with which novels reward their protagonists and mark the happy resolution of plot. Exceptions abound, of course. Seduction plots, such as those of *The Scarlet Letter* or *Adam Bede*, generate the most mid-narrative children, but the scandal of those children and their function in the novel is that their untimeliness proves a deviation from the marriage plot proper; the very appearance of such a child proves that the path to marriage has gone wrong. Likewise, for sentimental novels like *Uncle Tom's Cabin*, the tragic redemptive force of the angelic, typically feminine child who dies mid-narrative is that because she dies without having matured into parenthood, the untimeliness of her death endows her with the transcendent authority of spiritual guardian. In the case of Little Eva, for instance, Gillian Brown has argued that Eva's saintliness emerges from the uncanny maturity of a girl who "emblematizes the virtues of motherhood as well as of childhood," so that by her death, "Eva is the child who is the mother to the woman."[9] Such child saints die without reaching the closure of their own children because their sanctity depends on a sense that they have exceeded a normative sense of age and development.

For the more mundane and "deserving" protagonist, though, passing from being a child to having children marks the successful development of subjectivity and its accompanying agency. One of the most widespread readings of this movement from childhood to childbearing in U.S. literature has focused on independent development, reading the protagonist's decision to marry as a break from an unhealthy form of domesticity and the establishment of a new, more individualist model of kinship. As Cindy Weinstein has argued, the initial youth of the main character stages a scene of dependence and inherited scandal from which she is redeemed by the individual agency of liberal romance, contrasting that final expression of will with what she terms "the pain and disaster of the consanguineous family" of her youth.[10] For female protagonists especially, the expression of consent contained in the marriage plot provides the highest form of freedom available to them and the greatest proof that they have chosen their adult life, even as it presents heterosexual marriage as the exclusive and inevitable option. Gretchen Murphy, too, observes a particularly compact version of this pattern in her description of sentimental fiction's tendency for siblings-by-adoption to become romantic partners. For Murphy, this incestuous strain highlights the importance of the shift between a household of birth and a household of choice, arguing that "when the couples turn from siblings into lovers, they create a new social fiction that replaces an imperfect one imposed by a previous generation's choices. Their horizontal bonds represent a democratic, bourgeois resistance to symbolic patriarchal power."[11] In other words, the shift to marriage also marks a new orientation toward power that promises an escape from the weight of the past while retrospectively proving that the child-protagonist at the novel's opening had always possessed the seeds of that individuality.

To read the marriage plot as an answer to the initial childish dependency of the protagonist, though, also introduces a certain circularity: the philosophical problems of childhood are apparently solved through the promise of more children. This second generation may represent the offspring of a purportedly more democratic, bourgeois family structure, but the basic challenges raised by child dependency on liberal individualism remain. A number of critics, including Cindy Weinstein and Lauren Berlant, have pointed out that this seeming inevitability of the heterosexual romance as being both proof of many female protagonists' agency and their only option in life is the imposition of a norm as a celebration of private choice.[12] But this circularity also tempers the relationship of children to the larger social body as well. Nancy Armstrong observes that the tendency of British Victorian novels to unfold through cyclical waves of childhood allows for a mediation between isolated lives and the predictable repetitions of a community:

> The figure of reproduction obviously lends itself to a linear developmental narrative, where an individual starts off as less than a full and independent individual and progresses, as Moll, Jane Eyre, Pip, and other protagonists do, to a social level where his or her individuality can be socially recognized and sanctioned. To signal this achievement, the story cannot stop there but must reproduce itself. Moll writes her story; Jane has a child and writes her story; Pip vicariously reproduces himself through Biddy and Joe.[13]

The exceptionalist logic that seems to underpin such plots' promise to extract the course of a singular and particularly remarkable life softens in this closing gesture toward a future beyond the end of that life. By turning to reproduction, Armstrong argues, such novels reframe the trajectory toward marriage from concern merely over individualist consent into a leaning toward community. By ending *Great Expectations* with a miniature, second Pip—whom the narrating Pip recognizes with a start as "I again!"—the focus moves toward how stories *like* Pip's recur and form a predictable network of similar lives.[14] In this sense, childhood is a sign of communal continuity, marking the similar lives running parallel to and sequentially from the life of the protagonist.

Literary children, particularly that happy second generation, thus serve a two-fold and contradictory role: their innocence promises that the protagonist has successfully broken from the historical specters of bad kinship, and their futurity guarantees that this historical break will continue to resonate throughout their community. They demonstrate that the protagonist has made a life of her own, but they also guarantee that the effects of that life extend beyond her death. To put a finer point on the matter, such children act as the critical relays between the private and public spheres of the nineteenth-century novel, allowing a happy collective future to be extrapolated from the happily domestic end of a single life. Their ability to stand in as the proxy resolution for the political problems of the narrative relies on the continued vision of childhood as a zone of idyllic escape; without innocence, childhood offers no departure from either history or politics.

My discussion thus far has taken a non-intuitive route toward an observation that is routinely made about both British and American novels of the period, namely that the political stakes of reform novels are often twinned with plots about heterosexual romance and the successful culmination of those romances are taken as a resolution-by-proxy for the reform, or revolution, left undone in the narrative; the marriage plot preempts and replaces the political plot.[15] As with any truism, there has been a good deal of discussion about the limitations of such a model. In this case, one major pushback has centered around the model's reliance on a separation between the political and the private. Scholars such as Patricia Yaeger, Rosemarie Bodenheimer, and Barbara Leah Harman have pointed out that domesticity is by no means an apolitical space, and a shift in setting from factory to hearth can sometimes represent not so much a retreat from the political as politics by another means.[16] I heartily agree with these stipulations. However, rethinking this narrative reflex with attention to the narrative function played by children and their role as a synecdochial representation of a larger social solution left beyond the horizon of the novel allows for a stronger understanding of what *type* of childhood is necessary to support this interpretation. More importantly, it allows for an analysis of how the alternative models of childhood circulating in the period create different types of plot resolution and irresolution—particularly given that these childhoods are often reserved for children of color, queer children, and poor children. Just as recognizing the politics that can inhere in some versions of domestic life allows us to recognize implicit social commentary in novels whose endings otherwise appear timid or even reactionary, acknowledging that not all portraits of children emphasize innocence or futurity can help us re-read the conventional ending of a marriage-plot-generated child in a way that is both more historically accurate and more politically useful.

The child's ability to stand as a proxy resolution for the political problems of the narrative relies on a vision of childhood innocence and domestic exceptionality that never existed in Malthusianism. Far from being the "infant citizen" ideal described by Lauren Berlant as "not yet bruised by history," the child in Malthusianism represents a continuation and intensification of the political problems that preceded its birth.[17] As Armstrong argues, Malthus's focus on human desire in the aggregate takes a sharply contrary view of the reproductive drive that is common at the end of a novel; as she writes, under Malthusian frameworks, "reproduction ceases to rely on a linear progressive narrative and begins to observe the logic of repetition."[18] Distinguishing between the successive logic of reproduction and the impersonal amorphousness of repetition, Armstrong reads Malthus as dissolving the correlation between private and public satisfaction, describing his *Essay on the Principle of Population* as an "assault on the novelistic assumption that individual gratification on a mass scale would lead to collective well-being."[19] In other words, happy families are happy families, but there is no reason to think that they would lead to happy worlds, nor that happy families do not come without a cost of their own. Whereas novels often use individual characters as personifications of larger worlds, populations resist easy correlations between singular lives and collective bodies, so that no one birth can be messianic enough to answer the needs of this sprawling and tangled complexity.

THE CROWDS OF *DRED*

Excess pervades *Dred* at its most basic structure. Even from the distance of plot summary, *Dred* is an over-crowded novel. At the text's opening, the novel's center appears to be a fairly conventional coming-of-age story in which the motherless protagonist, Nina Gordon, must mature from the thoughtless flirtations that have resulted in her simultaneous engagements with three different men into the Christian and heterosexual maturity of marriage. The narrative quickly branches out, however, to the struggles of her enslaved half-brother Harry, who is desperately trying to keep the plantation afloat to protect his sister and to prevent those enslaved on the plantation from going to auction, while also trying to preserve his marriage with the naïvely perfect Lisette. After Nina's love interest, the aspiring lawyer and idealistic abolitionist Edward Clayton, arrives, the novel adds his struggles with the legal system to its plot lines, along with the characters of his parents and sister. Running alongside the family plots of the Gordons and the Claytons is a plot strand devoted to the difficulties of a poor white family squatting on the edge of the Gordon family. Over the scope of the narrative, Stowe also takes up two trials based on real events and a religious controversy, each centering on characters not yet mentioned here. Beside all of this is the connecting thread offered by the figure of Dred, a self-emancipated prophet and son of Denmark Vesey, who lives in the swamp near the Gordon planation and preaches to bring about divine justice by active revolution.

Dred's presence in the text and the centrality that the novel's title gives his otherwise peripheral role has drawn a number of critics to note how immediate the prospect of apocalypse appears to be throughout the novel and how inextricable Stowe's eschatology is from her abolitionism. Claudia Stokes describes the plot of *Dred* as enacting the "fulfilment of biblical prophecy" and as a considerable escalation of Stowe's millennialism, in that "where *Uncle Tom's Cabin* only foretells the imminent destruction of American civilization, *Dred* dramatizes such an event, as slavery unleashes chaos and lawlessness."[20] Samuel Otter concurs, declaring that "Stowe in *Dred* tells a different kind of story than she had in *Uncle Tom's Cabin*" because, as he explains, "in *Dred*'s swamp, facts are saturated with figures and the nation is on the verge of apocalypse."[21] Dred's oracular position seems clear, given his frequent declamations such as "the day of vengeance must come,"[22] but the parallel that Otter raises between "facts saturated with figures" and the apocalypse helps to suggest why the statistical imagination of population would mesh so closely with the mystic warnings of eschatology.[23] No single individual success or individual martyrdom can hope to be sufficient for the mass imagination of the novel; the cosmological ending that is promised by Dred, but always deferred, represents the only scale on which resolution could even be posited.

Within the comparisons that are inevitable to criticism about *Dred*, that character functions very differently than in *Uncle Tom's Cabin*. Where that novel's logic of salvation by messianic sacrifice—in which the goodness of Eva and Tom makes their sacrifices sufficient to organize the novel's emotional weight around their loss—employs characters as archetypes so that their singular fate also signals larger social changes, that metonymic chain is altogether messier in *Dred* because the crowd of characters to be represented and redeemed is always swelling. As one otherwise-sympathetic review published in the *National Era* in 1856 complained, "there is no one character that runs through the whole book, like Uncle Tom."[24] The lack of a clear central protagonist to whom readers can cling registers in modern criticism as well. In his explanation of the greater success of *Uncle Tom's Cabin*, Lawrence Buell largely attributes *Dred*'s problems to its more contradictory characters: Harry is too "torn by self-division" to be properly heroic, "Eva's adolescent quasi-analogue Nina Gordon remains so long a frivolous belle that her transfiguration into serious-minded plantation head seems unconvincing," and Clayton is "compromised" by his "impracticality and quixoticism" as well as by his association with "Nina's wobbliness."[25] In other words, all of the characters evoke clear types, but none can quite embody that type fully enough to become the almost-metaphysical icons that Eva, Tom, and Legree were. Collective identities in *Dred*, whether of femininity or Christianity or even human evil, are always multiplying and extending in too many directions for one character to embody so many lives.

One way to explain this shift is to frame it, as Buell does, as an increasing interest in realism and in the collision of that realism with romance.[26] What, though, might the "wobbliness" that disqualifies Nina from Eva's role as national saint and scapegoat tell us about the novel's multiplying body of characters, its persistent interest in finding an end that can satisfy our interest in them all, or its continual frustration of those hopes? What does the failure of the central child's innocence, the complication of a girl who has clear sexual desire and is a few years too old for that desire to be overlooked, reveal about Stowe's narrative project? Unlike the tidy allegories of *Uncle Tom's Cabin* that trade on infant utopianism and its underlying promise that domesticity can rescue politics, *Dred* is resolutely committed to endings that exceed the marriage plot and avoid treating childhood as a source of closure. A sweeping system of apocalypse looms over the text because the individualist resolutions of private romance only add to the problem of a system that feeds off reproduction. Amid the sprawling expanses of flawed characters, the birth of another white child only recapitulates the injuries structuring Stowe's domesticities.

Nowhere is this Malthusian influence stronger than in the plot that unfolds on the borders of both the plantations and the swamps in Stowe's depiction of the poor families squatting at the outskirts of the Gordon property. These families are, like the enslaved people that Stowe describes, alternately caricatured and pitied as the excess of the slave system, shown as perpetually unable to find wage labor in a slavery-based system, and always at risk of falling into slavery themselves—a point that Stowe makes quite directly, having Nina's aunt declare that "there is n't any help for them, unless, as I said before, they were made slaves; and then they could be kept decent."[27] The basic argument that slavery injured white labor was a common one among the more openly anti-Black critics of slavery, and although she never paints these poor whites as the single or even the central object of slavery's harm, Stowe's willingness to adopt this line of argument veers unsurprisingly close to its racism.

What this attention to these squatters does allow, though, is to provide a condemnation of the heartlessness of Malthusianism alongside a tacit endorsement of its population logic. Thus, the language with which the land-holding plantation owners discuss them echoes nothing so closely as Malthusian disregard at Ebenezer Scrooge-like levels. These opinions, voiced most often by Nina's uncle, John Gordon, and her two aunts, Maria Gordon and Mrs. Nesbit, frame poor whites as an impossibly entrenched demographic problem for which reform is impossible. Annihilation is, John Gordon declares, the only answer:

> "It's perfectly insufferable, what we proprietors have to bear from this tribe of creatures!" he said. "There ought to be hunting-parties got up to chase them down, and exterminate 'em, just as we do rats. It would be a kindness to them; the only thing you can do for them is kill them. As for charity, or that kind of thing, you might as well throw victuals into the hollow logs as try to feed 'em. The government ought to pass laws—we will have laws, somehow or other,—and get them out of the state."[28]

As a "tribe of creatures" and an infestation of "rats," the poor, for John Gordon, have moved past the perceived moral failings such as idleness, alcoholism, and dishonesty that have often been used to rationalize the view that their class has become both animalized and intrinsically plural. They are, as Aunt Nesbit put it, a "whole race" unto themselves.[29] Mass violence in the form of John Gordon's wish to "exterminate 'em," or mass displacement in the equally violent but more vague desire for "laws, somehow or other" to police them out of the state become the only resolution with a scale large enough to answer Gordon's framing of the problem on the level of population.[30]

This rejection of charity is quickly undone by the power of sympathy, to an extent. Nina's kindness to the children of a nearby family, Fanny and Teddy Cripps, is repeatedly held up as a sign of her developing goodness, and she becomes a model for Fanny in particular after the death of the children's mother.[31] Even her Uncle John immediately retreats from his position when he sees starving squatters face-to-face with an ambiguously worded declaration that "if people are going to starve, they mustn't come on to my place to do it. I don't mind what I don't see—I wouldn't mind if the whole litter of 'em was drowned to-morrow; but, hang it, I can't stand it if I know it!"[32] Stowe partly plays off the selfishness of this charity, in which blissful ignorance is presented as preferable to aid, by making John into a somewhat buffoonish character, blustering but soft-hearted and comically terrified of his wife, who in turn develops some minor willingness to give food to the squatting family.[33]

However, *Dred* remains deeply suspicious of the ability of this downward flowing benevolence to offer any meaningful counter to the systemic problems of either poor whites or enslaved peoples.[34] After giving food and shelter to the family he had intended to evict, John laments that "there must be some place for them in the world"; he echoes the family's own explanation that they squat because they "an't got nowhere else to be" but "have got be somewhere," but, more importantly, he acknowledges the inadequacy of his piecemeal offerings.[35] They may be coming to his house for dinner, but they have no place to stay. Instead, their reliance on John's goodness is immediately revealed as a vulnerability. John continues his so-called sympathy for the squatters by indignantly wondering "why can't we pass a law to take them all in with our niggers, and then they'd have some one to take care of them."[36] For John, power is the only vehicle for kindness.

His proposal of white slavery, though repugnant to Stowe for both racist and abolitionist reasons, is also the closest that she comes to a systemic recommendation. Its menace, as such, lies partly in its sense of looming inevitability. Even Nina's attention to the Cripps, well-intentioned as it might have been, is tied to the fact that the late Mrs.

Cripps was born a Peyton and therefore "one of the most celebrated families in Virginia," a reputation zealously guarded by the children's enslaved guardian Tiff.[37] Moreover, Nina's attention and tutoring in "proper" class behavior cannot actually do anything to "save" the children from their economic position; their only means to escape poverty and an increasingly abusive father and stepmother is a literal escape orchestrated by Tiff away from the South. In other words, their environment determined their situation in a way that neither education nor individual action could change. Departure is the only option.

In fact, for all that Nina's relatives caricature a hyper-violent strand of population control, Stowe herself adopts many of the demographic logics underpinning their thought. In her persuasive reading of *Dred*, Holly Jackson argues that the text is driven toward thinking of groups that extend beyond the nuclear family. Noting that one of the plot's closing gestures is, after Nina dies abruptly, to settle Clayton instead in a relationship with his sister and her friend, Jackson suggests that Stowe's true group ideal is "a more group-oriented affinity, . . . denying special significance to relationships that guarantee the reproductive futurity of the social order, the traditional maneuver of the marriage plot."[38] The groups that Jackson traces are largely positive, but her description of Stowe's tension between her "pronounced strain of genealogical determinism" and her "desire to dethrone the family" need not produce only the affirmative bonds of what Jackson terms "a nonkin model of political community."[39] However, this insistent focus on a relatedness that exceeds the personal attachments of family also hews closely to models of population in which new children are no longer the sign of transcendent intimacy so much as an almost mechanistically determined byproduct.

MALTHUS AND THE AMERICAS

If Stowe had been born in Britain, rather than simply a repeat visitor, turning to Malthus as a key for all this talk on reproduction would be a relatively familiar critical move. It is increasingly common for scholars to recognize the influence of Malthus over British literature in the nineteenth century. However, no comparably sized body of criticism exists in U.S. literary studies.[40] This absence is not for a lack of early U.S. readers. In their recent study *The New Worlds of Thomas Robert Malthus*, Alison Bashford and Joyce E. Chaplin demonstrate that Malthus was central to nineteenth-century understandings of empire far beyond British borders.[41] This was certainly true for the United States. As George Johnson Cady demonstrates, many of the first pieces of political economic writing in the United States make reference to Malthus, and a number of influential thinkers—such as Matthew Carey, Alexander H. Everett, and George Tucker, along with many others—wrote essays responding directly to Malthus's *Essay on the Principle of Population*.[42] Conversely, Malthus's ideas had their own American roots. Malthus's interest in the effect that marriage has on rates of reproduction drew much of its inspiration from Benjamin Franklin's 1755 essay on population growth in the Americas "Observations Concerning the Increase of Mankind,"[43] and Malthus's 1807 edition of *Essay on the Principle of Population* repeatedly cites Franklin as a source and interlocutor.

Critical inattention to Malthus's place in early American literature is instead more likely prompted by the unstable standing of the *Essay on Population* among U.S. readers. Malthusian ideas circulated quickly and widely among political elites like Thomas Jefferson[44] and John Adams, both of whom discuss them in their personal correspondence.[45] For more casual readers, too, periodicals such as the *Richmond Enquirer* ran essays summarizing and debating Malthusian principles and, by 1809, the first U.S. imprint of *Essay on the Principle of Population* had appeared in Washington, DC.[46] Yet, as historian Nicole Eustace argues, the considerable interest among Americans had more to do with celebrating the high birthrates of Anglo settlers in the United States than in worrying about the misery that Malthus ascribed to those births. As she observes, "Often, when Americans did offer any approval of Malthus, it was only to applaud his exact and methodical accounting of American population strength, not to agree with his argument that future increases should be curtailed."[47] Malthus, in other words, was more significant for many Americans as either a convenient antagonist for patriotic political economists or, in more hurried readings, as a source of pride and publicity for the country's growth, without regard for Malthus's larger claims.

By the time of Malthus's death in 1834, popular awareness of his *Essay on Population* thus hinged on a quite different reading of the text than the concerns about scarcity that drove British readers and that largely drive modern interpretations. Such readings often produced Malthus as a European foil for the heady optimism of U.S. settler colonialism, praising American fertility—as, for instance, did the obituary that forms my epigraph for this chapter. Such readings of Malthus are somewhat glib, but their dismissal of Malthusian population theory as irrelevant in the United States is not so superficial as it first seems. Indeed, the text of *Essay on Population* has its own conflicted relationship with the Americas that shaped this U.S. response, predicated on the still-uncertain status that the newly independent United States held to the British geographic imaginary. If the *Cincinnati Mirror*'s obituary for Malthus seems unimpressed by his predictions that rising populations were a danger rather than a strength, its blithe pride in the children of its western territories emerges from a mythology of settler colonialism that Malthus himself helped to reinforce, even as he doubted how long-lived its exceptionalism would be. The U.S. reaction to Malthus, as a result, was always mediated by its textual status as evidence and application in *Essay on Population*, as well as by the U.S. geopolitical standing as a former colony and ongoing empire.[48]

As a system that edges toward an equilibrium between births and starvation, Malthus's population theory traces a historical process tending toward a state close to stasis, arguing that the poor of England already live in this harshly balanced state of necessary scarcity in which greater resources would only lead to greater need. Attempts to alleviate their hunger must fail, he argues, because "the transfer of three shillings and sixpence a day to every labourer would not increase the quantity of meat in the country. There is not at present enough for all to have a decent share."[49] In his view, England's population had already grown to the edge of what it could sustain and any attempt at relieving the resulting suffering causes the lower classes to produce still more children and therefore still more need.[50] While granting the possibility that food supplies might increase and calling for some measures to promote agriculture, Malthus's conclusion is that no such reform could ever be sufficient. He writes, for instance, that "the demand for an increased quantity of subsistence is, with few exceptions, constant every where, yet we see how slowly it is answered in all those countries that have been long occupied."[51] Teleologies of progress bottom out in this state of a need that is "constant" and amelioration that comes "slowly," if at all. Nations "long occupied" reach what is essentially a saturation point, unable to change the condition of a significant portion of their population.

However, because he stations England at this late stage of population growth, Malthus turns to the Americans as a form of control, imaging the Anglo settlers of the Americas as roughly analogous to some earlier, as-yet-unpopulated Western Europe. Census data from 1740s New Jersey is set alongside that of England and France to suggest the latent reproductive potential of those nations, if they were not already under the stress of their existing populations. U.S. population figures also form the basis for half of his most famous formulation[52]—the notion that population increases exponentially: "In the United States of America, where the means of subsistence have been more ample, the manners of the people more pure, and consequently the checks to early marriage fewer, than in any of the modern states of Europe, the population has been found to double itself in twenty-five years. This ratio of increase, though short of the utmost power of population, yet as the result of actual experience, we will take as our rule, and say, that population, when unchecked, goes on doubling itself every twenty-five years or increases in a geometrical ratio."[53] Malthus centers U.S. reproduction as the nearest available approximation of ideal human fertility, substituting its rate of population increase as the universal rate of increase. However, in the same moment that Malthus founds his theories on U.S. data, he distances those settlers from the effects of his models. It is precisely because he asserts that land is available and unoccupied, despite his acknowledgements elsewhere of Native American populations, and that settlers are "more pure"—essentially, that the checks of misery do not apply or apply much less—that he can set up the United States as the normative model for human reproduction. His arguments therefore echo myths of American exceptionalism, presenting "the English North American colonies" not only as making "by far the most rapid progress" compared with contemporary colonies held by other European nations, but as being "probably without parallel in history" for its increase in number.[54] Malthus establishes the United States as the exception through which he proves the rule.

Although his rhetoric overlaps with the most chauvinistic strands of U.S. nationalism, *Essay on Population* makes clear that a decline into poverty and bare survival remains inevitable. In a work designed in large part as a counter to the utopian narratives of progress put forward by William Godwin and Marquis de Condorcet, Malthus is similarly cynical about imperial expansion as a means of avoiding the poverty of Europe. Hence, as much as he praises it above non-British colonies, Malthus makes clear that a U.S. decline into the same poverty and bare survival is inevitable. Disputing philosopher Richard Price's belief that American democracy made the United States into a special case, Malthus argues that "even civil liberty, all powerful as it is, will not create fresh land" and observers can be "perfectly sure" that the unparalleled population growth he claims "will not long continue."[55] What appears as exceptionalist is quickly reframed in Malthus as evidence that the United States is on the same trajectory as other nations, albeit at a different stage, and that nothing can be done to depart from this path toward misery. As he writes, "the situation of new colonies, well governed, is a bloom of youth that no efforts can arrest."[56] Thus, settler colonialism may stave off misery from the settlers, but the growth that Price saw as proof of a bright future, Malthus took as evidence that a future decline was inevitable.

What difference is made for U.S. readers of Malthus, therefore, is not a question of final results but a matter of temporal orientation. Where for Britain, Malthus's writing suggested an endless continuance of a suffering that was already present and mundane, for the United States, the coming of Malthusian conditions appeared as an imminent catastrophe. For British readers, *Essay on Population* predicts the impossibility of reform, promising that whatever policies might be put in place, the current situation of the country would be the perpetual situation of the country. For U.S. readers invested in Manifest Destiny, however, the core of Malthus was that their time as an alternative to and improvement on Europe was running out. As soon as they were unable to colonize further, the misery associated with the "Old World" would come for the New. Preempting Frederick Turner's "frontier thesis," the pro-slavery academic Thomas R. Dew proclaimed as early as 1836 that "the time must come when the powerfully elastic spring of our rapidly increasing numbers shall fill up our wide spread territory with a dense population—when the great safety valve of the west will be closed against us . . . then will come the great and fearful pressure upon the engine," threating mobocracy and an end to private property.[57] What had been a critique of the Poor Laws, in other words, took on the air of the apocalyptic, as the coming applicability of Malthusianism to the United States came to signify a secular end of days for the nation.

The debates that sprang up around population theory were accordingly slanted toward concerns, or even outright fears, about the nature of that terminal stage of history. Even many Malthusian opponents, most prominently the political economist Henry C. Carey, took Malthus's vision of an eventual scarcity caused by overpopulation as possible, arguing less with its content than its immediacy. As a result, anti-Malthusian writings could take on their own strand of apocalyptic language, but with the greater sense of distance and therefore complacency about that future. Carey writes, for instance, that "the time *may* arrive when the world will be so fully occupied that there will not be even room, but we may safely leave that distant future to the benevolent care of the Deity."[58] Similarly, an 1848 column for the *North American Review* declares Malthus's basic tenets of population to be "undeniable" but mockingly likens policy decisions based on those tenets to a "speculatist in natural philosophy" demonstrating that "the sun was gradually but surely expending its stock of light and heat" and therefore recommending "the instant necessity of economizing with the utmost care our fuel and oil."[59] While these scholars did also seek to counter the grounds of Malthus's arguments, a large part of their response was to defer his version of the future to some more distant horizon.

In contrast to its original application, U.S. writers therefore took up Malthusian analysis not to justify the present as inevitable but to argue for a deliberate management of how this future, stable population would be composed. As Dennis Hodgson argues, Malthusianism played a significant role in the U.S. debates over slavery, offering pro-slavery advocates evidence in favor of plantation-based paternalism as the only viable system for managing population. At the same time, as Hodgson demonstrates, anti-slavery writers used Malthus to portray slavery as forcing white populations to struggle for increasingly scarce resources against a purportedly faster-growing Black population.[60] For critics of immigration, too, this competitive population model supported a depiction of imperial expansion in the West under threat from the Irish, Scottish, and Southern European populations settling the West as well. In fact, one of the most famous such pamphlets, *A Plea for the West* (1835), was published by Stowe's father, Lyman Beecher. While Beecher does not cite Malthus directly and does retain the possibility of a utopian nation, his assertion that "the West is filling up as by ocean waves; and . . . the capital of the East and of Europe hold competition for her acceptance and use" retains a sense of finite territory and inevitably explosive populations.[61] For writers like Lyman Beecher, the chief relevance of Malthus in the nation is as an exhortation to seek racial, ethnic, and religious homogeneity in the United States lest this coming scarcity threaten white Protestantism's hold on national resources.

STOWE, MALTHUS, AND THE MARRIAGE PLOT

The popularity of citing Malthus during the debate over slavery by both pro- and antislavery advocates had cast Stowe as a tacit interlocutor of his population theory from the initial 1852 publication of *Uncle Tom's Cabin*. In an 1858 article titled "The Problem of Free Society" published in the *Southern Literary Messenger*, for example, readers are equally warned away from "the darkest fictions of Mrs. Harriet Beecher Stowe" and encouraged toward "the splendid work of Malthus on Population," signifying Stowe and Malthus's shared status as central figureheads for the intellectual debate over abolition.[62]

The first glimpses of Malthusianism in Stowe's own writing come in the years immediately after the publishing *Uncle Tom's Cabin*, when she found herself subject to two apparently unrelated strands of public criticism. The first was controversy over her novel's end, which exiles most of its surviving African American protagonists to Liberia. The second, now obscure, controversy arose during Stowe's 1853 speaking tour of Britain and Ireland promoting the antislavery movement and her novel. That scandal centered on the fact that many of Stowe's supposedly benevolent patrons were themselves implicated in the ongoing violence of the Highland Clearances. Her memoir of the trip, *Sunny Memories of Foreign Lands*, provoked special ire for its chapter-long endorsement of the Duchess of Sutherland, an aristocrat whose family had spearheaded the enclosure movement and who had hosted Stowe with an elaborate hospitality during her tour, culminating in the gift of a gold bracelet shaped like a shackle.[63]

Remarkably, for a text written partially to answer a public outcry already circulating in British and U.S. newspapers, *Sunny Memories*' defense of the Highland Clearances rests on a joint defense of the end of *Uncle Tom's Cabin*. In that memoir, Stowe argues that both displacements are the products of the same inexorable, and markedly Malthusian, laws: "As [British enclosure] progressed northward, the demand for labor in the great towns absorbed the surplus population; but when it came into the extreme Highlands, this refuge was wanting. Emigration to America now became the resource; and the surplus population were induced to this by means such as the Colonization Society now recommends and approves for promoting emigration to Liberia."[64] Stowe's history of Scottish overpopulation finding outlets in the United States directly mirrors Malthus's analysis of Scotland from later editions of *Essay on Population*, which claim that "half of the surplus births in Scotland is drawn off in emigrations."[65] Moreover, her attention to the balancing of "surplus population" against the "resource" of available land, whether in America or England, frames immigration as a natural flow of bodies—an imaginary that echoes Malthus's focus on human life understood en masse.

It is not necessarily surprising that Stowe's vision of Scotland turns on ideas of population: Karl Marx's complaint about her association with Sutherland centers, in part, on the idea that Sutherland "had well-digested her Malthus."[66] Complaints against the friendship between Sutherland and Stowe intensified with Stowe's publication of *Sunny Memories*, which explicitly contests accusations of cruelty in the press and judges the whole arrangement as an "almost sublime instance of the benevolent employment of superior wealth."[67] This praise for the Sutherland estate's policies is also underscored by Stowe's explanation of the supposedly unavoidable demographic effects of enclosure, suggesting that her friend's "well digested" Malthusianism found a ready audience.

Still, it is striking that these ideas of population evoke Liberia as a necessary term for explaining Anglo-Scottish history and point to the larger ramifications of this thinking in Stowe's literary work. In a chain of equivalence that suggests that the United States is to Scotland what Liberia is to the United States, Stowe links the two diasporas as moments of "surplus population" being pushed out beyond the nation. As this connection suggests, *Dred*'s refusal to let reproduction form the horizons of the novel has especial significance for the long-standing difficulty of reconciling Stowe's moments of radicalism with her novels' tendency toward much more conservative endings. *Uncle Tom's Cabin* has famously come under scrutiny for the ease with which the radical potential present in the midpoint of the text deflates into a comparatively placid ending in which white readers are left "feeling right" while Black characters are neatly banished to heaven or to the Liberian colonization project. In Martin Delany and Frederick Douglass's final published exchange about the value of *Uncle Tom's Cabin*, nearly the only point of agreement between the two is the error of the colonization plot.[68] As one contemporary African American reader summarized the close of *Uncle Tom's Cabin*, "Uncle Tom must be killed, George Harris exiled! Heaven for dead Negroes! Liberia for living mulattoes. Neither can live on the American continent."[69] The novel's resolution thus seems to uphold a white-only United States as the reward for white abolitionists, such that, as Isabella Furth argues, Liberian colonization "serves as a means of purging a retrograde element from the American utopia."[70] Rather than positing a solution to racial violence, Stowe offers her readers the appearance of closure by instead proposing a removal of raced bodies from the field of that violence.

The intensity of the criticism for this reliance on Liberia to solve the problems of the United States may well have come as a surprise to Stowe, because the ending that she gives George and Eliza is perhaps the most conventional and traditionally satisfying one available to the novel; they marry and raise children in a supposedly undeveloped land secluded from the political problems of the novel. Liberia, in that framing, emerges as a prop for a marriage plot that even Stowe recognizes as insufficient to the narrative. Before projecting their move to Liberia, Stowe displaces the family from Canada to France and, after political turmoil, from France back to the United States; only after showing the impossibility of a stable home in these places does the plot raise the prospect of Liberia.[71] The plot's basic structure, too, seems to suffer from the inadequacy of a conventionally novelistic ending, within which characters meet their good fortune through individual merit without any larger systemic change, in order to address the impossibly systemic nature of U.S. racial violence. Noting Stowe's movement to "two fictional codas and one non-fictional chapter" clustered at the end of *Uncle Tom's Cabin*, Christopher Diller observes that it is "almost as if she did not know where or how to conclude her story."[72]

The failure of conventional domestic endings for Stowe's Black characters points to the basic fact that African American families were under siege in the United States. This critique of marriage plot is made explicitly by several Black authors of the period. Harriet Jacobs's *Incidents in the Life of a Slave Girl* (1861) famously ends with the declaration, "Reader, my story ends in freedom; not in the usual way, with marriage," and states that she still does "not sit with [her] children in a home of [her] own" because what freedom she has is insufficient for that security.[73] Similarly, in his 1849 *Narrative of the Life and Adventures of Henry Bibb*, Bibb agonizes that the domesticity he was able to find under slavery was also co-opted by slavery, writing that "if ever there was any one act of my life while a slave, that I have to lament over, it is that of being a father and a husband of slaves. I have the satisfaction of knowing that I am only the father of one slave."[74] Within the area of the United States, the impossibility of using a marriage plot as a simple and sufficient resolution for Black families was a well-established point.

For the children of George and Eliza to signal the promise of an escape from oppression, Stowe cannot just establish a new household. She must imagine some space in which that household could be plausibly distanced from the public sphere, a move that, as Mark Rifkin has argued, historically relies on an imperialist vision of the world as empty space.[75] Stowe's syllogistic alignment of Scotland, Liberia, and the United States, however, reveals a concerned awareness that Britain was treating the United States in the same way that the Unites States was using Liberia—as a means of resolution for the displaced bodies that result from a "surplus population," regardless of whether the other space has already been populated.[76] Encountering Malthusianism as the resident of a settler-colonial nation shapes Stowe's interest in the putative elsewhere that many British Malthusians saw as a solution to population problems. This fundamentally changes the role of child characters for Stowe, because the marriage plot relies on an imperialist imaginary of open space that is impossible in Stowe's Malthusian world. The liberal vision of family as starting in a new space outside of existing politics breaks down upon encountering Stowe's awareness of colonial space as an already-occupied area.

The stakes of Stowe's interest in Malthus therefore warrant more than another rereading of *Dred* as an isolated text. They also push for a reconsideration of the ways that children can animate political novels, which in turn can also reorder our understanding of how nineteenth-century plots are able to encapsulate social problems that emerge at the level of population. The child seen by sentimentalism and the child seen by proponents of Malthusianism prompt dramatically different orientations toward history. The former's insistence on childhood as a separation from the social order of the "adult" world establishes the basis for liberal individualism's singular forgetfulness of the past by suggesting that each new individual arises from a vacuum. The latter, as grim and potentially dehumanizing as it can be, is able to imagine birth as the index of an accumulating time. In short, it lets us see children not as retreats into either domestic bliss or sentimental catharsis, but as products of and participants in their social world.

Whereas *Uncle Tom's Cabin* sought to accomplish this by falling back onto a trajectory moving from the national into the settler colonial, *Dred* takes on the far more difficult business of finding resolution when the household carries its politics with it. By presenting childhood as a product of inequality, Stowe prevents the founding of any new family from serving as a substitute for the systemic, legal problems of *Dred*. This failed departure from the reach of slavery into domestic bliss is the moment when the most surprising strand of Malthusianism creeps into Stowe's work, allowing her to see childhood's ongoing imbrication in slavery and to critique the novelistic endings that she herself had employed. If Malthusianism is premised on the interpretation of reproduction as having a dystopian bent, then the establishment of a new family is no longer an opening in the political sphere but a continuation and intensification of national decline. In the case of *Dred*, the U.S. relation to Malthusianism sets her characters on a fruitless search for new land in hopes of reaching that now-nonexistent space beyond politics. Finding none, they spiral inward toward the impossibly crowded wilderness of the swamp at the center of the novel. Through the site of this dense life, Stowe captures a different role for the child, recasting birth not as a departure from systemic history but as a continuation and crystallization of it.

THE FAMILY LIFE OF POPULATION

The most immediate impact that reading Stowe through this lens of population has is to highlight the frightening or even predatory relationships that can underwrite the white nuclear family. The condition of scarcity makes it especially clear that the family is a system of distributing resources, and that its members may not benefit equally. The children of impoverished families take on an accordingly threatening air, oscillating between piteous and monstrous. Their lack of education renders them, in the words of Harry, to be "wild white children," while at other times, they are "scared, cowering children . . . with features wasted and pinched blue with famine."[77] The burden that their birth represents to the family unit is also made surprisingly clear in Stowe's portraits of infancy as animalistic or even cruel. When, for instance, John Gordon confronts his squatters, one of his first sights is of a "miserable, haggard woman, with large, wild eyes, sunken cheeks . . . and long, lean hands, like bird's-claws," whose suffering is compounded by nursing: "at her skinny breast an emaciated infant was hanging, pushing, with its little skeleton hands, as if to force the nourishment which nature no longer gave."[78] The blurred boundary between animacy and death of "little skeleton hands" trying to draw food from a starving woman presents maternity as an almost gothic torment made all the more unsettling by the reversal of an infant actively at work "hanging, pushing" on the passive body of its mother.

Even in more traditionally sentimental scenes, in which children might be expected to be a locus of sympathy, Stowe decenters them, emphasizing instead the pain that they themselves can generate. In a portrait of the dying Susan Peyton, who had fallen from the genteel poverty of Nina Gordon into more dire straits by her marriage to John Cripps, for example, Stowe recirculates the language of sympathy without quite including her child: "The poor, frail creature in the bed seemed to be in one of those helpless hours of life's voyage, when all its waves and billows are breaking over the soul; and while the little new-comer was blindly rooting and striving at her breast, she had gathered the worn counterpane over her face, and the bed was shaken by her sobbings."[79] Because she had once held a higher class status, Susan is accorded more humanity and a clearer sense of interiority than the "haggard woman" John encounters; in place of "hands, like bird's-claws," she has a "soul" as well as a name.[80] Yet in the midst of this highly conventional language of sympathetic relation in which readers are invited to recognize "one of those helpless hours of life's voyage" as an experience they might have endured themselves, Peyton's child is pointedly excluded. Its label as a "new-comer" frames the infant as an intruder, while its thoughtless "rooting and striving" against the body of a weeping woman emphasizes the animal side of infancy. Where the reader can feel Susan's pain, the unnamed child shows no sign that he or she can; Stowe presents us with a baby whose drives are biological and distinctly outside of the circuits of sympathy. The infant's single-minded focus on physical survival transforms breastfeeding from a moment of sentimentalized interconnection between mother and child to a moment between reader and a woman under siege.[81]

Stowe's near-demonization of infancy allows her to extrapolate a critique of the harms that children can unconsciously do. Susan suffers partly from the negligent cruelty of her spouse but also directly as a result of her children. Though hungry herself, she routinely gives up her meals to feed them, an act simultaneously naturalized and made sinister by Stowe's explanation that the children, Fanny and Teddy, had "stood hungrily regarding her, as children will regard what is put on to a sick mother's plate."[82] They stand watching her, as they might watch her food, a slippage between being a mother and being consumed that is intensified by the detail that a "sick mother's plate" is under particular scrutiny, apparently because she is a weaker target. Their relationship, though it is framed as being much healthier than that with their father, more closely resembles parasitism than any ideal of maternal martyrdom, especially because Susan so explicitly regrets her role in the family. Her greatest emotional connection with her children is demonstrated when she hails the future adult version of Fanny, begging her daughter to find a different life than her own: "Go away! go away, child! O, I wish I had never been born! I wish you had never been born, nor Teddy, nor the baby! It's all nothing but trouble and sorrow! Fanny, don't you ever marry! Mind what I tell you!"[83] Domesticity and, in particular, the reproductive burden of so many unwanted births—Fanny's, Teddy's, the baby's—have destroyed Susan so thoroughly that her last words about the comfort of Jesus can only partially mitigate that her second-to-last words, "give me rest—*please* do!," plead for the quiet privacy of death.[84]

Though it is intensified and made visible by poverty, the dysfunction of the Cripps family extends throughout all the families of the text. The intra-family conflicts of the Cripps, all struggling for a share of the same pool of too little food, are echoed in the Gordon family despite their very different material circumstances. While the Cripps' hunger allows for a concrete demonstration of the costs that children exert on adults, the same set of pressures emerge in similarly damaging ways in the Gordon household in order to provide Nina with childhood. By insisting on the material labor underpinning childhood, Stowe's frighteningly selfish infants set the possibility of an angelic child at a slant.

THE COSTS OF WHITE GIRLHOOD

The mistrust of reproduction on the large scale also filters into the individual childhoods of *Dred*, and it does so most pointedly when it comes to white girls, such as *Dred*'s protagonist, Nina. By making obvious the forces necessary to produce children like Nina—the human costs of white girlhood—Stowe repositions the symbolic force of white girlhood. In her reading of Eva's role in *Uncle Tom's Cabin*, Hortense Spillers argues that the structuring logic behind Eva's death is a patriarchal compulsion to punish the girl for her desires that is then extended into the body of Tom.[85] *Dred* proceeds by an inverted logic, dramatizing the destruction of Black families and the suffering of Black children that is necessary before a white girlhood can even be imagined. By thus building the production of white childhood into the historical trajectory of slavery, Stowe prevents childhood from serving as a substitute for resolution; the white children of *Dred* are part of the problem and no source of utopian relief.

With a name that makes her link to girlhood almost allegorical, Nina has a decided aversion to leaving her childhood despite her late-teenaged years.[86] Though the text opens with her having accrued three engagements, marriage remains unappealing and confining to Nina, who declares, "I think it's a very serious thing, this being married. It's dreadful! I don't want to be a woman grown. I wish I could always be a girl, and live just as I have lived, and have plenty more girls come and see me, and have fun."[87] The erotics of this wish to remain forever in girlhood, surrounded by girls and steeped in fun, hinge on the pleasure of unproductiveness and stasis—the luxury to "live just as I have lived." Where heterosexuality leads toward maturity, labor, and seriousness, the experience of childhood permits a sense of sexuality without constraints or burdens. Like the otherwise unspeakable desire that Spillers locates in Eva's wanting of Tom, Nina's immaturity allows her a free-floating aura of sex not yet funneled toward family or home or the suffering of mothers like Susan Peyton. Unlike Eva, though, the other characters of *Dred* seem well aware of these desires.[88] As her then-fiancé Clayton remarks, "Nina isn't a woman; she is a *child*—a gay, beautiful, unformed child."[89] Nina's childishness is not contrary to her sexuality but is part of its allure.

However, much as childhood is not excluded from sexual desire, Stowe's child characters are, from birth, interwoven into larger systems of violence. Millie, the enslaved woman largely responsible for raising Nina, explains that she has endured the sale of her fourteen children with the profit going to raise the children of Nina's Aunt Harriet. For Millie, the production of angelic-seeming white girls is already reliant on the hidden sacrifice of Black children. As she says of Nina's cousin and counterpart, "When Miss Susy came home from boarding-school, she was a pretty girl; but I didn't look on her very kind, I tell you, 'cause three of my chil'en had been sold to keep her at school."[90] The equation is as direct as it is brutal; three Black girls must be erased for every white girl who enters the scene.

Millie's loss is extreme but it is not unique, for Nina's childhood is revealed to be yet another repetition in a cycle of such sacrifices. Nina's joyful carelessness about money is subsidized by her mixed-race brother Harry, who, having been charged by their dying father to act as guardian for his sister, has kept her out of bankruptcy by repeatedly using his own freedom-money to pay her bills. His continued enslavement is, by the most literal accounting, the cost of her continued innocence, a fact that Harry himself is aware of and tries to convey to Nina, declaring, "Love you? You have always held my heart in your hand! That has always been the clasp on my chain."[91]

As the case of Harry shows, the violence of these family ties extends beyond the physical into the affective. Millie shows immediate and sustained resistance to the sale of her children, but for a character like Harry, raised to conflate family and slavery by his father/owner, his investment—again, a literal as well as affective one—in maintaining Nina's childhood on conventional terms costs him his freedom, a fact that her eventual death has no redemptive power to counter.

The power that white childhood holds in *Dred* instead proves to be the power of extending slavery outside the institutions of enforcement, demonstrated most directly again by the Cripp household. Temporarily abandoned by their father after the death of Susan, the still-functionally enslaved Tiff takes charge of rearing Teddy and Fanny, acting as both parents while directing the children to adopt the manners of his former, higher-status enslavers, the Peytons. This parentage proves Tiff's affection for the children, his social awareness, and his considerable talent for adopting society's various roles as well as for undermining the essentialism of these roles; as Jackson describes it, "Fanny learns to be a white upper-class lady from a gender-bending black man."[92] Yet the forms that Tiff's household takes recapitulates slavery, seemingly because slavery shapes the only attachments to the children that he can imagine. As Stowe describes the home he runs, it is both a perfect, secluded happy family and a crystallization of slavery: "The interior of the poor cottage bore its wonted air of quaint, sylvan refinement; and Tiff went on with his old dream of imagining it as an ancestral residence, of which his young master and mistress were the head, and himself their whole retinue."[93] In fact, it is because their home is a temporary remove from the institutions of slavery, which would have otherwise put Mr. Cripps in charge, that Tiff is able to recreate this fantasy of an aristocratic Southern family.

To reduce this "dream" to false consciousness alone would patronize a character who, while often cloyingly subservient and caricatured, also maintains his own secret connections with Dred and successfully escapes with the children to the swamps and on to the North. Instead, Tiff occupies a more complicated stance, in which his expressions of devotion to Teddy and Fanny are important markers in his own identity. Labeled during their time in New York as "Tiff and his children," Fanny and Teddy are the family that Tiff made for himself, but because those family forms emerged in slavery, they never entirely depart from it. Even after the group resettles in Massachusetts, the language that Tiff uses to show his pride in a grown Fanny is rooted in Southern hierarchies: as he brags, she can socialize with families that are "e'enamost up to old Virginny."[94] He has successfully taught her to be as good, or almost as good, as slaveholders. Thus, while critic Tess Chakkalakal turns to the enslaved marriages of *Dred* for an example of family relationships formed without the state—arguing that "a marriage between slaves provided Stowe with the necessary terms to articulate the condition of an ideal marriage" because they are shown "existing apart from the law"—vertical family relationships between guardians and children become the opposite, a site where slavery can persist in new, extralegal forms.[95]

SURPLUS POPULATIONS AND NARRATIVE RESOLUTIONS

Stowe's attention to white childhood's ability to embody and reenact oppression warps the geography of *Dred* into new shapes and spaces, and it provides us alternative ways of interpreting her relatively conventional concluding moves. Most importantly, the retreat into family no longer reads as a retreat from systems of violence, and relocation to a new area involves its own potential for harm. By the time she wrote her defense of enclosure in Scotland and its comparison to African American colonization of Liberia, Stowe had already publicly recanted her apparent support for colonization schemes as well as her decision to end *Uncle Tom's Cabin* with its invocation.[96] Records of the American and Foreign Anti-Slavery Society in New York a year earlier report that Stowe wrote to them claiming her dislike for the American Colonization Society, the primary force in deporting African Americans to Liberia.[97] Meeting minutes also include a personal testimony from an acquaintance of Stowe's that "Mrs. Stowe had told him that if she were to write 'Uncle Tom' again, she would not send George Harris to Liberia."[98]

Stowe's regrets are most likely the immediate product of the work done by African American writers and activists. However, her regrets dovetail in interesting ways with her analogy between Scottish movements to the United States and African American movements to

Liberia, most notably that Stowe writes from the perspective of living in one of the spaces in which these supposed "surplus population" resettled. For Stowe, the comparison does seem to offer a reminder that if England can treat the United States as merely an outlet for excess population, treating Liberia as a tidy space of resolution fails to account for the ways that migrant populations raise new issues of their own or for the lives already in progress there.

As a result of this rethinking, the resolution of *Dred* reveals the novel's many children to be a bridge between the problems of families and geography. Recalling the child who complained that he "an't got nowhere else to be" but "have got be somewhere," the ending of *Dred* struggles with just where it can put its families that could offer real political difference.[99] Her answer is not an optimistic one. Rather than offering emigration as an oppositional way of life or a true alternative, Stowe frames these closing departures as continuations, albeit in different forms and different spaces, of the systems at work in the original nation.

Key to this attempted escape is the sprawling Great Dismal Swamp, which forms part of the novel's title. Martha Schoolman reads the swamp as a place of refuge and resistance, urging critics not to see it as what she calls the "ultimately normative project" of reinvesting in the nation, because the swamp is not straightforwardly national space though it lies within national boundaries.[100] Proposing instead a dialectic pattern of internal reform spurred by the pressure of revolutionary violence, Schoolman argues that *Dred* "triangulates the fantasy of a resistant region—the imaginary free place on the map—with the political drama unfolding in 1856."[101] Through depictions of marronage, Schoolman suggests that Stowe and other white abolitionists attempt to reconfigure the dynamics of their movement and build stronger interracial alliances outside the hierarchies of the United States. This is persuasive, but at the same time, what I want to highlight is that Stowe's vision of this withdrawal and the further withdrawal to Canada that awaits the swamp's residents does not so fully shed the structures of the nation, because for her, this movement toward a sheltering wilderness still follows the scripts of settler colonialism. In particular, they preserve the family structure that makes settler colonialism possible.

For Stowe, the dream of departing from the state in order to protect the family retains its ties to both empire and the marriage plot. The promise of the swamp is as explicitly literary as it is political. Hannibal, a self-emancipated man who becomes a leader among Dred's men, for instance, joins the ranks of Stowe's characters who use literacy to combat slavery. However, though he has a Bible, his reading of choice is instead *Robinson Crusoe*, because the novel offers him a glimpse of liberty that the Bible apparently cannot. Reading it, he imagines a precursor of his marronage: "There he yearned after the wild freedom of the desolate island. He placed his wife and children, in imagination, in the little barricaded abode of Robinson. He hunted and made coats of skin, and gathered strange fruits from trees with unknown names, and felt himself a free man."[102] Stowe does not discourage or discount Hannibal's dream, but she does suggest a parallel between her version of marronage and European colonization. The swamp provides that "wild freedom" but also tracks to the fantasies of empty land that inspired Defoe. Hannibal's desire is not just to be the man alone in nature, but the family alone. The domestic ideal of a "little barricaded abode," closed off from intrusion, runs closely parallel to the notion of the home as a sphere without politics, and in *Dred*, that ideal is inevitably tied to patterns of imperialism.

In her much-cited essay "Manifest Domesticity," Amy Kaplan challenges critics to remember the centrality of "women's work" in the home in defining and expanding national boundaries.[103] Stowe's move to consider the domestic even in exile performs a comparable maneuver in reemphasizing that because politics structure domesticity, an escape to a new home in a new space may export politics with it. As the novel finally embraces the cliché of the marriage plot, with Fanny's long-lost aunt returning to bestow Canadian land enough for the various characters to form a new settlement and wealth enough for Fanny's happy wedding to a family friend—a reversal so artificial and unlikely that Stowe herself marks its literariness, pronouncing the inheritance "so romantic a nature, that, had we not ascertained it as a positive fact, we should hesitate to insert it in our veracious narrative"—attention turns not to what is resolved but to what remains the same.[104] The final words of the novel, showing of a proud Tiff "trundling a little wicker wagon, which cradled a fair, pearly, little Miss Fanny, whom he informed all beholders was 'de very sperit of de Peytons'" return us to Tiff's role in Virginia pushing the original Miss Fanny and Miss Susan before her.[105] The hauntings of the enslaving Peytons lingers in the ambivalent repetition of white infancy.

As interested as *Dred* is in institutions, whether law, religion, or government, Stowe suggests that leaving these structures behind is not enough when slavery and racism have also saturated the narratives available for that departure. The making of a new family in the wilderness is itself a continuity of historical processes rather than a break in them and, if anything, threatens a hastening of collective misery that multiplies the social forms that it seeks to escape. The birth of a new Fanny gives the spirit of the Peytons a foothold in the new territory. Though it is a project that the novel never fully accomplishes, by re-embedding childhood in the systems of the past, *Dred* pushes for a reexamination of what it might mean to step outside the nation without the shield or confinement of imperial domesticity, to encounter the crowded world without reproducing it.

CONCLUSION

In the decades following the Civil War, interest in child welfare increasingly moved from being either a family or commercial concern to a prerogative of the state. The nation that had only begun including the names of minors in the census in 1850[1] had, by the end of the nineteenth century, developed laws against child labor, a system of public schooling, requirements for educating children, and a host of reformers fixated on policies to protect children, who were now seen as young citizens.[2] The rise of these "child savers," eager to secure and train waves of future citizens, was reinforced by the Fourteenth Amendment, which at least nominally gave a clear definition of how citizenship would be attached to future generations.[3] With this legal stabilization, attitudes around the potential wildness of white childhood (particularly of the wildness of white boys) grew more positive and was more likely to be seen as proof of personal freedom than of irredeemability.[4] Similarly, the debates around heritability between generations began to be dominated by Darwinian notions that held inheritance to be a fundamental property of all life—rather than a characteristic of social systems like family, aristocracy, or property.[5] All of this contributed to an increasingly popular belief that children were a national resource to be managed rather than a source of instability.

But this by no means is to say that unequal childhoods ended, simply that they took new forms. As Geoff K. Ward's *The Black Child-Savers* has shown, even at the height of passion for reforms aimed at children, progressives consistently allocated fewer, if any, resources for the welfare of African American children.[6] Social Darwinism, popularized in the United States by media like Horatio Alger novels, naturalized systemic inequality as the individual failures of children not "enterprising" enough to acquire property. The forcible removal and residential schooling of Native American children, already started during the antebellum period, intensified to devastating effects and, beginning around the 1880s, the rise in biological Darwinism fueled eugenic attempts to eliminate children of color and children with disabilities on a massive scale.[7]

It is equally apparent that the social differentiation of childhoods persists into the present. To name only a few examples, throughout the 1980s and early '90s, children of color and especially African American children could be labeled with the now-discredited diagnoses of the developmentally static "crack baby,"[8] or the terminally criminal "super-predator," labels that echo the earlier categories of "prodigy" and "incorrigible" in their use of medicine and law, respectively, to alienate and demonize.[9] Expansive definitions of "gang behavior" continue to police the most mundane behavior up to and into social contact among African American and Latinx children.[10] Correspondingly dehumanizing descriptions of children as "anchor babies" continue to be used to undermine the citizenship of Latinx and Asian American families, as well as that of immigrant children of color in general.[11] These discourses have direct and material effects on the lives of such children. Recent research shows that not only are hospitals less likely to give African American children effective pain medication[12] and police officers more likely to use force against Black children, white Americans more generally interpret African boys as being four-and-a-half years older than they are and as being less innocent than white or Latinx peers.[13] In other words, political rhetoric around childhood continues to rely as much on establishing differentiated categories of children as it does on an idealization of childhood.

Equally, though, childhoods portrayed as antisocial never truly were. As children of color were increasingly consolidated into the national population at the end of the nineteenth century and subjected to new types of violent institutional management as a result, writers moved to imagine life trajectories that ended beyond citizenship and the limits of supposed formal equality. Zitkala-Ša, a Yankton Dakota Sioux author, wrote about the violence she survived as a child in the residential school system and is careful to connect that childhood to an adulthood that exceeds citizenship. After describing the absolute psychological and spiritual misery of teaching at the Carlisle school, Zitkala-Ša provides autobiographical resolution by stepping away from reader expectations for resolution. She writes that, eventually, she came upon "a new way of solving the problem of my inner self," leaves Carlisle, and begins her own self-directed education in the East.[14] The solution grants the protagonist peace and direction, but she also does not share anything about what that idea is; the critical point is simply that she "liked it."[15] This turn places Zitkala-Ša's emergence into adulthood outside of known structures of civic rights or national belonging. While she fought for these rights throughout her career, they are also less important than her own sense of self.

Similarly, Pauline Hopkins's *Winona: A Tale of Negro Life in the South and Southwest* turns on the capacity for a reimagined childhood to also reinvent the terms of sociability.[16] Published serially in the *Colored American Magazine* starting in 1902, *Winona* combines history with adventure and romance to tell the story of two young half-siblings, Judah and Winona, as they are kidnapped into slavery and then escape and join forces with John Brown's troops to fight their former enslavers, eventually leaving in triumph to England to claim Winona's secret ancestral fortune. Throughout, Hopkins reminds readers that her young heroes have potential far beyond what the United States can offer them and that their heroism is rooted in their ability to form communities and kinships.

Childhood is slippery in *Winona* for a few reasons. First, Hopkins is ambiguous about her main characters' ages. At the start of the novel, we're introduced to Judah and Winona as "two children" and told that Judah has already started school and Winona will be sent to school later that year.[17] A reference two months later to "the new act for the rendition of fugitive slaves jes' passed by Congress" would tend to place the year around 1850 or perhaps 1851 in the novel's opening.[18] The fact that Winona's parents first meet sometime after 1842 would suggest that Winona is no more than eight years old at the novel's start.[19] Judah, arriving in 1842 as an orphaned "mite of humanity," is harder to pin down in age, but is treated as a protective older brother who is close in age to his half-sister. This timeline is complicated by the fact that, in the same point in the narrative that is marked as being around 1850–1851, Winona is also described by an observer as "not more than fourteen, but appearing younger."[20] After this point, there's a jump in the narrative that brings us two years into the future[21] into 1856,[22] when we're told that Winona is "only sixteen."[23] Even omitting the reference to the Fugitive Slave Act of 1850, Winona should not be older than fourteen at this point based simply on the years (1842 and 1856) we are explicitly given. The realities of serial publication likely play a role in this confusion. Hopkins was probably writing for a deadline—possibly an unpredictable deadline—and one inherent feature of serial novels is that, once a plot point, or year, has been introduced, it cannot be revised for later plot needs. However, much of this conflicting information comes from a single portion that was published together; part one of the novel as it originally appeared contained the information that Winona was born after 1842, that the present of the novel was around 1850, and that in this present, Winona is recognized as fourteen.[24] Even allowing for a rush on preparing this portion, it seems easier to ascribe intent to Hopkins's years than to wave them off as carelessness.

What this numerical juggling does is force readers to reconsider what they know about Winona and Judah's ages and from whom they know it. The years make perfect sense if Winona is actually seven or eight, which would leave the observer's description of her as "not more than fourteen, but appearing younger" as an inflation of her age, possibly motivated by the fact that the observer is white, is sexually attracted to her, and eventually becomes her husband.[25] The fact that this bad guess at Winona's age as fourteen sticks in the novel—so that two years later in the narrative, the narrator confirms that she is "only sixteen"[26]—elevates social age over chronological age. The people around Winona assume that she is fourteen and, to all intents and purposes, she becomes fourteen. Judah is simpler in that there is less contradiction about his age, but there is also far less information for both readers and characters. By staging both his mother's death and his adoptive mother's death before the beginning of the novel, Hopkins leaves open the possibility that no one living knows quite when Judah was born.[27]

The ambiguity in character age, however, does not erase childhood from Judah and Winona's worlds. What happens instead is that Hopkins redefines its nature to center individual dignity and collective interdependence. Childhood as a result looks very different, and Hopkins trains readers to recognize it gradually. One strategy for this is simply to label Winona and Judah "children,"[28] "precious child,"[29] and "childish"[30] throughout the full course of their adventures, reminding us of their ages amidst moments of intense bravery and sacrifice. Even Winona's romance with Warren Maxwell, a young British lawyer turned abolitionist rebel, is couched in reminders that she is young, and perhaps even too young for her relationship. Hopkins writes that "more and more Warren felt toward her as to a darling, irresistible child, and sometimes as to a young goddess far beyond him."[31] More subtle cues, though, come in gestures toward the fantastical—such as Judah's ability to tame wild horses with his "unflinching gaze"[32] or his participation in a daring escape in which lighting strikes an evil ship's captain and Judah catches his half-sister "as deftly as a ball is caught and tossed from one player to another"[33]—that momentarily realign the novel with the most roaring of adventures. Hopkins's repeated descriptions of Winona, too, as a "princess,"[34] "a young princess,"[35] and as a "queen" are references to Winona's inherent dignity and her secret ties to British aristocracy but are also suggestive of a fairy tale. In such moments, Hopkins evokes genres popular among younger readers and ties them to characters who are themselves young.

Perhaps most importantly, Hopkins highlights how her characters' status as children rallies new communities and new ways of being social around them. In her reading of transracial adoption in abolitionist literature as a source of radical love, Brigitte Fiedler proposes that scholars focus not only on the behavior and descriptions of African American child characters, but also on how white characters respond to them, in order to deemphasize "black worthiness of love" and instead center the obligations owed by white people.[36] From this perspective, the most immediate feature of Winona and Judah's childhoods are the connections that others immediately make with them. When the two children's father is murdered, Warren and Ebenezer Maybee, the local innkeeper, each attempt to find households for them, and, as Warren suggests, the impulse is natural and reflexive: "It was a time that would have made any one a friend to those helpless children."[37] Warren is being naïve, of course, because the men who murdered the children's father enslave Winona and Judah shortly thereafter, but what Warren articulates is the same obligation that Fiedler describes; the failure of the enslavers to honor it is further evidence of their evil rather than evidence against Warren's statement.

Winona, especially, forms the center of a novel that is as much about the invention of new forms of sociability as it is about her personal growth as an individual. Nazera Sadiq Wright has demonstrated the centrality of Black girlhood as a figure of social and political change for Black writers in the nineteenth century; Winona, too, figures as an anchor for the community around her and the kinship at the core of the novel *Winona*.[38] Crucially, Hopkins crafts this kinship into a continually shifting and open framework that has little to do with biology. A sequence of adoptions shapes the backstory of the novel. A British nobleman framed for murder escapes to the shores of Lake Erie and is adopted into the Seneca Nation, takes on the name "White Eagle," and eventually becomes a leader. He, in turn, aids people escaping from slavery through the Underground Railroad. One woman arrives with the infant Judah, having adopted him after his own mother died. She stays and marries White Eagle. They both act as adoptive parents for Judah and then have their own child, Winona. Though Winona's mother dies in childbirth, Nokomis, a Native woman (presumably Seneca, though it is not specified), steps in as a surrogate mother. By the time of the novel's start, Judah is being raised by his third maternal figure and by an adoptive father who has himself been adopted into a new society.

Even the plot of the novel, which appears from one angle like a tale of two exceptional children who are enslaved and able to escape through their own heroic efforts, also identifies part of that heroism in the children's ability to form networks of supporters around themselves. When Warren coincidentally arrives at the planation where Judah and Winona are enslaved and offers help, Judah responds with joy but also with the assurance that he had expected this help, declaring, "I knew you would be here soon: I dreamt a year ago that I saw you coming out of a cloud of intense blackness."[39] This foretelling shifts the weight of the scene from any potential expectation of gratitude from Judah to reaffirming the debt that Warren owes to two children he meet in passing two years ago. Warren's arrival and pledge to help is closer to overdue than extraordinary. Over time, the trio expands to include Maybee, who then brings them in touch with John Brown and his many supporters as a band that lives and works together to fight slavery.

The impulse to help Winona and Judah arises almost spontaneously, but what sustains this new group is mutual assistance and obligation to each other. While this may sound like a fairly typical use of childhood dependency as a center for sympathy, Judah and Winona are fully included in giving aid within this exchange. Warren and Maybee help the two siblings escape slavery, but Hopkins gives more space to a different rescue—that of Warren from a Missouri prison, where he has been held for supporting abolitionism. Winona disguises herself as a boy and is willingly captured and jailed as a fugitive so that she can tend to Warren's gunshot wounds, making Warren declare that she has "saved [his] life."[40] Similarly, at a crucial interval in John Brown's raid on the prison, as the heroes are cornered and held at gunpoint, Judah intervenes and tackles the villain—saving the group as a whole.[41] This reversal, in which two young African American characters save a wounded and helpless white man from the grasp of slave law also reverses the notion of childhood dependency into a universal interdependency. The children's need may provide the impetus for this family formation, but their own strengths as individuals allow them to help as well.

This is a politics of care that recalls Harriet Wilson's demands that Frado receive good treatment from her town. It also echoes Susan Paul's vision of a community of intertextual saints—with one small boy helping other small children, when he is vulnerable and suffering—or even William Apess's search for a community in which action matters more than intention. For all of these writers, the sociality that emerges from these childhoods is one with borders other than those of the nation, whether it is Wilson's township or Apess's passing through borderlands or Paul's spiritual connections across space and time. It also calls to mind Derrick R. Spires's work on the theorization of citizenship by early Black print culture. As he describes the model of community imagined by Absalom Jones and Richard Allen, citizenship reinvented outside the government could be "a permeable civic space, resembling more a dynamic web of associations based in mutual aid than a single sphere, a neighborhood rather than a market."[42] This non-convergence with national scales is especially highlighted in Hopkins's novel because it tracks the converging genocides of the Atlantic slave trade and the dispossession and murder of Native Americans. As Augusta Rohrbach has noted, *Winona* "posits the devastation of Native Americans as the occasion for its narrative."[43] Part of the importance of this choice is that it centers the joint injuries that U.S. white supremacy has done to Black and Native peoples and the potential for solidarity between them. Another part, though, has to do with reshaping the significance of Winona and Judah's childhoods away from pre-determined civic frameworks.

The family that these characters form is not an analog to the nation. Instead, they exist in opposition to and flight from the nation. Hopkins imagines the revolutionary community that works with John Brown as extralegal and entirely orderly: "In the Brown camp the great family of fugitives dwelt together in guileless and trusting brotherhood under the patriarchal care of Captain Brown, who daily praised the Eternal Sire, and one soul of harmony and love was infused into each individual dweller."[44] While Hopkins does use norms of masculinity and femininity throughout the text, I read her reference to the "patriarchal care of John Brown" as an insistence that this group is a family, as well as an invocation of Biblical models of family that stretched well beyond the limits of nuclear family. This "great family of fugitives" are fugitive either because they are self-emancipated or because they have fought to emancipate others, but in the midst of this flight, Hopkins describes the greatest possible stability, granting them "one soul of harmony and love." Literally chased by the United States government, the kinship that Winona and Judah experience in John Brown's camp is antithetical to the biological, nuclear families that had become models of the nation in miniature.

The geography of the novel accordingly exists between defined countries. Winona and Judah's family begins in the space that the Seneca Nation left, on the border between Canada and the United States, until they eventually cross into Canada and end in England. Mary Grace Albanese has noted a similar line of focus on the new types of family that "flourish outside the logics of traditional lines of kinship and genealogical reproduction, and beyond the imperial geographies of the United States"[45] in Hopkins's 1902 novel *Of One Blood*. Though *Winona* closes with Judah and Winona each joyfully marrying into new and loving families, neither of these happy endings mention them parenting children. Instead, the novel ends with a different type of reproduction and a distinct future. In her final chapter, Hopkins presents Aunt Vinnie, an African American woman working as a cook at Maybee's inn, telling and retelling Winona's adventures to "groups of curious neighbors, white and black who never tired of hearing her tell the story."[46] Tacitly including her readers in these crowds of eager listeners, Hopkins places Winona's extraordinary childhood as the grounds for new kinds of non-biological reproduction, for stories being told over and over to form new populations from their audiences.

Winona traces what are perhaps the most important afterlives of these antebellum childhoods—the power to transform exclusion into new ways of being. As Hopkins makes clear, if Winona and Judah are not the future of the United States, it is because they deserve something better. New types and categories for the "antisocial child" continue to emerge in the present world of intensified school-to-prison pipelines (and in schools that blur the line between classroom and prison[47]), in the captivity and deportation of children seeking U.S. asylum, and any number of other abuses. Attending to the forms of childhood that these institutions imagine provides a critical means of tracing their spread into popular culture and recognizing their connections with earlier stereotypes. Just as vital, though, is the ability to attend to narratives of childhood that do not look like childhood in ways that are immediately apparent or that are written to subvert these narratives. Submerged forms of alternative childhood, good and bad, remain throughout literature and print culture and can both enable criticism of their harmful contemporary legacies or provide new options to imagining what childhood can be.

NOTES

Introduction

1. Carl Linnaeus, "Mammalia Primates: Homo," in *Systema Naturae*, tenth ed. (Stockholm: Laurentii Salvii, 1758), 20–24, Internet Archive, accessed October 20, 2015, https://archive.org/details/cbarchive_53979_linnaeus1758systemanaturae1758.
2. Ibid., 22–23.
3. Ibid., 20. The 1766 edition adds three children to this list, two female and one male. Although feral childhood may have been more readily accorded to boys, gender was not a central organizing principle in the structure of Linnaeus's taxonomy.
4. Alys Eve Weinbaum, *Wayward Reproductions: Genealogies of Race and Nation in Transatlantic Modern Thought* (Durham, NC: Duke University Press, 2004).
5. John Locke, *Two Treatises of Government*, ed. Peter Laslett (London: A. Millar et al., 1764; New York: Cambridge University Press, 2009), 177.
6. Kathryn Bond Stockton, *The Queer Child, or Growing Sideways in the Twentieth Century* (Durham, NC: Duke University Press, 2009).
7. Though this is only a few names among many possible references, I am especially indebted to the work of Saidiya Hartman, P. Gabrielle Foreman, Nazera Sadiq Wright, Aimee Meredith Cox, and Sandrina de Finney.
8. Marie Jenkins Schwartz, *Born into Bondage: Growing Up Enslaved in the Antebellum South* (Cambridge: Harvard University Press, 2001), 5. As a point of comparison, Schwartz further notes that this demographic pattern was not present in slave-holding nations in Latin America, which relied on the transport and purchase of new adults to maintain their labor force.
9. Wilma King, *Stolen Childhood: Slave Youth in Nineteenth-Century America*, second ed. (Bloomington: Indiana University Press, 2011), 73.
10. Dawn Peterson, *Indians in the Family: Adoption and the Politics of Antebellum Expansion* (Cambridge: Harvard University Press, 2017).
11. James D. Schmidt, "'Restless Movements Characteristic of Childhood': The Legal Construction of Child Labor in Nineteenth-Century Massachusetts," *Law and History Review* 23, no. 2 (2005): 315–50.
12. Robin Bernstein, *Racial Innocence: Performing American Childhood from Slavery to Civil Rights* (New York: New York University Press, 2011); Anna Mae Duane, *Suffering Childhood in Early America: Violence, Race, and the Making of the Child Victim* (Athens: University of Georgia Press, 2010).
13. For representative works in this vein, see Marah Gubar, *Artful Dodgers: Reconceiving the Golden Age of Children's Literature* (New York: Oxford University Press, 2009); Claudia Nelson, *Precocious Children and Childish Adults: Age Inversion in Victorian Literature* (Baltimore: Johns Hopkins

University Press, 2012); or Jacqueline Rose's foundational *The Case of Peter Pan* (Philadelphia: University of Pennsylvania Press, 1992).

14. For further discussion, see Ian Baucom, *Out of Place: Englishness, Empire, and the Locations of Identity* (Princeton, NJ: Princeton University Press, 1999).
15. This 1790 law was replaced in 1795 by another law of the same name, which preserved these central points and added a more detailed description of the requirements for naturalizations, including a renunciation of previous political loyalties and hereditary titles. See *The Public Statutes at Large of the United States of America* (Boston: Little, Biddle, and Co., 1845), 414–15.
16. Kristin A. Collins, "Illegitimate Borders: *Jus Sanguinis* Citizenship and the Legal Construction of Family, Race, and Nation," *Yale Law Journal* 123, no. 7 (2014): 2136.
17. *Public Statutes*, 103.
18. Collins, "Illegitimate Borders," 2139.
19. Carrie Hyde, *Civic Longing: The Speculative Origins of U.S. Citizenship* (Cambridge: Harvard University Press, 2018).
20. Martha Jones, *Birthright Citizens: A History of Race and Rights in Antebellum America* (New York: Cambridge University Press, 2018).
21. This literary wave, of course, was not without some precedents. The most popular of whom was likely Capitola Black of *The Hidden Hand*, though I would suggest that Capitola's dramatized search for her origin story hints at a more fraught relationship with genealogy than Twain or Alcott's protagonists have.
22. Kenneth B. Kidd, *Making American Boys: Boyology and the Feral Tale* (Minneapolis: University of Minnesota Press, 2004).
23. Even as stories of feral children grew less popular in the United States, Linnaeus himself remained as a scientific authority. His *Systema Naturae* was widely available in early American libraries, enthusiasts formed Linnaean societies, and, as Alison M. K. Klaum demonstrates, Linnaean ordering shaped the largely female-authored genres of floral art instruction and floral poetry. The lectures in botany prepared by Almira H. Lincoln in 1829 may have best captured the ubiquity of Linnaean thought in their explanation to adolescent readers that "the classification of Linnaeus was received with scarcely a dissenting voice" and that "what this system was, you have not now to learn, since it has been the basis of your botanical studies" ("History of Botany"). Lincoln may have overstated the official acceptance of Linnaeus, but her essential point remains that U.S. taxonomic thinking drew reflexively from Linnaean thought. See Alison M. K. Klaum, "Seeing Botanically: Linnaean Influence in Popular Antebellum Flower Books and the Library Company of Philadelphia's Visual Collections," *Pennsylvania History: A Journal of Mid-Atlantic Studies* 79, no. 3 (Summer 2012): 298–314; Almira H. Lincoln, "History of Botany: Familiar Lectures on Botany," *Ladies' Magazine* 2, no. 10 (October 1829): 472.

24. Nathaniel Hawthorne, *The Scarlet Letter* (Boston: Ticknor, Reed & Fields, 1850; New York: Penguin Books, 2003), 84.
25. Ibid., 82.
26. Ibid., 99.
27. The parallels between Una Hawthorne and Pearl were first explored in depth in T. Walter Herbert's "Nathaniel Hawthorne, Una Hawthorne, and *The Scarlet Letter*: Interactive Selfhoods and the Cultural Construction of Gender," *PMLA* 103, no. 3 (1988): 285–97.
28. Charles Loring Brace, *The Dangerous Classes of New York and Twenty Years' Work among Them* (New York: Wynkoop & Hallenback, 1872), 322.
29. In my emphasis on the perceived irredeemability of some children, I also focus on an earlier and distinct period noted in Kenneth Kidd's excellent study of feral children and late nineteenth- and twentieth-century boyhood, which argues that the association between wildness and a normative child development out of that wildness structures much of our ideas about adult freedom. See Kidd, *Making American Boys*.
30. Michel Foucault, *Security, Territory, Population: Lectures at the Collège de France, 1977–78*, ed. Michel Senellart, trans. Graham Burchell (New York: Picador, 2009): 231.
31. See Lee Edelman, *No Future: Queer Theory and the Death Drive* (Durham, NC: Duke University Press, 2004); Elizabeth Freeman, *Time Binds: Queer Temporalities, Queer Histories* (Durham, NC: Duke University Press, 2010); and Lauren Berlant, *The Queen of America Goes to Washington City: Essays on Sex and Citizenship* (Durham, NC: Duke University Press, 1997).
32. Jack Halberstam, *In a Queer Time and Place: Transgender Bodies, Subcultural Lives* (New York: New York University Press, 2005), 5.
33. José Esteban Muñoz, *Cruising Utopia: The Then and There of Queer Futurity* (New York: New York University Press, 2009), 95.
34. Holly Brewer, *By Birth or Consent: Children, Law, and the Anglo-American Revolution in Authority* (Chapel Hill: University of North Carolina Press, 2012).
35. Duane, *Suffering Childhood in Early America.*
36. Bernstein, *Racial Innocence.*
37. Nazera Sadiq Wright, *Black Girlhood in the Nineteenth Century* (Chicago: University of Illinois Press, 2016).
38. See, for instance, Saidiya Hartman, *Wayward Lives, Beautiful Experiments: Intimate Histories of Social Upheaval* (New York: W. W. Norton & Co., 2019); and the edited collection *Who Writes for Black Children?: African American Children's Literature before 1900*, ed. Katharine Capshaw and Anna Mae Duane (Minneapolis: University of Minnesota, 2017).
39. Benedict Anderson, *Imagined Communities: Reflections on the Origin and Spread of Nationalism* (New York: Verso, 2006), 246.

Chapter 1: Bound Children

1. The spellings of the surname "Barns" and "Barnes" are used interchangeably in the indenture; I have chosen the former for consistency in this chapter. [Indenture of Cynthia Barns to Samuel Richmond], Pomfret, CT: 1822, "Indentures. 1710–1857." Winterthur Manuscript Collection, Coll 288. Winterthur Museum, Library, and Garden, Winterthur, Delaware.
2. William Apess, *A Son of the Forest: The Experience of William Apes [sic], A Native of the Forest Comprising a Notice of the Pequod Tribe of Indians* (New York: Published by the Author, 1829); Harriet Wilson, *Our Nig; or, Sketches from the Life of a Free Black*, ed. P. Gabrielle Foreman and Reginald H. Pitts (Boston: Geo. C. Rand & Avery, 1859; New York: Penguin, 2005).
3. Nazera Sadiq Wright, *Black Girlhood in the Nineteenth Century* (Chicago: University of Illinois Press, 2016) 79–83.
4. For Krupat's early discussion, see Arnold Krupat "The Indian Autobiography: Origins, Type, and Function," *American Literature* 53, no. 1 (1981): 22–42. For a more recent overview of the genre and further discussion of Apess in relation to it, see Kendall Johnson, "Imagining Self and Community in American Indian Autobiography," *The Columbia Guide to American Indian Literatures of the United States since 1945*, ed. Eric Cheyfitz (New York: Columbia Press, 2006), 357–410.
5. Ana Mae Duane, *Suffering Childhood in Early America: Violence, Race, and the Making of the Child Victim* (Athens: University of Georgia Press, 2010); Laura L. Mielkle, "Containing Native Feeling: Sentiment in the Autobiographies of William Apess, Mary Jemison, and Black Hawk," *Moving Encounters: Sympathy and the Indian Question in Antebellum Literature* (Amherst: University of Massachusetts Press, 2008), 70–92.
6. For an overview of this tendency, as well as a persuasive pitch that gothic narratives be included as well, see Julia Stern, "Excavating Genre in *Our Nig*," *American Literature* 67, no. 3 (September 1995): 439–66.
7. Apess, *Son of the Forest*, 67, 68.
8. Jed Esty, "The Colonial Bildungsroman: *The Story of an African Farm* and the Ghost of Goethe," *Victorian Studies* 49, no. 3 (2007): 409.
9. British common law established the threshold at twenty-one, setting the standard precedent for U.S. law. See William Blackstone and Edward Christian, *Commentaries on the Laws of England* (Portland, ME: Thomas B. Wait & Company, 1807), 451. Some state laws, however, did create slightly different definitions. While common law infancy was generally categorized without reference to sex, many states legislated that female infancy would instead end at the age of eighteen. See John Bouvier and Francis Rawle, "Infancy," *Bouvier's Law Dictionary*, vol. 1 (Boston: Boston Book Company, 1897), 1029. Similar differentiations occur in Pennsylvania laws from the 1830s

regarding the indenture of minors in the custody of the states; see chapter two for this discussion.

10. James Kent, *Commentaries on American Law*, vol. II (New York: O. Halsted, 1832), 227.
11. William B. Wedgwood, *The Government and Laws of the United States* (New York: J. W. Schermerhorn & Co., 1867), 143.
12. "Infant, n.1 (and adj.)," Oxford English Dictionary Online, Oxford University Press, accessed August 15, 2015, https://www.oed.com/view/Entry/95211?rskey=CfQCUM&result=1&isAdvanced=false.
13. David Booth, *An Analytical Dictionary of the English Language* (London: James Cochran and Co., 1835), 25. Emphasis in original.
14. Blackstone, *Commentaries*, 21.
15. Ibid.
16. Ibid. His argument that child criminals have historically been treated as a distinct class from adults does, however, includes a number of exceptions and finely parsed distinctions that, much like the current U.S. system, rests in large part on whether the court believes the child to have adult understanding or active malice. For instance, although the age of majority for Blackstone is generally twenty-one, he records the burning of a thirteen-year-old girl for "killing her mistress" and the hanging of a ten-year-old boy for murder on the grounds that he attempted to hide the body and thus showed guilt (ibid., 23).
17. Ibid., 465.
18. Joseph Slaughter, *Human Rights, Inc: The World Novel, Narrative Form, and International Law* (New York: Fordham University Press, 2009), 103.
19. Franco Moretti, *The Way of the World: The Bildungsroman in European Culture*, second ed. (London: Verso, 2000), 18–19.
20. Much as the child provides a site at which the body cannot be cleanly separated from the subject in antebellum thought, the physical and social coming of age of the child also offers a point at which individualism crosses into its own variety of species thinking. For example, Ralph Waldo Emerson crosses into a botanical account of human life, noting that "we fancy men are individuals; so are pumpkins; but every pumpkin in the field goes through every point of pumpkin history." See Ralph W. Emerson, *Works of Ralph Waldo Emerson* (New York: George Routledge and Sons, 1883), 136
21. Blackstone, *Commentaries*, 22.
22. See Franco Moretti's preface to the second edition of *Way of the World* for a longer discussion of the bildungsroman's tendency to avoid poor or working-class protagonists. Note also that although I list these categories of gender, race, and class mobility as distinct, they are certainly interrelated, as Harriet Wilson makes clear.
23. Viviana A. Zelizar, *Pricing the Priceless Child: The Changing Social Value of Children* (New York: Basic Books, 1985), 59.

24. Jacqueline S. Reiner, "Re-forming Character: Work," *From Virtue to Character: American Childhood, 1775–1850* (New York: Twayne Publishers, 1996), 131.
25. Xiomara Santamarina, "The View from Below: Menial Labor and Self-Reliance in Harriet Wilson's *Our Nig*," *Belabored Professions: Narratives of African American Working Womanhood* (Chapel Hill: University of North Carolina, 2005), 76.
26. Wilson, *Our Nig*, 38.
27. Ibid., 23.
28. Ibid., 17.
29. Ibid., 65.
30. [Indenture of Cynthia Barns].
31. Wilson, *Our Nig*, 60.
32. I slightly differ here from Barbara A. White's reading. In her analysis of the autobiographical content of *Our Nig*, White considers Frado's limited education and her social context and concludes that the girl's indenture was likely real. I generally agree, but my emphasis instead is on how artificial such an indenture appears within the narrative itself. See Barbara A. White, "*Our Nig* and the She-Devil: New Information about Harriet Wilson and the 'Bellmont' Family," *American Literature* 65, no. 1 (1993): 19–52.
33. Wilson, *Our Nig*, 70.
34. Ibid., 60.
35. Priscilla Wald, "'As from a Faithful Mirror': *Pierre*, *Our Nig*, and Literary Nationalism," *Constituting Americans: Cultural Anxiety and Narrative Form* (Durham, NC: Duke University Press, 1995), 165.
36. Ibid.
37. Wilson, *Our Nig*, 58.
38. Ibid., 11.
39. Ibid., 34.
40. Ibid., 34.
41. Ibid., 17.
42. Ibid., 12.
43. Ibid., 31.
44. Ibid., 14.
45. Ibid., 14.
46. Apess, *Son of the Forest*, 16.
47. Ibid., 34.
48. Ibid., 35.
49. [Indenture of Mariah Elizabeth Perry to Humphrey Dillon], Bedford, PA: 1834. "Records of Negro and Mulatto Children and Miscellaneous Slave Records," Pennsylvania Historical and Museum Commission, Pennsylvania State Archives, accessed June 20, 2015, http://www.phmc.state.pa.us/bah/dam/rg/di/r47-SlaveRecords/r47-SlaveRecords-Bedford

/r47-SlaveRecords-Bedford3rdGroup.htm. For Dillon's occupation, see *History of Bedford, Somerset, and Fulton Counties* (Chicago: Waterman, Watkins, & Co., 1884), 250.

50. Although child signatures or marks are sometimes included in indentures, there was no requirement at that time in Pennsylvania that the child consent to the contract; as Pennsylvania's compilation of state law, *Purdon's Digest*, reports in 1853, "it is not necessary that the infant should join in the indenture." See John Purdon, George M. Stroud, and Frederick C. Brightly, *Purdon's Digest: A Digest of the Laws of Pennsylvania* (Philadelphia, James Kay, Jun. & Brother, 1853), 39. That law had changed by 1860 to require infant consent and participation in the contract, though the law's application to indentures from poor houses and houses of refuge is far from clear. See William T. Haines, *Township and Local Laws of the States of Pennsylvania* (West Chester, PA: Edward F. James, 1860), 309.
51. Although provisions for the upkeep of workers did appear in adult indentures, the substation of such bare supplies as food and drink for wages or land was more associated with child apprenticeship. See Christopher Tomlins, *Freedom Bound: Law, Labor, and Civic Identity in Colonizing English America, 1580–1865* (New York: Cambridge University Press, 2010), 242.
52. Thomas Hobbes, *Leviathan: Or, The Matter, Forme & Power of a Commonwealth, Ecclesiasticall and Civill* (Cambridge: Cambridge University Press, 1904), 90. *Google Books*, accessed June 2016, https://www.google.com/books/edition/Leviathan/20c6AAAAMAAJ?hl=en&gbpv=1.
53. Ibid., 90.
54. Ibid., 91.
55. James Kent's *Commentaries on American Laws* (1832) notes, for instance, that an infant "may bind himself as an apprentice, it being an act manifestly for his benefit." See Kent, *Commentaries*, 242. Similarly, indentures could be dissolved by the court system if they lacked education for the apprentice; see *Butler v. Hubbard*, 5 Pick, 250 (Massachusetts 1827) for one such ruling.
56. Though his age is not given explicitly, the specificity of his term of service—"Nine years three month[s] and twenty days"—suggests that it has been set based on the time to his majority, mostly likely to his twenty-first birthday. See [Indenture of Isaac Pennell Jr. to Joseph Dunn], Radnor, PA: 1817. Van Pelt Special Collections, Misc Mss Box 14 Folder 32, University of Pennsylvania, Philadelphia.
57. [Indenture of Oliver Gautier to Stephen Dutilh], Philadelphia, PA: 1785. Van Pelt Special Collections, Misc Mss Box 6 Folder 27, University of Pennsylvania, Philadelphia.
58. Wilson, *Our Nig*, 65.
59. Ibid., 67.
60. Ibid., 67.
61. Ibid., 100.

62. Ibid., 79.
63. Ibid., 67.
64. Ibid., 68.
65. Ibid., 68.
66. Ibid., 65.
67. Ibid., 67.
68. Ibid., 66.
69. Ibid., 67.
70. Peter L. Bayers, "William Apess's Manhood and Native Resistance in Jacksonian America," *Melus* 31, no. 1 (Loss, Melancholia, Resistance) (Spring 2006): 125.
71. Apess, *Son of the Forest*, 54.
72. Ibid., 54.
73. Ibid., 57.
74. Ibid., 66.
75. Ibid., 112.
76. Ibid., 22.
77. Jean-Jacques Rousseau, *The Social Contract*, trans. Maurice Cranston (New York: Penguin, 1968), 153.
78. John Locke, *Two Treatises of Government*, ed. Peter Laslett (London: A. Millar et al., 1764; New York: Cambridge University Press, 2009), 348.

Chapter 2: The Incorrigible Child

1. The organizational layout of these documents requires an unorthodox citation method. To preserve specificity, I have cited first with the relevant case number and then, when relevant, with the date of the cited remark. All inmate records have been taken from New York House of Refuge, Inmate Case Histories, 1824–1935, A2064, Vol. 1, Microfilm Roll 1, New York State Archives, Albany, NY (hereafter "Case Histories").
2. Nathaniel Hawthorne, *The Scarlet Letter* (Boston: Ticknor, Reed & Fields, 1850; New York: Penguin Books, 2003), 86.
3. See William Blackstone, St George Tucker, and Edward Christian, *Blackstone's Commentaries: With Notes of Reference, to the Constitution and Laws, of the Federal Government of the United States; and of the Commonwealth of Virginia*, vol. 4 (Philadelphia: W. Y. Birch, and A. Small, R. Carr, 1803), 11. Accessed September 14, 2015, https://www.google.com/books/edition/_/BwwoAQAAMAAJ?hl=en&gbpv=0.
4. See, for instance, the 1826 Assembly Act founding the Pennsylvania House of Refuge and authorizing it to commit children indefinitely for "incorrigible and vicious conduct," and the 1838 case, *Ex parte Crouse*, confirming the extant practice of doing so without the extension of habeas corpus. See Ardemus Steward, *Stewart's Purdon's Digest: A Digest of the Statute Law of*

the State of Pennsylvania from the Year 1700 to 1903 (Philadelphia, George T. Bisel Co., 1905), 1854; and *Ex parte* Crouse, 4 Whart. 9, 11 (Pa. 1839).

5. "The Fundamental Ideas of Geometry," *Yale Literary Magazine* (New Haven: Herrick & Noyes, 1847), 193–96.
6. Annalisa Coliva, "Self-Knowledge: Fragile or Robust?," *The Self and Self-Knowledge* (New York: Oxford University Press, 2012), 202.
7. Richard Briggs Stott, *Workers in the Metropolis: Class, Ethnicity, and Youth in Antebellum New York City* (Cornell, NY: Cornell University Press, 1990), 71.
8. Walter Kamphoefner, *The Westfalians: From Germany to Missouri* (Princeton, NJ: Princeton University Press, 2014), 84.
9. For a discussion of the legal details of this transition, see James D. Schmidt's "'Restless Movements Characteristic of Childhood': The Legal Construction of Child Labor in Nineteenth-Century Massachusetts," *Law and History Review* 23, no. 2 (2005): 315–50.
10. Quoted in Hugh D. Hindman, *The World of Child Labor: An Historical and Regional Survey* (Armonk, NY: M. E. Sharpe, 2009), 464.
11. Timothy A. Hacsi, *Second Home: Orphan Asylums and Poor Families in America* (Cambridge, MA: Harvard University Press, 1997), 19–21.
12. Gustave de Beaumont and Alexis de Tocqville seized on this point as a proof of the benevolent, educational value of the House. See Gustave de Beaumont and Alexis de Tocqueville, *On the Penitentiary System in the United States: And Its Application in France; with an Appendix on Penal Colonies, and Also, Statistical Notes* (Philadelphia: Carey, Lea & Blanchard, 1833), 112.
13. For a discussion of individualization in Houses of Refuge and in antebellum prisons more broadly, see Michael Meranze, *Laboratories of Virtue: Punishment, Revolution, and Authority in Philadelphia, 1760–1835* (Chapel Hill, NC: University of North Carolina Press, 1996). For context on juvenile justice's historical consideration of child character, see Holly Brewer, "Understanding Intent: Children and the Reform of Guilt and Punishment," *By Birth or Consent* (Chapel Hill: University of North Carolina Press, 2012), 181–230.
14. David J. Rothman, *Discovery of the Asylum: Social Order and Disorder in the New Republic* (New Brunswick, NJ: Transaction Publishers, 1971), 262.
15. Gillian Brown, *The Consent of the Governed: The Lockean Legacy in Early American Culture* (Cambridge, MA: Harvard University Press, 2001), 17.
16. "Art. XIV.—Library of Education," *American Annals of Education* 1, no. 8 (August 1831): 393.
17. "Short Reviews and Notices of Books," *Methodist Quarterly Review* 34 (January 1852): 146.
18. The institution would not officially open until January 1, 1825, but then-Superintendent Joseph Curtis began mustering and profiling the first group of inmates shortly before that date.

19. John Locke, *Some Thoughts Concerning Education*, ed. John W. and Jean S. Yolton (New York: Oxford, 1989), 84.
20. Ibid., 82.
21. Ibid., 96.
22. Ibid., 95.
23. Ibid., 101.
24. James Salazar, *Bodies of Reform: The Rhetoric of Character in Gilded Age America* (New York: New York University Press, 2010), 14.
25. Locke, *Some Thoughts Concerning Education*, 61.
26. Amos Bronson Alcott, *Observations on the Principles and Methods of Infant Instruction* (Carter and Hendee, 1830), 5.
27. Lydia Maria Child, *The Mother's Book* (New York: C. S. Francis, 1844), 1.
28. John A. Gere, *The Government of Children* (New York: Lane & Scott, 1851), 59.
29. Ibid., 59–60.
30. Ibid., 82.
31. Locke, *Some Thoughts Concerning Education*, 113.
32. Ibid., 138.
33. Richard H. Brodhead, "Sparing the Rod: Discipline and Fiction in Antebellum America," *Representations*, no. 21 (1988): 67–96. For further exploration of this dynamic, see Elizabeth Barnes, *Love's Whipping Boy: Violence and Sentimentality in the American Imagination* (Chapel Hill: University of North Carolina Press, 2011).
34. Child, *The Mother's Book*, 36. Emphasis in original.
35. Ibid., 37.
36. Ibid., 171.
37. Heman Humphrey, *Domestic Education* (Amherst, MA: J. S. & C. Adams, 1840), 60.
38. See Brodhead, "Sparing the Rod," 68.
39. Elizabeth Palmer Peabody, *Record of a School: Exemplifying the General Principles of Spiritual Culture* (Boston: J. Munroe, 1835), 145.
40. Alcott, *Observations*, 21.
41. For a discussion of John Brown's use of a similar method of discipline with his son, see Elizabeth Barnes, "Fathers of Violence: Frederick Douglass, John Brown, and the Radical Reproduction of Sensibility," *Love's Whipping Boy*, 83–122.
42. Child, *The Mother's Book*, 4. Emphasis in original.
43. Ibid., 4.
44. Ibid., 37.
45. "Second Annual Report, &c.," *Documents Relative to House of Refuge Instituted by the Society for the Reformation of Juvenile Delinquents in the City of New-York in 1824*, ed. Nathaniel Hart (New York: Mahlon Day, 1832), 25.

46. Even this list is not nationally comprehensive, missing at least the incorporation of a New Orleans House nine years prior to the report's publication ("Records of Correctional Institutions"). See "Art. Iii.—Houses of Refuge and Reformation," *Pennsylvania Journal of Prison Discipline and Philanthropy (1845-1856)*, April 1854: 75.
47. "Second Annual Report, &c.,", 84–85.
48. Quoted in John Sergeant, *An Address Delivered Before the Citizens of Philadelphia, at the House of Refuge, on Saturday, the Twentyninth of November, 1828* (Philadelphia: Jesper Harding, 1828): 39–40.
49. Beaumont and Tocqueville, *On the Penitentiary System*, 111.
50. *The Design and Advantages of the House of Refuge* (Philadelphia: Brown, Bicking, and Guilbert, 1840), 4.
51. "Crime among the Young," *New York Evangelist (1830-1902)*, December 5, 1835: 278. For a similar instance of delinquency as a subject of didactic literature, see also "The Children's Column: What I Saw: Or, Little Lee's-Sin," *Christian Advocate and Journal (1833-1865)* January 3, 1850, which takes a juvenile theft as occasion for individual moral speculation and readerly instruction.
52. E. C. & J. Biddle, ed., *Prize Essays on Juvenile Delinquency* (Philadelphia: Philadelphia House of Refuge, 1855), 6.
53. Thomas Lake Harris, *Juvenile Depravity and Crime in Our City: A Sermon* (New York: C. B. Norton, 1850), 6. Emphasis in original.
54. Alan Richardson, *Literature, Education, and Romanticism: Reading as Social Practice, 1780-1832* (New York: Cambridge University Press, 2004), 14.
55. Ralph Waldo Emerson, "Nature," *Essays and Poems by Ralph Waldo Emerson* (New York: Spark Educational Publishing, 2004), 7–13.
56. Harvey Newcomb, *How to Be a Man: A Book for Boys: Containing Useful Hints on the Formation of Character* (Boston: Gould and Lincoln, 1856), 179–80.
57. Curtis resigned as superintendent in 1826 and was succeeded by N. C. Hart, who remained in the position until 1837. Because the two held converging attitudes regarding delinquency, and to highlight the institutional nature of their narrative voice, for this case I refer to the author of a given entry by title rather than personal name. For more on the transition and on the distinctions between Curtis's and Hart's philosophies, see Negley Teeters, "The Early Days of the Philadelphia House of Refuge," *Philadelphia History: A Journal of Mid-Atlantic Studies* 27, no. 2 (April 1960): 165–87.
58. Case Histories, Inmate 5, January 17, 1825.
59. Case Histories, Inmate 5, September 31, 1825, August 1, 1828.
60. Case Histories, Inmate 5, September 31, 1825, August 1, 1828.
61. This type of immurement for entirely financial reasons was technically against the original spirit of the institution, but was not especially unusual—for John A. Mead, for example, the superintendent ponders, "I rather think this boy has been sent here in consequence of the poverty of his mother"

(See Inmate 214; December 2, 1826)—and by the 1838 Pennsylvania case, *Ex parte Crouse*, the right to treat children as delinquent for having parents considered to be inappropriate guardians was legal precedent.

62. Case Histories, Inmate 138, 5 April 1831.
63. Case Histories, Inmate 385, October 27, 1831; Inmate 454, June 11, 1828; Inmate 323, February 1, 1828.
64. Case Histories, Inmate 116, [no date], January 1828, October 15, 1830.
65. Case Histories, Inmate 400, March 31, 1831; October 27, 1831; September 10, 1832.
66. Case Histories, Inmate 9, April 30, 1825.
67. Case Histories, Inmate 442, May 17, 1828.
68. Case Histories, Inmate 69, April 16, 1826.
69. I refer here chiefly to the suggestive case of James Dillon, a boy whose record consists of two remarks. The first, made two months after his entrance to the House, declares him "the most extraordinary we have yet to deal with" and "in every respect disobedient and disrespectful," despite multiple beatings, so that he was eventually sent to the main prison to subdue him. After an unusually long period of two and half years without any documentation, the silence is broken by an abrupt declaration that James is "an unfit subject" due to "Epileptic fits" and has been sent off to the almshouse. See Case Histories, Inmate 53, June 16, 1825, November 30, 1827.
70. Case Histories, Inmate 136, January 1828.
71. Case Histories, Inmate 416, April 24, 1829.
72. Case Histories, Inmate 35, March 14, 1825.
73. Case Histories, Inmate 78, December 12, 1828.
74. Case Histories, Inmate 80, December 12, 1828.
75. House officials were also quite canny about the institutional benefits of disposing of the most difficult inmates, as the superintendent records express when a mother complained about her son's indenture at sea: "I told her that after a two years trial we were unable to qualify him for anything except the Floridas or Navy—and that the managers had no idea of keeping hopeless boys, they must make room for more hopeful cases, etc." (Case Histories, Inmate 454; October 21, 1829).
76. Case Histories, Inmate 45, April 8, 1825.
77. Sigmund Freud, "A Preface to Aichorn's *Wayward Youth*," *Wayward Youth*, by August Aichhorn (New York: Viking Press, 1935), v.
78. Ibid., vii.
79. Worth noting, too, is that nothing more is said about how psychoanalysis might be "adapted to meet the need" of these unsuitable objects of analysis, except in the form of general education.

Chapter 3: Prodigious Births

1. This sense of the term *prodigy* has been a long-standing part of disability studies as an early modern category of disability. For a fuller account of

this history, see, among others, Rosemarie Garland-Thomson, "Staring at the Other," *Disability Studies Quarterly* 25, no. 4 (2005), http://dx.doi.org/10.18061/dsq.v25i4.610.

2. For further discussion of Melville's own approach to race, see Fred V. Bernard, "The Question of Race in *Moby-Dick*," *Massachusetts Review* 43, no. 3 (2002): 384–404; Christopher Freeburg, *Melville and the Idea of Blackness: Race and Imperialism in Nineteenth-Century America* (New York: Cambridge University Press, 2012); Carolyn L. Karcher, *Shadow over the Promised Land: Slavery, Race, and Violence in Melville's America* (Baton Rouge: Louisiana State University Press, 1980); Samuel Otter, *Melville's Anatomies* (Berkeley: University of California Press, 1999); and Geoffrey Sanborn, *The Sign of the Cannibal: Melville and the Making of the Postcolonial Reader* (Durham, NC: Duke University Press).

   For broader discussions of Melville and disability, see David T. Mitchell and Sharon L. Snyder, "The Language of Prosthesis in *Moby-Dick*," *Narrative Prosthesis: Disability and the Dependencies of Discourse* (Ann Arbor: University of Michigan, 2001), 119–40; and Harriet Hustis, "'Universal Mixing' and Interpenetrating Standing: Disability and Community in Melville's *Moby-Dick*," *Nineteenth-Century Literature* 69, no. 1 (2014): 26–55.

3. In this respect, prodigy acts as a cousin to infantilization but is less interested in the subject themselves than in their relationships or lack thereof.

4. Herman Melville, *Moby-Dick* (New York: Harper & Brothers, 1851; New York, NY: Signet Classic, 1998), 115, 399.

5. For a broad overview of medical and social approaches to inheritance, see Staffan Müller-Wille and Hans-Jörg Rheinberger, *A Cultural History of Heredity* (Chicago: The University of Chicago Press, 2012).

6. As many several scholars in queer theory have demonstrated, childhood has long been central to the temporalities of heterosexual reproduction, marking not only the orientation toward the futurity of a Messianic birth but also the more quotidian organizations of family and nation. Jack Halberstam, for instance, enumerates a reproductive time that dictates a proper age by which an adult should marry, a family time that centers on perceived needs of children for stable scheduling, and a time of inheritance that tracks the slower drift of property and culture between generations. See Jack Halberstam, *In a Queer Time and Place: Transgender Bodies, Subcultural Lives* (New York: New York University Press, 2005), 5. For Elizabeth Freeman, this generational logic allows for the equation of family futurity with national and racial teleologies, using individual births to suture public and private temporalities. See Elizabeth Freeman, *Time Binds: Queer Temporalities, Queer Histories* (Durham, NC: Duke University Press, 2010). Yet, as even Lee Edelman's pointed critique of child-centered politics points out, this affiliation of childhood with futurity on any scale rests in the reading of the child as a symbol of the citizen to come, rather than as a subject who is already immediate in the present. The infant's material dependency must transform into a symbolic promise of an adult future. The prodigy, on the

other hand, particularly as it emerges from medical discourse, is stuck in an all-too-recalcitrant body and, through this language of freakishness, is estranged from community with others and any sense of continuity with his or her history.

7. Habiba Ibrahim, "Any Other Age: Vampires and Oceanic Lifespans," *African American Review* 49, no. 4 (Winter 2016): 313.
8. Melville, *Moby-Dick*, 115, 511.
9. Herman Melville, *Redburn* (New York: Modern Library, 2002), 69
10. Melville, *Moby-Dick*, 115.
11. Ibid., 420.
12. Hortense Spillers, "Mama's Baby, Papa's Maybe: An American Grammar Book," *Diacritics* 17, no. 2 (1987): 68.
13. Jayna Brown, *Babylon Girls: Black Women Performers and the Shaping of the Modern* (Durham, NC: Duke University Press, 2009), 24.
14. Ibid., 86.
15. Harriet Beecher Stowe, *Uncle Tom's Cabin: Or, Life Among the Lowly* (Boston: John P. Jewett and Company, 1852; New York: Penguin Classics, 1981), 3.
16. Lois Brown, "Introduction," in Susan Paul, *Memoir of James Jackson, The Attentive and Obedient Scholar, Who Died in Boston, October 31, 1833, Aged Six Years and Eleven Months*, ed. Lois Brown (Cambridge, MA: Harvard University Press, 2000), 1.
17. Jacob D. Wheeler, *Reports of Criminal Law Cases* vol. III (New York: Gould and Banks, 1825), 200. Later in the case, a witness would define *sambo* as the racial category for a person who is half "black" and half "mulatto," though it is not certain that this is the sense in which Williams used the term (Ibid., 364).
18. Ibid., 195–98.
19. Ibid., 211–12.
20. Ibid., 202.
21. For instance, in an 1825 manual on the presentation and analysis of medical evidence by Scottish surgeon and editor of the *London Medical Repository* James Gordon Smith, Mitchill's testimony is mocked with the note that, "Surely, American judicature, *outré* as we are taught to believe it, could not allow this to pass as *evidence* [emphasis in original]." Williamson's comments on prodigies and perjuries, in contrast, are applauded as doing "great honor" to their speaker and as being an exemplar of "forensic wit." See James Gordon Smith, *An Analysis of Medical Evidence* (London: Thomas and George Underwood, 1825), 365, 363.
22. See "The Siamese Brothers," *Boston Medical and Surgical Journal* 2, no. 29 (1829): 459; and "The Belgian Giant," *Boston Medical and Surgical Journal* 15, no. 45 (1840): 36.
23. Georges Louis Leclerc, Comte de Buffon, *A Natural History of the Globe: Of Man, of Beasts, Birds, Fishes, Reptiles, Insects, and Plants*, ed. John Wright (Boston: Gray & Bowen, 1831), 178–80. Alongside a number of British

editions, versions of this passage were published under Buffon's name in Boston in 1831 as part of *A Natural History of the Globe*, in Brattleboro, MA, in 1834 as part of *A System of Natural History*, and in New York in 1857 as part of *Buffon's Natural History of Man, the Globe and Quadrupeds*.

24. Kant's work was not frequently printed in the United States; however, his work was discussed in periodicals of the time, including *Littell's Living Age* and *Biblical Repository and Princeton Review*. Immanuel Kant, "On the Different Races of Man," *Race and the Enlightenment: A Reader*, ed. Emmanuel Chukwudi Eze (Malden, MA: Blackwell Publishing Ltd., 2009), 40.
25. Georges Louis Leclerc Buffon (comte de), *Barr's Buffon. Buffon's Natural History: History of Man Continued*, ed. J. S. Barr (London: H. D. Symonds, 1797), 345.
26. Johann Friedrich Blumenbach, *Anthropological Treatises of Blumenbach and Hunter*, trans. Thomas Bendyshe (London: Longman, Green, Longman, Roberts & Green, 1865), 108.
27. Immanuel Kant, "Physical Geography," *Race and the Enlightenment*, 60.
28. "The 'Lancet' and the Color of Newly Born Negro Children," *Medical News*, December 10, 1898, 766.
29. Samuel Adolphus Cartwright, "Natural History of the Prognathous Species of Mankind," *Cotton Is King, and Pro-Slavery Arguments*, ed. E. N. Elliot (Augusta, GA: Pritchard, Abbott & Loomis, 1860), 708.
30. Ellen Samuels, "Examining Millie and Christine McKoy: Where Enslavement and Enfreakment Meet," *Signs* 37.1 (2011): 56. The McKoys were enslaved conjoined twins displayed in circuses and medical journals since infancy and who might easily have joined the prodigies considered in this chapter.
31. Historian Marie Jenkins Schwartz cites an example of an antebellum doctor who announced that a large baby had been gestated for eleven months. See Marie Jenkins Schwartz, *Birthing a Slave: Motherhood and Medicine in the Antebellum South* (Cambridge, MA: Harvard University Press, 2010), 129.
32. John Archer, "Facts Illustrating a Disease Particular to the Female Children of Negro Slaves: And Observations, Showing that a White Woman by Intercourse with a White Man and a Negro May Conceive Twins," *Medical Repository*, ed. Samuel Latham Mitchill and Edward Miller, vol. 1 (New York: Collins and Perkins, 1810), 323.
33. Archer, "Facts Illustrating," 323. For other examples of other medical accounts tracking superfetation by race, see John Stearn, "Article VII. A New Theory of Conception," *New York Medical and Physical Journal* 4, no. 3 (July, August, September 1825): 360–68; "Superfoetation," *Medico-chirurgical Review* 1, no. 1 (June 1824): 181–82; or, for a British example, A. T. Thomson, "Lectures on Medical Jurisprudence: Pregnancy," *London Lancet* 1, no. 699 (January 21, 1837): 578–82.
34. This sensationalism can also have more explicit presence in the clinical tone of the report. An account from the *Dublin Journal of Medial and Chemical Science* republished in the *American Journal of Medical Sciences* shows its alarm through excitable punctuation: "One child was white, the

other evidently a half caste . . . The same difference of color was strikingly evident in the umbilical cords of the infants! but not in the membranes or placenta. On inquiry it appeared that she was in the habit of intimacy with a negro, shortly after or at the time she had conceived by her husband!" See "Instance of Superfœtation," *American Journal of the Medical Sciences* vol. xiii (Philadelphia: Carey, Lea, & Blancard), 220.

35. Chris C. Yates, "Account of a Monster," *Philadelphia Medical Museum* 4, no. 4 (1808): 254.
36. Ibid.
37. Todd Savitt, "The Use of Blacks for Medical Experimentation and Demonstration in the Old South," *Journal of Southern History* 48, no. 3 (1982): 331–48.
38. Steven M. Stowe, *Doctoring the South: Southern Physicians and Everyday Medicine in the Mid-Nineteenth Century* (Chapel Hill: University of North Carolina Press, 2004), 55.
39. Deborah Kuhn McGregor, *From Midwives to Medicine: The Birth of American Gynecology* (New Brunswick, NJ: Rutgers University Press, 1997), 49–50.
40. For more on the role of Black women in the early development of obstetrics and gynecology, particularly in the work of J. Marion Sims, see also Terri Kapsalis, "Mastering the Female Pelvis: Race and the Tools of Reproduction," in *Public Privates: Performing Gynecology from Both Ends of the Speculum*, ed. Terri Kapsalis (Durham, NC: Duke University Press, 1997).
41. Schwartz, *Birthing a Slave*, 220.
42. Ibid., 218.
43. Ibid., 223.
44. Spillers, "Mama's Baby," 68.
45. Stowe, *Doctoring the South*, 7.
46. Mitchill cites "a case, called the Black Case, in Haddington's poems." I have not been able to trace the poem in question, but Mitchill summarizes it as a white woman giving birth to a Black child after her husband spills ink in her shoes. See Wheeler, *Reports of Criminal Law Cases*, 209.
47. "Coffee," *London Medical and Surgical Journal*, ed. Michael Ryan, vol. 5 (London: Thomas and George Underwood, 1830), 175. Accessed October 2014, https://www.google.com/books/edition/The_London_Medical_and_Surgical_Journal/y-gEAAAAQAAJ?hl=en&gbpv=0.
48. "Adulteration of Beer," *London Medical and Surgical Journal*, ed. Michael Ryan, vol. 7 (London: Thomas and George Underwood, 1831): 348.
49. An 1831 article on the "Medical Institutions of Naples" in the *North American Medical and Surgical Journal*, for instance, punctuates its descriptions of various Italian hospitals with recollections of patient performances the author saw and the individual doctors he met (17–62).
50. For further discussion of this interconnection, see Sari Altschuler's *The Medical Imagination: Literature and Health in the Early United States* (Philadelphia: University of Pennsylvania Press, 2018).

51. Nancy Bentley, "The Fourth Dimension: Kinlessness and African American Narrative," *Critical Inquiry* 35, no. 2 (Winter 2009): 271.
52. A survey of the eighteen issues of the *London Medical and Surgical Journal* leading up to the issue with "Skinning" reveals no other explicitly literary pieces, but does show multiple articles on medicine in Ireland, the West Indies, and the United States. There are also a few lengthy excerpts from biographies written about notable thinkers that might have helped make Barrington's memoirs less incongruous in a medical journal.
53. See, for instance, Philadelphia's *Ariel: A Semi-monthly Literary and Miscellaneous Gazette*, September 1, 1832, 152.
54. Jonah Barrington, "Skinning a Black Child," *Ariel: A Semi-monthly Literary and Miscellaneous Gazette*, September 1, 1832, 152.
55. [Untitled Review of *Personal Sketches of His Own Times* by Sir Jonah Barrington], *Athenæum* 244 (1832): 409, 411.
56. Jonah Barrington, "Skinning a Black Child," *London Medical and Surgical Journal* 1, no. 26 (1832): 818.
57. If Barrington's introduction of the Black servant in the opening of the tale, immediately before a paragraph on the inexplicable variation of skin color among newborns, is not enough to tip off the reader, the child's eventual death after a "horning" from one of his father's cows more than hints that a cuckolding is in play.
58. Barrington, "Skinning," 152.
59. Ibid.
60. Ibid.
61. Ibid.
62. Ibid.
63. Henry Clay Lewis, "Stealing a Baby," *The Swamp Doctor's Adventures in the South-West* (Philadelphia: T. B. Peterson and Brothers, 1858), 131–37.
64. Ibid., 137.
65. Ibid., 134.
66. Ibid., 135, 137.
67. Ibid., 133.
68. Melville, *Moby-Dick*, 512, 500.
69. Ibid., 115.
70. Ibid., 115.
71. Ibid., 402
72. See, for example, Stephen Best's discussion of the public reception of the pianist known as Blind Tom in *Fugitive Properties*. Contemporary reviewers, he argues, treat Tom's music as so strangely distanced from Tom himself that the musician appears only as an uncanny conduit for a thoroughly external gift. Thus, the beauty of the performance came to a measure of how strange the audience found its source.
73. For a longer discussion of the racialization of the connections between individual and group identity, see Sharon Holland's "When Characters Lack Character: A Biomythography," *PMLA* 123, no. 5 (2008): 1494–502.

74. Susan Paul, *Memoir of James Jackson: The Attentive and Obedient Scholar, Who Died in Boston, October 31, 1833, Aged Six Years and Eleven Months*, ed. Lois Brown (Cambridge, MA: Harvard University Press, 2000).
75. Diana Walsh Pasulka, "A Communion of Little Saints: Nineteenth-Century American Child Hagiographies," *Journal of Feminist Studies in Religion* 23, no. 2 (2007): 57.
76. Paul, *Memoir*, 92, 74, 76.
77. Ibid., 83.
78. Ibid., 88. Emphasis in original.
79. Ibid., 93.
80. See Max Cavitch, *American Elegy: The Poetry of Mourning from the Puritans to Whitman* (Minneapolis: University of Minnesota Press, 2006), 144. Another factor in the categorization of *The Memoir* as a primarily abolitionist text may well be what Cavitch terms the "antebellum crisis in the economic value of the child" (Cavitch, *American Elegy*, 18). As Cavitch argues, the presence of enslaved and therefore commodified children in the U.S. forced even writers who were only explicitly discussing white children into a reconsideration of the links between property loss and child death—a crisis that the mourning of a child potentially eligible for slavery must certainly intensify.
81. Paul, *Memoir*, 69.
82. Ibid., 71, 87.
83. Ibid., 103.
84. Ibid., 97.
85. Ibid., 102.
86. Ibid., 107, 108.
87. Ibid., 71.
88. Brown, "Introduction," 39–40.
89. Paul, *Memoir*, 73.
90. Ibid.
91. Brown, "Introduction," 11.
92. Paul, *Memoir*, 67.
93. Ibid., 75.
94. Ibid., 82.
95. Ibid., 72.
96. Ibid., 74.
97. Ibid., 76–66.
98. Ibid., 87.
99. Ibid., 99.
100. Ibid., 67.
101. Ibid., 67–68.
102. Langston Hughes, "Genius Child," *Selected Poems of Langston Hughes* (New York: Vintage Classics, 1990), 83.

103. Brown, "Introduction," 58.
104. Melville, *Moby-Dick*, 51, 24.
105. Ibid., 22.
106. Ibid., 22, 51, 462.
107. Ibid., 51.
108. Ibid., 51.
109. Ibid., 61.
110. Ibid., 60.
111. Ibid., 416.
112. Ibid., 420.
113. José Esteban Muñoz, *Cruising Utopia: The Then and There of Queer Futurity* (New York: New York University Press, 2009), 95.

CHAPTER 4: TOO MANY CHILDREN

1. "Death of Malthus," *Cincinnati Mirror and Western Gazette of Literature, Science, and the Arts* 4, no. 16 (February 14, 1835): 131.
2. Ibid.
3. Ibid.
4. For further discussion, see Robin Bernstein, *Racial Innocence: Performing American Childhood from Slavery to Civil Rights* (New York: New York University Press, 2011).
5. Harriet Beecher Stowe, *Dred: A Tale of the Great Dismal Swamp*, ed. Judie Newman (Halifax, England: Ryburn BAAS American Library, 1992).
6. Thomas K. Malthus, *An Essay on the Principle of Population*, ed. Antony Flew (Harmondsworth, England: Penguin Classics, 1983).
7. Most notably, Robin Bernstein has suggested that idealized child purity, coded as white, is the defining trait of antebellum literature's depiction of childhood. See, additionally, Lauren Berlant, Kathryn Bond Stockton, and Lee Edelman for broader theoretical readings of child innocence as a pernicious form of utopianism, and Anna Mae Duane, Viviana Zelizer, and Karen J. Sánchez-Eppler for more detailed examinations of such qualities in the nineteenth century.
8. Henry James, "The Art of Fiction," *Theory of Fiction: Henry James*, ed. James E. Miller (Lincoln: University of Nebraska Press, 1972), 382.
9. Gillian Brown, "Getting in the Kitchen with Dina: Domestic Politics in *Uncle Tom's Cabin*," *American Quarterly* 36, no. 4 (Autumn, 1984): 519.
10. Cindy Weinstein, *Family, Kinship, and Sympathy in Nineteenth-Century American Literature* (New York: Cambridge University Press, 2004), 130.
11. Gretchen Murphy, "Revising the Law of the Mother in the Adoption-Marriage Plot," *Nineteenth-Century Literature* 69, no. 3 (2014): 354.
12. See Weinstein, *Family, Kinship, and Sympathy;* and Lauren Berlant, *The Female Complaint: The Unfinished Business of Sentimentality in American Culture* (Durham, NC: Duke University Press, 2008).

13. Nancy Armstrong, *How Novels Think: The Limits of British Individualism from 1719–1900* (New York: Columbia University Press, 2005), 109.
14. Charles Dickens, *Great Expectations* (London: Chapman and Hall, 1861; New York: Modern Library, 2001), 430.
15. For a foundational discussion of this trope, see Ruth Yeazell, "Why Political Novels Have Heroines: *Sybil*, *Mary Barton*, and *Felix Holt*," *Novel* 18, no. 2 (Winter 1985): 126–44.
16. See Patricia Yaeger, *Dirt and Desire: Reconstructing Southern Women's Writing, 1930–1990* (Chicago: University of Chicago Press, 2009); Rosemarie Bodenheimer, *The Politics of Story in Victorian Social Fiction* (Ithaca, NY: Cornell University Press, 1991); and Barbara Leah Harman, *The Feminine Political Novel in Victorian England* (Charlottesville: University of Virginia Press, 1998).
17. Lauren Berlant, *The Queen of America Goes to Washington City: Essays on Sex and Citizenship* (Durham, NC: Duke University Press, 1997), 6.
18. Armstrong, *How Novels Think*, 115.
19. Ibid., 128.
20. Claudia Stokes, *The Altar at Home: Sentimental Literature and Nineteenth-Century American Religion* (Philadelphia: University of Pennsylvania, 2014), 104.
21. Samuel Otter, "Stowe and Race," *The Cambridge Companion to Harriet Beecher Stowe* (New York: Cambridge University Press, 2004), 35.
22. Stowe, *Dred*, 518.
23. Otter, "Stowe and Race," 35.
24. "The Review," *National Era* 10, no. 510 (October 9, 1856): 162, *Uncle Tom's Cabin & American Culture*, University of Virginia, accessed October 2020, http://utc.iath.virginia.edu/notices/noar01cpt.html.
25. Lawrence Buell, *The Dream of the Great American Novel* (Cambridge, MA: Harvard University Press, 2014), 242.
26. Ibid.
27. Stowe, *Dred*, 150.
28. Ibid., 251.
29. Ibid., 151.
30. Ibid., 251.
31. Ibid., 297–98.
32. Ibid., 258.
33. Ibid., 289.
34. Although I do not address it here for reasons of space, *Dred* has long been understood as practicing a particularly legal- and rights-oriented form of sentimentalism, underscoring this suspicion of what any single individual's feelings might lead them to do. For a classic discussion of this interplay between feeling and law, see Gregg D. Crane, "Dangerous Sentiments: Sympathy, Rights, and Revolution in Stowe's Antislavery Novels," *Nineteenth-Century Literature* 51, no. 2 (September 1996): 176–204.

35. Stowe, *Dred*, 254, 252.
36. Ibid., 254.
37. Ibid., 131.
38. Holly Jackson, *The Ends of the Family in American Literature, 1850-1900* (New York: Oxford University Press, 2013), 85.
39. Ibid., 77.
40. Molly Farrell's *Counting Bodies: Population in Colonial American Writing* (New York: Oxford University Press, 2016) deals with the topic for an earlier period. Rare essays have taken up the question in the nineteenth century—Beryl Rowland's "Sitting Up with a Corpse: Malthus according to Melville in 'Poor Man's Pudding and Rich Man's Crumbs,'" *Journal of American Studies* 6, no. 1 (April 1972): 69–83, for example, offers one such analysis—but there has been nothing approaching the sustained attention shown in British studies, particularly after the end of the eighteenth century.
41. Alison Bashford and Joyce E. Chaplin, *The New Worlds of Thomas Robert Malthus: Rereading the 'Principle of Population'* (Princeton, NJ: Princeton University Press, 2016).
42. See, for instance, Lauren Campbell, "Mary Shelley's Malthusian Objections in *The Last Man*," *Nineteenth-Century* 67, no. 2 (September 2012): 177–203; Philip Connell, "Wordsworth, Malthus, and the 1805 *Prelude*," *Essays in Criticism* 50 (2000): 242–67; Dallin Lewis, "Prophesying the Present: Shelley's Critique of Malthus in *A Defense of Poetry*," *European Romantic Review* 25, no. 5 (2014): 575–90; Maureen Noelle McLane, "Literate Species: Populations, 'Humanities,' and *Frankenstein*," *ELH* 63, no. 4 (1996): 959–88; and Emily Steinlight, "Hardy's Unnecessary Lives: The Novel as Surplus," *Novel* 47, no. 2 (June 2014): 224–41.
43. Nicole Eustace, *1812: War and the Passions of Patriotism* (Philadelphia: University of Pennsylvania Press, 2012), 7.
44. Thomas Jefferson, "Letter to Doctor Priestly, Washington, January 29, 1804," *The Works of Thomas Jefferson*, ed. H. A. Washington, vol. IV (New York: Townsend MacCoun, 1884), 526.
45. Though Adams does not disagree with the content of Malthus's arguments, he was somewhat cynical about their novelty, declaring in a letter to John Taylor, "that the first want of man is his dinner, and the second his girl, were truths well known to every democrat and aristocrat long before the great philosopher Malthus arose to think he enlightened the world by the discovery." See John Adams, "Letters to John Taylor of Caroline, Virginia in Reply to his Strictures of Some Parts of the American Constitution," *The Works of John Adams, Second President of the United States*, ed. Charles Francis Adams, vol. 6 (Boston: Charles C. Little and James Brown, 1851), 516.
46. Eustace, *1812*, 13–15.
47. Ibid., 17.

48. For an example of the way that Malthus's use of early U.S. demographics as evidence could inspire pride, take an 1822 article in the *North American Review*, which declares that "it was not, however, until the publication of the American censuses, that the world was enabled to judge with any degree of accuracy, in how short a period this doubling could be accomplished. . . . Most of the writers who have attempted to answer Mr. Malthus, at least those whose works have lived long enough to cross the Atlantic, have been content to acquiesce in the truth of the geometrical increase." "ART. XIII.—An Inquiry Concerning the Power of Increase in the Numbers of Mankind," *North American Review* 12, no. 37 (1822): 290, *Google Books*, accessed October 2020, https://books.google.com/books?id=86FKAAAAcAAJ&pg=PP13#v=onepage&q&f=false.
49. Malthus, *Essay on Population*, 94.
50. He writes of the English Poor Laws that their "obvious" effect is "to increase the population without increasing the food for its support. A poor man may marry with little or no prospect of being able to support a family in independence." See Malthus, *Essay on Population*, 97.
51. Ibid., 100.
52. Though Malthus cites another demographer, Richard Price, for the data behind this rate, the assertion that U.S. populations doubled every twenty-five years appears earlier in Franklin's 1755 essay "Observations on the Increase of Mankind" (Franklin, "Observations," 9).
53. Malthus, *Essay on Population*, 74.
54. Ibid., 105.
55. Ibid., 197.
56. Ibid., 198.
57. Thomas R. Dew, *An Address on the Influence of the Federative Republican System of Government upon Literature and the Development of Character* (Richmond, VA: Office of the "Southern Literary Messenger," 1836), 19. For additional discussion of Dew's Malthusian pessimism, see Hodgson, "Malthus and American Slavery," 760–761.
58. Henry C. Carey, *The Past, the Present, and the Future* (Philadelphia: Carey and Hart, 1848), 77.
59. "Principles of Political Economy," *North American Review* 67, no. 141 (October 1848): 396, Google Books, accessed October 2020, https://books.google.com/books?id=maFKAAAAcAAJ&printsec=frontcover&source=gbs_ge_summary_r&cad=0#v=onepage&q&f=false.
60. Dennis Hodgson, "Malthus' Essay on Population and the American Debate over Slavery," *Comparative Studies in Society and History* 51, no. 4 (2009): 742–70.
61. Lyman Beecher, *A Plea for the West* (New York: Leavitt, Lord, and Co., 1835), 30–31.
62. "The Problem of Free Society," *Southern Literary Messenger* 26, no. 6 (June 1858): 401.

63. Julie Newman, "Stowe's Sunny Memories of Highland Slavery," *Special Relationships: Anglo-American Affinities and Antagonisms*, ed. Janet Beer and Bridget Bennett (New York: Manchester University Press, 2002), 29.
64. Harriet Beecher Stowe, *Sunny Memoires of Foreign Lands*, vol. 1 (Boston: Phillips, Sampson, and Company, 1854), 303.
65. Thomas R. Malthus, *An Essay on the Principle of Population* (London: J. Johnson, 1803), 334, Google Books, accessed October 6, 2020, https://www.google.com/books/edition/An_essay_on_the_principle_of_population/-stOAAAAcAAJ?hl=en&gbpv=0.
66. Karl Marx, "The Duchess of Sutherland and Slavery" [February 8–9, 1853], *Dispatches for the New York Tribune: Selected Journalism of Karl Marx*, ed. James Ledbetter (New York: Penguin Books, 2007), 116. Donald McLeod's parodic response to *Sunny Memories*, *Gloomy Memories in the Highlands of Scotland* (1857), echoes Marx in its condemnation of the "monstrous sophistry" that allowed Sutherland to espouse a "desire to liberties and blessings upon the American slaves, which they so sternly and Malthusian-like deny to their own people." See Donald McLeod, *Gloomy Memories in the Highlands of Scotland* (Toronto: Thompson & Co., 1857), 112.
67. Stowe, *Sunny Memories*, 313.
68. Martin Delany, "Mrs. Stowe's Position," and Frederick Douglass, "The Letter of M.R. Delany," *Frederick Douglass' Paper* (May 6, 1853): 1. Both are available on *Uncle Tom's Cabin & American Culture*, University of Virginia, 2012, http://utc.iath.virginia.edu/africam/afar03rt.html.
69. Quoted in Isabella Furth, "Manifest Destiny, Manifest Domesticity, and the Leaven of Whiteness in *Uncle Tom's Cabin*," *Arizona Quarterly* 55, no. 2 (Summer 1999): 31–55, 45.
70. Ibid., 48.
71. Stowe, *Dred*, 608.
72. Christopher Diller, "Introduction," *Uncle Tom's Cabin*, ed. Christopher Diller (Buffalo, NY: Broadview Press, 2009), 27.
73. Harriet Jacobs, *Incidents in the Life of a Slave Girl, Written by Herself*, ed. Jean Fagan Yellin (Boston: Thayer and Eldridge, 1861; Cambridge, MA: Harvard University Press, 1987), 201.
74. Henry Bibb, *Narrative of the Life and Adventures of Henry Bibb: An American Slave* (New York: By the Author, 1849; Mineloa, NY: Dover Publications, 2005), 22.
75. Mark Rifkin, *Settler Common Sense: Queerness and Everyday Colonialism in the American Renaissance* (Minneapolis: University of Minnesota, 2014).
76. Before Marx took up the term, the phrase "surplus population" was common shorthand for the terms of Malthusian debate. For instance, Dickins's 1843 *A Christmas Carol* uses Ebenezer Scrooge's complaint that charity that only promotes "surplus population" to cue readers to Scrooge's Malthusianism. See Frank Christianson, *Philanthropy in British and American Fiction: Dickens,*

Hawthorne, Eliot, and Howells (Edinburgh: Edinburgh University Press, 2007): 80.

77. Stowe, *Dred*, 155, 252.
78. Ibid., 251.
79. Ibid., 127.
80. Ibid., 251.
81. This notion of a child, even an infant, without a natural connection to her or his mother's pain challenges a common antebellum belief that the infant affect is instinctively aligned with what the mother is feeling. See chapter one of this volume for instances of this belief and a longer discussion of its implications.
82. Stowe, *Dred*, 137.
83. Ibid., 127.
84. Ibid., 142.
85. Hortense Spillers, "Changing the Letter: The Yokes, the Jokes of Discourse, or, Mrs. Stowe, Mr. Reed," *Black, White, and in Color: Essays on American Literature and Culture* (Chicago: University of Chicago Press, 2003): 176–202.
86. Nina's biological age is not clearly marked in the text. At its opening, Clayton refers to her as eighteen. However, by the time of her death, which comes some three or four months along the time of the plot, the narrator refers to her as seventeen. See Stowe, *Dred*, 61, 460.
87. Ibid., 118.
88. As a college friend of Clayton describes her on one occasion, Nina is "a spicy little puss" and, on another, she appears full of mysterious animation: "She's alive, every inch of her! She puts me in mind of a sweet-brier bush, winking and blinking, full of dew-drops, full of roses, and brisk little thorns, beside! Ah, she'll keep him awake!" See Stowe, *Dred*, 384 and 391.
89. Ibid., 59.
90. Ibid., 236.
91. Ibid., 199.
92. Holly Jackson, *The Ends of the Family in American Literature, 1850–1900* (New York: Oxford University Press, 2013), 81.
93. Stowe, *Dred*, 499.
94. Ibid., 676.
95. Tess Chakkalakal, *Novel Bondage: Slavery, Marriage, and Freedom in Nineteenth-Century America* (Champaign: University of Illinois Press, 2011), 33.
96. I here follow the distinction made by Martin Delaney and others between "colonization," signifying a coercive and white-led removal of African Americans to Africa, and "emigration," a voluntary and Black-led renunciation of the United States. The distinction does, however, break down somewhat in my discussion of Malthusian framings of these processes, as the notion of individual agency gives way to aggregate forces.

97. Timothy B. Powell, *Ruthless Democracy: A Multicultural Interpretation of the American Renaissance* (Princeton, NJ: Princeton University Press, 2000), 123.
98. Quoted in Powell, *Ruthless Democracy*, 123.
99. Stowe, *Dred*, 252.
100. Martha Schoolman, *Abolitionist Geographies* (Minneapolis: University of Minnesota Press, 2014), 170.
101. Ibid., 170.
102. Stowe, *Dred*, 639.
103. Amy Kaplan, "Manifest Domesticity," *American Literature* 70, no. 3 (1998): 581–606.
104. Stowe, *Dred*, 671.
105. Ibid., 678.

CONCLUSION

1. Ronald Vern Jackson and Gary Ronald Teeples, "Preface," *Massachusetts 1850 Census Index*, ed. Ronald Vern Jackson and Gary Ronald Teeples (Bountiful, UT: Accelerated Indexing Systems, Inc., 1978).
2. Paula S. Fass, "Foreword," *Children and Youth During the Gilded Age and Progressive Era* (New York: New York University Press, 2014), vii–ix.
3. For a discussion of this legal precedent and its many exemptions, see Kristin A. Collins, "Illegitimate Borders: *Jus Sanguinis* Citizenship and the Legal Construction of Family, Race, and Nation," *Yale Law Journal* 123 (2013): 2134–235.
4. See Kenneth Kidd, *Making American Boys: Boyology and the Feral Tale* (Cambridge, MA: Harvard University Press, 2004), or the collected works of Mark Twain.
5. Darwin's 1859 *Origin of Species*, for example, promises that the terms of social relation used by natural scientists, such as "affinity, relationship, community of type, paternity" will, under his theory, "cease to be metaphorical, and will have a plain signification." He continues, suggesting that all typology will be unified under a single understanding of inheritance: "Our classifications will come to be, as far as they can be so made, genealogies; and will then truly give what may be called a plan of creation." See Charles Darwin, *Darwin: A Norton Critical Edition*, ed. Philip Appleman (New York: W. W. Norton Co., 2001), 172.
6. Geoff K. Ward, *The Black Child-Savers: Racial Democracy and Juvenile Justice* (Chicago: University of Chicago Press, 2012).
7. Steffan Müller-Wille and Hans-Jörg Rheinberger, *A Cultural History of Heredity* (Chicago: University of Chicago Press, 2012), 95–100.
8. For a longitudinal study undermining the reality of the "crack baby" narrative, see Laura M. Betancourt, et al., "Adolescents with and without Gestational Cocaine Exposure: Longitudinal Analysis of Inhibitory Control, Memory

and Receptive Language," *Neurotoxicology and Teratology* 33, no. 1 (2011): 36–46.

9. For discussion and critique of the "super-predator" theory in criminology, see Soo Ah Kwon, *Uncivil Youth: Race, Activism and Affirmative Governmentality* (Durham, NC: Duke University Press, 2013), 39–42.
10. See Donna Murch, "Crack in Los Angeles: Crisis, Militarization, and Black Response to the Late Twentieth-Century War on Drugs," *Journal of American History* 102, no. 1 (June 2015): 162–73.
11. For a discussion of this trend, see Priscilla Huang, "Anchor Babies, Over-Breeders, and the Population Bomb: The Reemergence of Nativism and Population Control in Anti-Immigration Policies," *Harvard Law and Policy Review* 2 (2008): 385.
12. Monika K. Goyal., et al., "Racial Disparities in Pain Management of Children with Appendicitis in Emergency Departments," *JAMA pediatrics* 169, no. 11 (2015): 996–1002.
13. Phillip Atiba Goff, et al., "The Essence of Innocence: Consequences of Dehumanizing Black Children," *Journal of Personality and Social Psychology* 106, no. 4 (2014): 526–45.
14. Zitkala-Ša, *American Indian Stories, Legends, and Other Writings*, ed. Cathy N. Davidson and Ada Norris (New York: Penguin Books, 2003), 112.
15. Ibid.
16. Pauline Elizabeth Hopkins, *Winona: A Tale of Negro Life in the South and Southwest, The Magazine Novels of Pauline Hopkins*, ed. Hazel Carby (New York: Oxford University Press, 1988), 285–438.
17. Ibid., 289, 292.
18. Ibid., 314.
19. Ibid., 290.
20. Ibid., 301–2.
21. Ibid., 320.
22. Ibid., 315.
23. Ibid., 355.
24. I take this information about part one of *Winona* from *Beyond the Digital Color Line: About the Colored American Magazine*, a digitization and curation of the *Colored American Magazine* directed by Brian Sweeney and Eurie Dahn.
25. Hopkins, "Winona," 301–2.
26. Ibid., 355.
27. Enslavement's erasure of exact age is perhaps most famously referenced in Frederick Douglass's "I have no accurate knowledge of my age," in his 1845 *Narrative*. For two discussions of this relationship, see Habiba Ibrahim, "Any Other Age: Vampires and Oceanic Lifespans," *African American Review* 49, no. 4 (Winter 2016): 313–27; and Lloyd Pratt, "The Deprivation of Time in African American Life Writing," *Archives of American Times:*

Literature and Modernity in the Nineteenth Century (Philadelphia: University of Pennsylvania Press, 2011), 157–86.

28. Hopkins, *Winona*, 430.
29. Ibid., 431.
30. Ibid., 355.
31. Ibid., 404.
32. Ibid., 324.
33. Ibid., 343–44.
34. Ibid., 359.
35. Ibid., 341.
36. Brigitte Fiedler, "'Those People Must Have Loved Her Very Dearly': Interracial Adoption and Radical Love in Antislavery Children's Literature," *Early American Studies: An Interdisciplinary Journal* 14, no. 4 (2016): 769.
37. Hopkins, *Winona*, 310.
38. Nazera Sadiq Wright, *Black Girlhood in the Nineteenth Century* (Champaign: University of Illinois Press, 2016).
39. Hopkins, *Winona*, 336.
40. Ibid., 388.
41. Ibid., 393.
42. See Derrick R. Spires, *The Practice of Citizenship: Black Politics and Print Culture in the Early United States* (Philadelphia: University of Pennsylvania Press, 2019), 56.
43. Augusta Rohrbach, "To Be Continued: Double Identity, Multiplicity and Antigenealogy as Narrative Strategies in Pauline Hopkins' Magazine Fiction," *Callaloo* 22, no. 2 (1999): 489.
44. Hopkins, *Winona*, 373.
45. Mary Grace Albanese, "Unraveling the Blood Line: Pauline Hopkin's Haitian Genealogies," *J19* 7, no. 2 (Fall 2019): 243.
46. Hopkins, *Winona*, 436.
47. As Lizbet Simmons argues, the pipeline metaphor suggests a cleaner break between the two institutions than there is in reality: "The current punitive dynamic in public schooling problematizes the linear rubric of a school-to-prison pipeline, since schools and prisons have in many ways merged, making the pipeline itself collapse in a state of punitive rupture." Lizbet Simmons, *The Prison School: Educational Inequality and School Discipline in the Age of Mass Incarceration* (Oakland: University of California Press, 2017), 29.

INDEX